THE LIFE

OF

DR. SAMUEL A. MUDD

CONTAINING HIS LETTERS FROM FORT JEFFERSON, DRY TORTUGAS
ISLAND,

WHERE HE WAS IMPRISONED FOUR YEARS FOR ALLEGED
COMPLICITY

IN THE ASSASSINATION OF ABRAHAM LINCOLN

WITH

STATEMENTS OF MRS. SAMUEL A. MUDD, DR. SAMUEL A. MUDD,

AND EDWARD SPANGLER REGARDING THE ASSASSINATION

AND

THE ARGUMENT OF GENERAL EWING

on the Question of the Jurisdiction of the Military Commission,

and on the Law and Facts of the Case

ALSO "DIARY" OF JOHN WILKES BOOTH

EDITED BY HIS DAUGHTER

NETTIE MUDD

1906

Contents

PUBLISHER'S NOTES

Whether one considers him innocent or guilty, Dr. Samuel Alexander Mudd's role at the center of one of the saddest and most dramatic incidents in American history cannot be challenged. As detailed by Nettie Mudd below, the Mudd's had met John Wilkes Booth prior to the assassination. They forever denied Dr. Mudd's involvement in the conspiracy to assassinate Abraham Lincoln.

Nettie Mudd was not the last of the family to try to clear the doctor's name. As late as the Jimmy Carter and Ronald Reagan presidential administrations, a Mudd descendant was petitioning for the conviction to be overturned. Jimmy Carter was apparently sympathetic but stated he had no authority to set aside the conviction. Reagan stated he had come to the conclusion that Mudd was innocent of wrongdoing but also did not act.

The United States Supreme Court in 2003 refused the case, stating that the deadline for filing had been missed.

MARY ELEANOR "NETTIE" MUDD

Mary Eleanor Mudd was born on January 10, 1878 in Waldorf, Maryland, and was the baby of the Mudd family of nine children. In 1900 she was living with a sister, working as a bookkeeper. On December 9, 1906 the 28-year-old Nettie married 62-year-old Baltimore lawyer, Daniel Eldridge Monroe. Monroe's wife had died in 1869, leaving him to raise five daughters and two sons. On September 27, 1907, Nettie gave birth to twins, William Eldridge Monroe and Sarah Frances Monroe, who died soon after birth. Nettie and Eldridge had two more children, James Victor Monroe, born November 7, 1908, and Frances Dyer Monroe, born October 12, 1910.

Eldridge Monroe died in 1914 and Nettie remained in Baltimore, raising her children and again working as a bookkeeper. She died on December 31, 1943.

PREFACE

The assassination of Abraham Lincoln startled and shocked the civilized world as few events have done in the whole course of human history. It occurred at a time when, by reason of the termination of the Civil War with the surrender of Lee at Appomattox, there was promise and hope of a more kindly feeling between the people of the two great sections of the country who, during a period of four years, had been arrayed against each other in deadly strife. The victors had granted magnanimous terms to the vanquished. The conciliatory and generous spirit shown by the Commanding General of the victorious armies in the hour of his crowning success, and to which he afterward gave expression in the famous declaration, "Let us have peace," awakened hopeful response in the hearts of the conquered people.

It was at this point of time, when better and brighter days seemed to be dawning for the whole country that the tragedy of Lincoln's death aroused throughout the land, North and South, an excitement unparalleled in the nation's history. The victim of the assassin had become almost deified in the minds of the Northern people. The people of the South had learned to respect and honor him for his lofty virtues as a man, while conscientiously condemning the administrative policies for which he stood. When the estimation in which he was held by the people is considered, it is not a matter to cause surprise, although to be deplored, that the news of the assassination excited for the time a feeling of bitterness more intense than had existed at any period during the bloody years of the Civil War. This feeling, deplorable but not altogether unnatural under the circumstances, was so extreme that, at first, a large number of the Northern people were disposed to place the responsibility of Lincoln's murder on the whole of the Southern people and to have inflicted upon them all vindictive punishment. This monstrous idea ultimately gave place to the one not less vicious, yet perhaps less far-reaching, that victims, guilty or innocent, must be sacrificed to avenge the crime of the assassination of the President. To the honor of the victorious Union army it should be stated that few of the soldiery shared in this desire for indiscriminate revenge. Among those high in authority in the administrative affairs of the nation, however, in a spirit diametrically at variance with that spirit of magnanimity and kindness that had uniformly characterized the course of President Lincoln, the determination was deep seated that victims must be offered up for sacrifice.

One of these victims was Dr. Samuel A. Mudd, whose sufferings to satisfy the demands thus born of prejudice and passion, are set forth in this volume, edited by his daughter, then unborn. In this work she has not sought to produce effect by ingenuity of argument, or to deduce conclusions from premises admitted or assumed. She has simply presented to the reader the facts as contained in the argument of General Ewing, made in defense of her father before the Military Commission before which he was tried; the statement of her mother; the statement of Spangler, one of the alleged "conspirators," who was imprisoned in Fort Jefferson for nearly five years; and the statement of Dr. Mudd, written while he was in prison but which he was not allowed by the authorities to give to the public, and which is now for the first time published; together with the letters of her father, written during the long period of his incarceration, and also the letters of various other persons relating directly or indirectly to the alleged "conspiracy." Upon these facts, without comment, she rests the question of the guilt or innocence of her father, and submits the matter to the consideration of an impartial public.

The letters of Dr. Mudd, written not for general perusal, but for the eyes alone of those very "near and dear" to him, reveal the character of the man more accurately perhaps than it could be revealed in any other manner. That he suffered intensely is apparent; that this suffering, which was caused chiefly by his anxiety concerning the welfare of his wife and little children, should have embittered him as the period of his imprisonment, which he regarded as absolutely unjust, was lengthened out from year to year, is neither surprising nor censurable. This bitterness appears only in his later letters. He was a man of culture, of quiet tastes, unostentatious, retiring. He preferred the peaceful surroundings of his home, the association and love of the members of his family, and the friendly intercourse of his neighbors, to any participation in the stirring and momentous events that were transpiring in his war-ridden country.

From such peaceful scenes and surroundings of his home he was, on the 24th of April, 1865, rudely torn, a prisoner charged with complicity in one of the most wicked and monstrous crimes that ever cast a stain upon the pages of the world's history. At first he seems to have scarcely regarded his arrest seriously, but as a mistake, incidental to the disturbed condition of the time, that would be speedily corrected. He believed that he would soon be restored to his family, and was particularly solicitous, not about his own fate, but that, during his brief absence from home, the work on the farm should be properly attended to. In the first letter he wrote to his wife, after his arrest, dated from the Carroll Prison, he does not speak of any personal discomfort or apprehension, but advises her to "try and get some one to plant our crop," "hire hands at the prices they demand," "urge them on all you can and make them work," and expresses the hope that his absence may be of short duration. This letter is clearly that of an innocent man, conscious of his innocence, and believing in his early and complete vindication.

His hopes, however, were not to be realized. "The frenzy of madness that ruled the hour," referred to by the eminent advocate for the defense, and himself a distinguished Union soldier, decreed otherwise. He was declared guilty by the military tribunal, and was ultimately sentenced to be confined for life in Fort Jefferson, on the Dry Tortugas Island, than which no more desolate place of imprisonment could have been found within the limits of the then United States, or where his banishment from his family would have been more complete. It seems clearly to have been the purpose of the Federal authorities to place him beyond the reach of the processes of the civil courts.

Now is shown forth the nobility of his character. He bears his misfortunes, as is testified by the distinguished attorney who

4

defended him, with "Christian fortitude." He is conscious of his innocence, knows his punishment to be unjust, yet believes that justice will ultimately triumph. Hope was still active and alluring. His anxiety was something apparently apart from himself and his personal interests and welfare, but existed solely on account of his wife and children. In his letter, written on shipboard when he was being carried to the place where he was to endure the severest privations as a prisoner, probably for life, he tells his wife "not to give up hope—take care of the little ones." All through his letters there breathes the spirit of true Christian heroism. His faith in the goodness and wisdom of a Supreme Power seems never to have been shaken. True, as time passed on and the rigors of his imprisonment were intensified rather than relaxed, and he realized more acutely the hardships of his unjust punishment, he showed occasionally a tendency toward misanthropy. He came to doubt both the gratitude and justice of man, but never appears to have doubted the goodness of God.

In a letter written on Christmas Day, 1865, to his wife, he says: "What have I done to bring so much trouble upon myself and family? The answer from my inmost heart—nothing. I am consoled to know that the greatest saints were the most persecuted and the greatest sufferers, although far be it from classing myself with those chosen friends of God. * * * I have endeavored to the best of my ability to lead as spotless and sinless a life as in my power." Again, on January 1, 1866, he writes to his wife: "I can stand anything but the thought of your dependent position; the ills and privations consequent pierce my heart as a dagger."

As time passed on and he was again and again disappointed in his hopes of an early release, his desire to again be with his family becomes more intense, until it seems to dominate his every thought. In one of his letters to his wife he says: "I have but one desire, namely: to be with you, and to see our dear little children properly trained and educated." One will therefore hesitate to blame him, when the harshness and injustice of his imprisonment are considered, for making an effort to escape. This he did in the latter part of the year 1865, although he had positively declared in the earlier months of his incarceration, his purpose not to try to escape, as any effort on his part to do so might seem to indicate a consciousness of guilt. The effort, however, when made was abortive, and resulted in his being subjected to greater hardship of treatment in his imprisonment than he had hitherto endured. He stated, after his release from prison, that he had intended to escape and reach some point where the writ of *habeas corpus* was in force and available and then surrender himself to the authorities, an order that the writ might be invoked in his behalf and the legality of his trial and sentence by the military court tested.

After his unsuccessful effort to escape he seems to have been subjected to cruelties almost beyond the power of human endurance. Yet we find him, during the visitation of the dreaded yellow fever to the island, ready and willing to sacrifice his life for the relief of his persecutors. Rarely has there been shown in the life of any man greater heroism and self-abnegation than that shown by Dr. Mudd in his course while the fever prevailed among the soldiers who held him in captivity. To minister to them as he did was an exhibition of magnanimity and self-sacrifice worthy of the highest praise that can be ascribed to human conduct. Yet he was to show that he had reached a loftier plane of human excellence than that evidenced by his mere ministrations to the stricken yellow fever sufferers. He had through months of wearying, harassing imprisonment, longed to get beyond his prison walls. The time came when nearly every man of the garrison was helpless from fever, when he could have Left the island, with no man to hinder him. Yet hear what he says: "By the hand of Providence my fetters have been broken, yet I run not, preferring to share the fate of those around me and to lend what aid in my power to breaking down the burning fever, overcoming the agonizing delirium, and giving all the hope and encouragement possible to the death-stricken victims of the pestilence." In this quotation from a letter to his brother-in-law, dated October 1, 1867, and intended not for public perusal, Dr. Mudd's character stands forth as a living exemplification of the loftiest Christian charity. When we find that only a little time had elapsed after he had written this letter, as he states in a letter dated

December 7, 1867, he was still in chains, under rigorous guard and required to do menial labor, can any one censure him for indulging in some harshness of expression concerning those responsible for his misfortunes?

Nor can one deny to his wife the highest measure of praise for her noble, womanly conduct during all the trying ordeals through which she was required to pass. Her trials will never be known save to herself and the God in whom she unfalteringly trusted. We are given some idea of the depth of her suffering, of the laceration of her woman's heart, in her letter of January 28, 1866, to President Johnson. In "Rachel mourning for her children and would not be comforted," no lower note of human anguish is sounded than that touched in the heart of this wife and mother, as shown in this appeal for justice to her husband and the father of her little children. Few can read this letter without emotion; none can read it without a measure of profound sympathy, and a yet larger measure of admiration, for the faithful woman who wrote it.

Through all the period of her husband's incarceration, with resources exhausted in his defense, dependent for the maintenance of herself and her children on the product of a farm for the tilling of which it was almost impossible to procure labor, with anxieties almost innumerable pressing upon her, she bravely struggled on, persistently striving to secure her husband's release, and writing cheering words to him, bidding him hope. To women such as she, for their example alone, the world owes a debt of gratitude not easily cancelled.

In conclusion—just forty-one years have elapsed since the death of President Lincoln; the sectional bitterness engendered by the civil war has passed away; we have in truth a reunited country; North and South alike honor the name of Lincoln. Has not the time arrived to fully vindicate the name of Dr. Samuel A. Mudd, who was so cruelly and unjustly called upon to suffer—and to remove from that name even the faintest shadow of doubt that may exist regarding his complicity in the great crime committed in Ford's Theater, in Washington, forty-one years ago?

D. ELDRIDGE MONROE.

BALTIMORE, *April 14, 1906.*

INTRODUCTION

Abraham Lincoln, President of the United States, while attending a play in Ford's Theater in Washington, on the evening of the fourteenth of April, 1865, was fatally shot by John Wilkes Booth. In jumping from the box in the theater, occupied by the President, and in which the infamous act was committed, to the stage, Booth fractured a bone in his leg. He nevertheless escaped through a rear entrance to the theater, and mounting a horse, which he had provided should be kept in readiness, escaped by way of the bridge across the Eastern Branch of the Potomac River, into southern Maryland. With his features disguised, and in company with David E. Herold, he reached the residence of Doctor Samuel A. Mudd, in Charles County, thirty miles south of Washington, about 4 o'clock on the morning after the assassination. Dr. Mudd set the broken bone in Booth's leg. As will appear by the following chapters neither Dr. Mudd nor any member of his family knew of Booth's identity. Both he and Herold gave assumed names. They left about 2 o'clock of the same day, and ultimately succeeded in crossing the Potomac into Virginia. They were discovered in a barn on the farm of a man named Garrett, near Port Royal, Virginia, on the morning of Wednesday, April 26, 1865. United States officers and soldiers surrounded the building. Herold surrendered. Booth refused to surrender. The barn was then set on fire. Booth approached the door of the barn, as the flames surrounded him, and was shot and killed by Sergeant Corbett.

In addition to David E. Herold, George A. Atzerodt, Mrs. Mary E. Surratt, Lewis Payne, Samuel Arnold, Michael O'Loughlin, Edward Spangler, and Dr. Samuel A. Mudd were subsequently arrested charged with complicity in the crime of assassinating the President, "and the attempted assassination of the Honorable William H. Seward, Secretary of State, and in an alleged conspiracy to assassinate other officers of the Federal Government at Washington." By an order issued by President Johnson, dated May 1, 1865, the Adjutant-General was "directed to detail nine competent military officers to serve as a Commission for the trial of the accused." It was strenuously contended, by many of the most eminent lawyers of the country, that the civil courts alone had jurisdiction to try the accused, and that their trial by the Military Commission was illegal.

The following officers were detailed on the Commission: Maj.-Gen. David Hunter, U. S. V.; Maj.-Gen. Lew Wallace [later famous for writing the novel *Ben Hur*], U. S. V.; Brevet Maj.-Gen. August V. Kautz, U. S. V.; Brig.-Gen. Alvin P. Howe, U. S. V.; Brig.-Gen. Robert S. Foster, U. S. V.; Brevet Brig.-Gen. James A. Ekin, U. S. V.; Brig.-Gen. T. M. Harris, U. S. V.; Brevet Col. C. H. Tompkins, U. S. V.; Lieut.-Col. David R. Clendenin, Eighth Illinois Cavalry. Brig.-Gen. Joseph Holt was Judge-Advocate and Recorder of the Commission, assisted by Judge-Advocates Burnett and Bingham. The Commission held its sittings in a room in the old Arsenal Building, in Washington. The Commission met May 9, 1865, but adjourned to the loth, to enable the accused to employ counsel.

The trial began on the latter date, and ended on the 30th day of June, 1865, when the Commission announced its decision. Mrs. Mary E. Surratt, David E. Herold, George A. Atzerodt, and Lewis Payne were declared to be guilty, and sentenced to be executed July 7, 1865, between the hours of 10 o'clock A. M and 2 o'clock P. M. Dr. Samuel A. Mudd, Samuel Arnold, and Michael O'Loughlin were declared to be guilty, and were sentenced to be confined for life, at hard labor, in the penitentiary at Albany, New York. Edward Spangler was declared to be guilty, in a lesser degree, and sentenced to be confined in the penitentiary at Albany, at hard labor, for a term of six years. The penitentiary sentences were subsequently modified, by changing the place of imprisonment from Albany to Fort Jefferson, on the Dry Tortugas Island, Florida. President Johnson approved the findings of the Commission on the 5th day of July, 1865.

On the 7th day of July, 1865, Mrs. Surratt, Herold, Atzerodt and Payne were executed by hanging. Strenuous efforts were made to save the life of Mrs. Surratt, but without avail. A writ of *habeas corpus* was issued in her behalf, by Judge Wylie of the Supreme

Bench of the District of Columbia, on the application of her legal advisers, returnable at ten o'clock on the morning set for her execution. The military authorities, however, refused to surrender her. The story of the imprisonment of Dr. Mudd, and incidentally that of Arnold, Spangler, and O'Loughlin, is told in the following chapters. Much information in relation to the incidents connected with, and growing out of, the assassination of President Lincoln, and not heretofore published, is also given.

BIRTHPLACE AND CHILDHOOD

Dr. Samuel Alexander Mudd, known in history as one of the "Lincoln conspirators," was born on a large plantation in Charles County, Maryland, nearly equidistant five miles between the villages of Waldorf and Bryantown, fifteen miles from the county seat, La Plata, and twenty-five miles from Washington. His father, Henry Low Mudd, was a wealthy planter and slave owner. His estate, for more than a mile, extended along the "Old Mill Swamp," gradually rising on the east side of a stream known as the Sakiah. The surface of the land increased in elevation from the "Swamp" until, with a steep upward sweep, it ascends to a high hill, sloping toward the north and south, the summit crowned with locusts and wide-spreading oaks; from these it derived the name it bears, "Oak Hill."

On the top of the hill was built the old homestead. In architecture it was not different from other houses in the vicinity. Wide, old-fashioned halls and spacious rooms, substantially furnished, formed a comfortable abode and place of entertainment for the family and visiting guests. At the north wing of the house was the schoolroom, where many lessons were learned, perhaps many childish tears were shed, and many airy castles were built never to be realized. Above this was the home chapel. Bed chambers occupied the remainder of the second floor.

Viewed from the nearest point in the valley, it presented in appearance a large structure without any architecturally definite shape. Outside it looked well enough. It seemed to the eye roomy and hospitable. A large lawn, sloping to the public road, was dotted with shrubbery, which contrasted prettily with the white background formed by the painted weatherboarding of the house.

Here on December 20, 1833, was born Dr. Samuel A. Mudd, who in after years was destined to involuntarily play so conspicuous a part in one of the most important events in the nation's history. Amid these rural scenes he passed his infancy and childhood. Even from his earliest years, he was always thoughtful of others, always distinguished for his gentleness and kindness. When attending the public school, which he began to do when a little boy of seven years of age, such was his uniform courtesy and consideration for others that the companions of his early childhood remained his friends for life.

After a year or two in the public school, his father secured a governess for the instruction of his children, and he then continued his studies at home with his sisters. Here under the tuition of Miss Peterson, the governess, he made rapid progress in his studies. At the age of about fourteen years he entered St. John's College, in Frederick City, Maryland, where he spent two years. He then entered Georgetown College, in the District of Columbia, where he completed his collegiate course. He was particularly interested in the study of languages and became proficient in Greek, Latin, and French; and was also a musician of recognized ability, performing with skill on the violin, piano, flute and other instruments. After leaving Georgetown College he studied medicine and surgery in the University of Maryland, Baltimore, where he graduated in March, 1856. During his last year at the University he practiced in the hospital attached to that institution, and in recognition of his services received from the faculty a complimentary certificate of merit at the time he received his diploma.

Again, his college life ended, we find him in his old home, amid the friends and scenes of his childhood. Here on his father's estate may have been seen more than a hundred slaves, who made the evenings merry with song, and with banjo and violin accompaniment. Scattered over various sections of the farm may also have been seen the "quarters" of these humble colored folk, who were always treated with the kindest consideration by their master and mistress, and who would say of these white friends, after they had passed from earth, "God bless my old Marse and Miss; I hope dey is in heaven." Here my father began his public life as a practicing physician; always keeping his old friends by his loyalty and uprightness, and continuously adding to the list some new ones. It is not too much to say, nor should it be charged to filial partiality, that to know him was in truth to love him. He was the friend of the needy, the consoler and comforter of those in distress and trouble.

He never paused to consider whether those needing his ministrations could or could not remunerate him. He gave freely of his best to all alike.

About eighteen months after he established himself in practice he married Miss Sarah Frances Dyer, whom he always in after years, as will appear by his letters, addressed as "Frank," his schoolmate and childhood's love, having been engaged to her four years. At the time they became engaged she had just graduated from the Visitation Convent, Frederick City, Maryland. Cardinal Bodeni, the first delegate sent to the church by the Pope of Rome, conferred on her the graduating honors. It may be of some interest to the young people of this day to learn how so important a matter as the matrimonial engagement was arranged at that time. There is perhaps little variation between the method of engagement at that time and that of the present. My mother, after my earnest solicitation to learn more of this important event, at last consented to say, "There was nothing romantic in our little love affair. I was only seventeen and Sam eighteen years of age, so it was impossible to think of getting married just then. When Sam asked me, 'Frank, are you going to marry me?' answered, 'Yes, when you have graduated in medicine, established a practice for yourself, and I have had my fun out, then I'll marry you. You need not get jealous; I vow I will never marry anyone else.' This seems to have settled matters, and on the 26th of November, 1857, they were married in her home, which was only a few miles distant from where my father then lived. During the two years following they resided at the home where they were married, with her elder brother, Mr. Jere Dyer, who was a bachelor, and whose name appears frequently in the succeeding chapters. After this they moved into their own home, which my mother still occupies. From this to the time of the Civil War life moved on smoothly, she being busy with her household duties and the care of her little ones, and he being fully occupied in attending to his practice and to the farm.

While Maryland never seceded from the Union, the war brought much distress and sorrow to many homes and hearts within her borders. Her people, especially in the southern part of the State, where the number of slaves was large, were subjected to many of the inconveniences and hardships suffered by the people in the States of the Confederacy. The negroes, very soon after the war commenced, became imbued with the idea of freedom, and as this idea gained stronger hold in their minds their efficiency as servants diminished.* When President Lincoln issued the Emancipation Proclamation on January 1, 1863, declaring the freedom of the slaves in the States that had seceded, the moral effect on the negroes in Maryland was such that they were of little value to their owners. Their demoralization as laborers was almost complete. Subsequently, when slavery was abolished in the State by constitutional provision, they almost uniformly refused to work for their former owners, even for highly remunerative wages. Of course, in my father's home, there were experienced these conditions. He had to pay twice the value of their services to the emancipated colored people in order to make even a partial crop, or to retain them as servants about his dwelling.

*Should anyone find this amazing? Working for another in slavery is hardly an inducement to ambition.—Ed., 2015

This was the state of affairs on my father's farm at the time Booth fired the fatal shot, in Ford's Theater, by which the life of the President was destroyed. The fact that these conditions did exist made it much harder for my father to bear his imprisonment. He was devoted to his family. He knew that my mother would find it to be almost impossible to obtain labor to cultivate the farm. He was at all times, during his long imprisonment, burdened, indeed almost tortured, by the fear that she and the children might come to want.

MY MOTHER'S STATEMENT

The following very full statement was written by my mother:

The first time I ever saw John Wilkes Booth was in November, 1864. My husband went to Bryantown Church, and was introduced to Booth by John Thompson, an old friend from Baltimore, who asked my husband if he knew of any one who had a good riding-horse for sale; to which he replied, "My next neighbor has one." After this they made arrangements for Booth to come up to our home that evening to see about buying this horse. There was company in the house and supper was just over, when my husband came in and asked me to prepare for a stranger. My husband came in with the stranger and made the necessary introductions. The conversation was on general topics. Nothing relative to the Administration or the war was spoken of by any one present. After supper, Booth joined the visitors and remained in general conversation until bedtime, which was about 9.30 o'clock. I did not see Booth again until at the breakfast table the next morning.

After breakfast the horses were ordered, Booth tied his at the gate, and my husband threw the bridle rein of his horse over his arm and walked along with Booth across the field to Squire George Gardiner's. Booth soon returned, came in and got his overcoat which he had thrown over the back of a chair in the parlor, said good-by, and rode away. The horse he purchased was sent to him at Bryantown that evening. After he had gone I went to the parlor to put things in order. Lying on the floor by the chair that had held his overcoat was a letter, not enclosed in an envelope, that had fallen from his pocket. I picked it up and almost involuntarily glanced at the headlines. These lines convinced me that some poor man's home had been wrecked by the handsome face and wily ways of Booth. The letter was from New York; but I did not look at the name of the writer, and I do not know to this day who she was. I laid it on the table, hoping to be able to find some means of returning it to him. As he never returned, I subsequently threw it in the fire.

About 4 A. M on the 15th of April, 1865, I heard a rap on the door, and as my husband was not feeling well he asked me if I would not go and see who it was. I replied, "I would rather you would go and see for yourself." He arose and went to the door in his night clothes. I heard some one talking in the hall, and footsteps as they passed into the parlor. My husband returned and told me there was a man out there with his leg broken. He asked me to tear some strips for bandages. I did so. Afterward I heard my husband and a third man assisting the injured man up-stairs. The Doctor returned, and went to bed himself. At 6 o'clock I arose, called the servants to get breakfast, and at 7 waked my husband. He sent a servant to tell the man who called himself "Tyson" (and who afterward proved to be Herold) to come to breakfast. I then prepared breakfast for the sick man, put it on a tray, and sent it to his room by a servant; told her to place it on the table by his bed and come down: Tyson and my husband then came to the table, and while at breakfast Tyson asked the Doctor if he knew many persons in the lower part of the county near the river. To which he replied in the negative. Tyson spoke of a good many families that he knew. The Doctor knew some of the parties spoken of, others he did not know. This led me to ask Tyson, "Are you a resident of the county?" He replied, "No, ma'am, but I have been frolicking around for five or six months." He looked so boyish that I remarked, "All play and no work makes Jack a bad boy. Your father ought to make you go to work." He answered me, "My father is dead, and I am ahead of the old lady."

At this time he seemed not to have a care in the world. Turning to my husband he asked the distance to the river. The Doctor replied, "About eighteen or twenty miles." Tyson then remarked, "We are on our way to the river; which is the nearest road we could take?" There was a road leading across the Sakiah which my husband usually took in attending to his practice, and as it was the shortest way, told him of it. Afterward I saw the Doctor standing in the back yard pointing across the swamp. Tyson then came into the house and went up-stairs, I presume to sleep. I heard no more from either of the strangers till dinner. When the doctor returned to dinner Tyson came down, and I sent the servant up to the sick man's room with his dinner. The servant returned and brought down the dinner and breakfast dishes, and I found he had not eaten anything during the day.

At dinner Tyson asked the Doctor if he thought he could procure a carriage in the neighborhood to carry his friend away. My husband replied, "I am going to Bryantown to get the mail and see some sick, and if you will ride along with me to the village, perhaps you can get a carriage there." As they were leaving the house I asked my husband if I could go up and see the sick man. "Yes, certainly you can," he replied. As he had taken nothing to eat during the day, I took up to his room some cake, a couple of oranges, and some wine on a tray. I placed the tray on the table by the bed, asked him how he was feeling and if I could do anything for him. His reply was, "My back hurts me dreadfully. I must have hurt it when the horse fell and broke my leg." I asked him if he would take the cake and wine; he refused. He then wished to know if the Doctor had any brandy. I told him no, but that he had some good whiskey, and offered to get him some, but he declined. I remarked, "I guess you think I have very little hospitality; you have been sick all day and I have not been up to see you;" and again asked if I could do anything for him, to which he did not reply—his face being all the time turned to the wall. I then left the room.

I went down to the kitchen, where the servants were preparing for the "Easter Sunday dinner." After a short while Tyson rapped from the outside on the kitchen window. I went to the front door, opened it, and asked if he succeeded in procuring a carriage. He replied, "No, ma'am; we stopped over at the Doctor's father's and asked for his carriage, but tomorrow being Easter Sunday, his family had to go to church, and he could not spare it. I then rode some distance down the road with the Doctor, and then concluded to return and try the horses."

He went up-stairs. I heard them moving around the room and in a short time they came down, the man calling himself Tyler (who afterward proved to be Booth) hobbling on a stick which our old gardener, Mr. John Best, an Englishman, had sent up to him at the

18

request of Tyson. When they came down I was standing in the hall at the foot of the stairs. Tyler wore heavy whiskers; these proved to be false, and became partially detached as he came down the stairs. So much of his face as could be seen presented a picture of agony. I told Tyson if he must go to do so, but to please leave his friend here, we would take care of him, although the discovery of the false whiskers aroused my suspicions. Tyson's reply was, "If he suffers much we won't go far. I will take him to my lady-love's, not far from here." They passed out of the door. Tyson helped Tyler to get on his horse, then mounted his own horse and they rode away. I did not see either of them after this.

About an hour afterward my husband returned and told me of the assassination of the President, and that there were soldiers in Bryantown looking for the assassin. A short while after this he remarked, "Frank, those men were suspicious characters. I will go to Bryantown and tell the officers." I agreed with him as to the suspicious character of the men, and told him about the false whiskers, but begged him not to go—I was afraid to remain in the house without him; and as the next day was Sunday, asked him to send word to the soldiers from church, which he did, Dr. George D. Mudd, of Bryantown, being the messenger. He heard no further from them, and on Monday went to see his sick patients. Tuesday he did the same thing, going out in the morning and returning about twelve o'clock. In the afternoon Dr. George Mudd came to the house with some soldiers and asked a description of the two men.

My husband, in my presence, gave them all the information he could. They then left and returned on Friday, when there was another conversation in the hall. My husband told them there was a boot, which he had cut from the man's leg, found in the room after he left, and went up-stairs to get it. The servant while cleaning the room had thrown it under the bed. My husband did not find the boot, and I sent Martha, the house-girl, to get it for him. He brought down the boot, and gave it to the officer in command, who took it and examined it. On the inside was written, "J. Wilkes." One of them said, "A part of the name has been effaced"; so I asked if I could see it. The officer held it in his hand while I looked at it. Then I remarked, "No, that is only a dash, there was no other name there." When they left they required my husband to go with them to Bryantown. I do not know what happened at Bryantown, but that night my husband came home, and was requested to return the next morning, which he did. Again he returned in the evening. The next day, being Sunday, he went to church. On Monday an officer with three soldiers came to our house. They had two colored men from the farm of the Doctor's father, who were riding two horses also taken from his father's place.

Then they called for two hired hands on our farm, made them get horses from the stable; one of them saddled the Doctor's horse, and then they all left for Washington. When the officer saw how grieved I was (I am sorry I do not know his name, for he showed some heart and feeling), he returned to the house and said to me, "Do not grieve and fret that way, I'll see that your husband soon returns to you"; but it was four long years before he saw his home. About a week after his departure from home I received the following brief note from him:

"Carroll Prison, April 29, 1865.

"My dearest Frank:

"I am very well. Hope you and the children are enjoying a like blessing. Try and get some one to plant our crop. It is very uncertain what time I shall be released from here. Hire hands at the prices they demand. Urge them on all you can and make them work.

"I am truly in hopes my stay here will be short, when I can return again to your fond embrace and our little children."

A few days later a company of soldiers were stationed on our farm. They burned the fences, destroyed the wheat and tobacco crops; pulled the boards off the corn-house, so that the corn fell out on the ground, and all the corn that the horses could not eat was trampled under their hoofs in such a way as to render it unfit for use. The meat-house was broken open and the meat taken out. All that they could not eat was left scattered on the hillside where they had pitched their camps. A day or so after their arrival my husband's sister came over to see me. She wanted some garden seeds, and asked me to go down with her to the old gardener, Mr. John Best, to get them for her. When we went out no soldiers were in sight. We carried a basket, and the old man tied up some seeds in packages, put them in the basket, and then asked us to go to see his garden. A few moments after we entered the garden we were surrounded by soldiers. One officer came over and demanded to know what we had in the basket. The little packages of seeds were unwrapped, the contents examined. With a crest-fallen look he remarked, "I thought you were carrying food to Booth."

A couple of days after this a negro regiment from Popes Creek came up the Sakiah Swamp in search of Booth. When they were opposite the house they turned and entered the valley leading up the hill at the back of the house. They passed around the house, which was guarded by two young men, left by William P. Wood, keeper of the old Capitol Prison in

Washington. These young men were instructed to shoot any one who dared to enter the yard. The negro regiment did not stop to search the house or its surroundings. Mr. Wood and two other detectives had their headquarters in the house, and went out during the day in search of Booth, returning at night. One night Mr. Wood did not return, and the officers in command of the troops on the farm placed a guard around the house and forbade any one leaving or entering the house. I was alone with four little children and a colored woman.

Some of the soldiers came around the house and began talking impudently to the colored woman. I called her in, locked the door, and drew down the curtains, not knowing whether I would be dead or alive the next morning. I lighted the lamp in the dining-room, put the children to bed, and with the colored woman sat there till two o'clock in the morning. At this time I heard a rap at the door, and a familiar voice call me. It was a cousin of mine, Sylvester Mudd, who had risked his life by coming within the lines, knowing I was alone. I could not have been more glad to see an angel from heaven than I was to see him. The next day the information came that Booth and

Herold had been captured. The bugle was sounded, the roll called, and the soldiers left on their march to Washington.

For a little while there was a lull in the storm. My husband, previous to his trial, was placed in the old Carroll Prison in Washington with the others, none of whom he had ever seen before except Herold; and the only time he had ever seen him was when he came to our house with Booth on the morning after the assassination of the President.

I engaged General Ewing to defend my husband. He was not only a lawyer of ability, but had distinguished himself for bravery in the Union army during the war. In this case he proved himself not only a lawyer of merit, but a true friend during my husband's trial and imprisonment. Whenever he saw the least shadow of hope, he would write me nice friendly and cheering letters, which I sometimes think must have kept me from despair.

During the trial, which commenced on May 10, 1865, the Doctor's friends and myself were shocked and surprised at the base and false testimony permitted to be given against him. Daniel Thomas, one of the leading witnesses for the prosecution, was an outcast from his home. His brother swore he would not believe him on his oath. Years afterward he was arrested and convicted on the charge of the commission of pension frauds, and died in the penitentiary. His reason for giving the false evidence was to secure a part of the large reward offered by the Government for the capture and conviction of Booth and those thought to be his accomplices. Norton, Evans, a number of the negroes, and several others, also swore notoriously false.

With all this false testimony his life was spared, but he was sentenced to a life imprisonment on a lonely, dreary island in mid-ocean. Several times during the trial I had occasion to go to Washington. On more than one of these occasions, while I was at General Ewing's office, I met Mrs. Browning, wife of Secretary of Interior Browning, a member of President Johnson's Cabinet. One day she told me that her husband and herself took breakfast at a restaurant in Washington, where General Lew Wallace, a member of

22

the Military Commission that condemned my husband, also breakfasted. In the course of the conversation she had with General Wallace at the breakfast table he remarked, "If Booth had not broken his leg, we would never have heard the name of Dr. Mudd." Mrs. -Browning said to him, "Why don't you then send Dr. Mudd home to his wife and children?" General Wallace then replied, "The deed is done; somebody must suffer for it, and he may as well suffer as anybody else." In order to be perfectly fair, my daughter wrote to Mrs. Wallace as to the correctness of this statement, and received the following note in reply:

"Crawfordsville, Ind., September 18, 1905.

"Dear Miss Mudd:

"Mrs. Wallace says she has no remembrance of hearing General Wallace say anything about Dr. Mudd that was like the sentence you quote.

"Truly yours,

"H. WALLACE, *Secretary.*"

A few days after my return from Washington, after the date of this conversation with Mrs. Browning, I saw an ambulance drive up to the house. Lieutenant Baker and Daniel Thomas got out of it and came in. Lieutenant Baker said, "Mrs. Mudd, we came to take you to Washington. I presume you know Daniel Thomas." I replied in the presence of both, "Knowing Mr. Thomas as I do, and not knowing you, I must look upon you as a gentleman; and if I must go to Washington, it will be under your protection and not that of Daniel Thomas." I then told Lieutenant Baker that my brother, Jere Dyer, would visit my home, from Baltimore, that evening, and that I would go to Washington the next day with my brother if that would be satisfactory. He replied, "I will trust you." They then left.

That evening my brother came, and the next day we took the stage for Washington, there being no railroad in this portion of the State at that time. When the stage arrived at Capitol Hill, Washington, I heard the clanking of swords, and an officer came up to the stage and asked if Mrs. Mudd was there. My brother answered, "Yes." The officer then called a carriage, and my brother and myself were driven to General Baker's office. In a few moments after our arrival there, the General, who was a brother of the lieutenant who came with Thomas to my home, entered the room and spoke to both of us, then left, I presume to consult with some one else. When he returned he told me to go to a hotel and send the hotel bill to him. I asked him if I could not go to the home of my cousin, Mr. Alexander Clark. To which he replied, "Yes, but return here to-morrow morning at ten o'clock."

The next morning, at the hour mentioned, I went to General Baker's office, and was not kept waiting many minutes before he came in. I told him if there was any information I could give him, please to let me get through as soon as possible, as I had left four little children at home, and no responsible person to take care of them. Without asking me a question he remarked, "Mrs. Mudd, stay over till two o'clock, and if I do not send for you, you can go home." No messenger came, and my brother hired a carriage and brought me home.

SWORN STATEMENT OF DR. SAMUEL A. MUDD

MY MOTHER (CON'T) I only saw my husband once after he was taken from home, and that was after his trial. I went to Washington, procured a pass from the War Department, and went to the old Arsenal. This was the day before the hanging of Mrs. Surratt, Herold, Atzerodt, and Payne. The workmen were then building, in the yard below, the scaffold on which they were to be hung. General Dana sent a messenger up to the second floor with me, and in a few moments my husband was brought from a cell. He was in his shirt sleeves and wore a pair of carpet slippers without socks. He said one of the guards told him who was to be hung, and what his sentence was. There were several guards in the room where we were. I noticed that his ankle was sore, and I asked if it was caused by the chains he had to wear. He paused a few moments, then answered, hesitatingly, as though afraid to say otherwise, in presence of the guards, "No." As I was leaving the Arsenal I met a poor girl who was weeping bitterly, and was told it was Anna Surratt, who had returned from the White House, where she went to plead for the life of her mother, but had been refused admittance to the President.

I came home, and only a few days later read in the papers that Spangler, Arnold, O'Laughlin and my husband were on their way to the Dry Tortugas. Two days after this I received a letter from the Doctor, which was written on board the ship and mailed at Charleston, where a short stop was made. In this letter he asked me not to give up hope; to take care of the little ones and at some future day he would be at home with us. This seemed to give me courage, and I began to work with renewed efforts to try to secure his release.

About the 2d of August I went to Washington to see Secretary of War Stanton, and asked him if I could not send my husband money and clothes to make him comfortable. He gazed at me in silence for a few moments, then said, "As long as Dr. Mudd is in prison the Government will furnish him with what it thinks necessary for him to have, and he can have no communication whatsoever with the outside world." I turned my back and walked out, not even saying good morning. In a short while I received the following letter from

25

Secretary Stanton, written by E. D. Townsend, Assistant Adjutant-General:

"War Department,

"Adjutant-General's Office, "Washington, Sept. 30, 1865.

"Mrs. Dr. Mudd,

"Bryantown, Charles County, Md.

"Madam: Your application of the 2d of August to know if you would be allowed to communicate with your husband, Dr. Mudd, and if so by what means, and whether you are at liberty to send to him clothing and articles of comfort and money, from home, has been considered by the Secretary of War.

"Dr. Mudd will be permitted to receive communications from you, if enclosed, unsealed, to the Adjutant-General of the Army at Washington. The Government provides suitable clothing and all necessary subsistence in such cases, and neither clothing nor money will be allowed to be furnished him.

"I am, Madam, very respectfully "Your obedient servant,

"E. D. Townsend,

"Assistant Adjutant General."

The following is a sworn statement written by my husband while he was a prisoner in Fort Jefferson, and which he was not permitted by the authorities to have published. He sent it to me in a letter about the 1st of October, 1865. This statement was made to correct erroneous statements, which had appeared in the public press, allegedly quoting my husband.

August 28, 1865.

1st. That I confessed to having known Booth while in my house; was afraid to give information of the fact, fearing to endanger my life, or made use of any language in that connection—I positively and emphatically declare to be notoriously false.

26

2d. That I was satisfied and willingly acquiesced in the wisdom and decision of the Military Commission who tried me, is again notoriously erroneous and false. On the contrary I charged it (the Commission) with irregularity, injustice, usurpation, and illegality. I confess to being animated at the time but have no recollection of having apologized.

3d. I did confess to a casual or accidental meeting with Booth in front of one of the hotels on Pennsylvania avenue, Washington, D. C., on the 23d of December, 1864, and not on the 15th of January, 1865, as testified to by Weichman. Booth, on that occasion, desired me to give him an introduction to Surratt, from whom he said he wished to obtain a knowledge of the country around Washington, in order to be able to select a good locality for a country residence. He had the number, street, and name of John Surratt, written on a card, saying, to comply with his request would not detain me over five minutes. (At the time I was not aware that Surratt was a resident of Washington.) I declined at first, stating I was with a relative and friend from the country and was expecting some friends over from Baltimore, who intended going down with me to spend Christmas, and was by appointment expected to be at the Pennsylvania House by a certain hour—eight o'clock. We started down one street, and then up another, and had not gone far before we met Surratt and Weichman.

Introductions took place, and we turned back in the direction of the hotel. Arriving there, Booth insisted on our going to his room and taking something to drink with him, which I declined for reasons above mentioned; but finding that Weichman and Surratt were disposed to accept—I yielded, remarking, I could not remain many minutes. After arriving in the room, I took the first opportunity presented to apologize to Surratt for having introduced to him Booth—a man I knew so little concerning. This conversation took place in the passage in front of the room and was not over three minutes in duration. Whilst Surratt and myself were in the hall, Booth and Weichman were sitting on the sofa in a corner of the room looking over some Congressional documents. Surratt and myself returned and resumed our former seats (after taking drinks

27

ordered), around a center table, which stood midway the room and distant seven or eight feet from Booth and Weichman. Booth remarked that he had been down in the country a few days before, and said he had not yet recovered from the fatigue. Afterward he said he had been down in Charles County, and had made me an offer for the purchase of my land, which I confirmed by an affirmative answer; and he further remarked that on his way up he lost his way and rode several miles off the track. When he said this he left his seat and came over and took a seat immediately by Surratt; taking from his pocket an old letter, he began to draw lines, in order to ascertain from Surratt the location and description of the roads. I was a mere looker on. The conversation that took place could be distinctly heard to any part of the room by any one paying attention. There was nothing secret to my knowledge that took place, with the exception of the conversation of Surratt and myself, which I have before mentioned. I had no secret conversation with Booth, nor with Booth and Surratt together, as testified to by Weichman. I never volunteered any statement of Booth having made me an offer for the purchase of my land, but made an affirmative response only to what Booth said in that connection.

Booth's visit in November, 1864, to Charles County was for the purpose, as expressed by himself, to purchase land and horses; he was inquisitive concerning the political sentiments of the people, inquiring about the contraband trade that existed between the North and South, and wished to be informed about the roads bordering on the Potomac, which I declined doing. He spoke of his being an actor and having two other brothers, who also were actors. He spoke of Junius Brutus as being a good Republican. He said they were largely engaged in the oil business, and gave me a lengthy description of the theory of oil and the process of boring, etc. He said he had a younger brother in California. These and many minor matters spoken of caused me to suspect him to be a Government detective and to advise Surratt regarding him.

We were together in Booth's room about fifteen minutes, after which, at my invitation, they walked up to the Pennsylvania House, where the conversation that ensued between Weichman and myself as testified to by him is in the main correct—only that he, of the two, appeared the better Southern man, and undertook to give me facts from his office to substantiate his statements and opinions. This was but a short time after the defeat of Hood in Tennessee. The papers stated that over nine thousand prisoners had been taken, and that the whole of Hood's army was demoralized and falling back, and there was every prospect of his whole army being either captured or destroyed. To this Weichman replied that only four thousand prisoners had been ordered to be provided for by the Commissary-General, and that he was far from believing the defeat of Hood so disastrous. I spoke with sincerity, and said it was a blow from which the South never would be able to recover; and that the whole South then laid at the mercy of Sherman. Weichman seemed, whilst on the stand, to be disposed to give what he believed a truthful statement. I am in hopes the above will refresh his memory, and he will do me the justice, though late, to correct his erroneous testimony.

To recapitulate—I made use of no such statement as reported by the "Washington Correspondent of the *New York Times,"* only in the sense and meaning as testified to by Dr. George D. Mudd, and as either misunderstood or misrepresented by Colonel Wells and others before the Commission.

I never saw Mrs. Surratt in my life to my knowledge previous to the assassination, and then only through her veil. I never saw Arnold, O'Loughlin, Atzerodt, Payne alias Powel, or Spangler—or ever heard their names mentioned previous to the assassination of the President. I never saw or heard of Booth after the 23d of December, 1864, until after the assassination, and then he was in disguise. I did not know Booth whilst in my house, nor did I know Herold; neither of whom made himself known to me. And I further declare they did not make known to me their true destination before I left the house. They inquired the way to many places and desired particularly to go to the Rev. Mr. Wilmer's.

I gave a full description of the two parties (whom I represented as suspicious) to Lieutenant Lovett and three other officers, on the Tuesday after the assassination. I gave a description of one horse—

the other I never took any notice of, and do not know to this day the color or appearance. Neither Booth's nor Herold's name was mentioned in connection with the assassination, nor was there any name mentioned on the Tuesday after the assassination, nor was there any name mentioned in connection with the assassination, nor was there any photograph exhibited of any one implicated in the infamous deed. I was merely called upon to give a description of the men and horses and the places they inquired. The evidence of the four detectives—Lovett, Gavacan, Lloyd, and Williams—conflict (unintentionally) vitally on this point; they evidently prove and disprove the fact as they have done in every instance affecting my interest, or upon points in which my welfare was at issue. Some swore that the photograph of Booth was exhibited on Tuesday, which was false. I do not advert to the false testimony; it is evident to the reader, and bears the impress of foul play and persecution somewhere—it may be owing to the thirst after the enormous reward offered by the Government, or a false idea for notoriety. Evans and Norton evidently swore falsely and perjured themselves. Daniel I. Thomas was bought by the detectives--likewise the negroes who swore against me. The court certainly must have seen that a great deal of the testimony was false and incompetent—upon this I charge them with injustice, etc.

Reverend Evans and Norton—I never saw nor heard their names in my life. I never knew, nor have I any knowledge whatsoever, of John Surratt ever visiting Richmond. I had not seen him previous to the 23d of December, 1864, for more than nine months. He was no visitor to my house.

The detectives, Lovett, Gavacan, Lloyd, and Williams, having failed to search my house or to make any inquiries whether the parties left anything behind on the Tuesday after the assassination, I myself did not think—consequently did not remind them. A day or two after their leaving, the boot that was cut from the injured man's leg by myself, was brought to our attention, and I resolved on sending it to the military authorities, but it escaped my memory and I was not reminded of its presence until the friday after the assassination, when Lieutenant Lovett and the above parties, with a squad of cavalry, came again and asked for the razor the party shaved with. I was then reminded immediately of the boot and, without hesitation, I told them of it and the circumstances. I had never examined the inside of boot leg, consequently knew nothing about a name which was there contained. As soon as I handed the boot to Lieutenant Lovett, they examined and discovered the name "J. Wilkes" they then handed me his photograph, and asked whether it bore any resemblance to the party, to which I said I would not be able to recognize that as the man (injured), but remarked that there was a resemblance about the eyes and hair. Herold's likeness was also handed me, and I could not see any resemblance, but I had described the horse upon which he rode, which, one of the detectives said, answered exactly to the one taken from one of the stables in Washington.

From the above facts and circumstances I was enabled to form a judgment, which I expressed without hesitation, and I said that I was convinced that the injured man was Booth, the same man who visited my house in November, 1864, and purchased a horse from my neighbor, George Gardiner. I said this because I thought my judgment in the matter was necessary to secure pursuit promptly of the assassins

ARGUMENT OF GENERAL THOMAS EWING

[Thomas Ewing was brother-in-law to General William Tecumseh Sherman. When Sherman was severely criticised by Secretary of War Edwin Stanton over surrender terms offered by Sherman to Confederate General Johnston, Thomas Ewing agreed to John Ford's request (Ford was owner of the theater where Lincoln was shot) to represent some of the defendants in the assassination trial.]

May it please the Court: The first great question that meets us at the threshold is—Do you, gentlemen, constitute a court, and have you jurisdiction, as a court, of the persons accused, and the crimes with which they are charged? If you have such jurisdiction, it must have been conferred by the Constitution, or some law consistent with it, and carrying out its provisions.

I. The 5th article of the Constitution declares: "That the judicial power of the United States shall be vested in one Supreme Court, and in such *inferior courts* as Congress may from time to time ordain and establish"; and that "the judges of both Supreme and *inferior courts* shall hold their offices during good behavior."

Under this provision of the Constitution, none but courts ordained or established by Congress can exercise judicial power, and those courts must be composed of judges who hold their offices during good behavior. They must be independent judges, free from the influence of Executive power. Congress has not "ordained and established" you a court, or authorized you to call these parties before you and sit upon their trial, and you are not *"judges"* who hold your offices during good behavior. You are, therefore, no court under the Constitution, and have no jurisdiction in these cases, unless you obtain it from some other source, which overrules this constitutional provision.

The President cannot confer *judicial* power upon you, for he has it not. *The executive,* not the judicial, power of the United States is vested in him. His mandate, no matter to what man or body of men addressed, to try, and, if convicted, to sentence to death a citizen,

32

not of the naval or military forces of the United States, carries with it no authority which could be pleaded in justification of the sentence. It were no better than the simple mandate to take A, B, C, D, E, F', and G H, and put them to death.

2. The President, under the 5th amendment to the Constitution, may constitute courts pursuant to the Articles of War, but he cannot give them jurisdiction over citizens. This article provides that "no person shall be held to answer for a capital or otherwise infamous crime, unless on a presentment or indictment of a grand jury, *except in cases arising in the land or naval forces, or in the militia when in actual service in time of war or public danger.*

The presentment or indictment of a grand jury is a thing unknown to and inconsistent with your commission. You have nothing of the kind. Neither you nor the law officers who control your proceedings seem to have thought of any such thing. These defendants did not and do not belong to the *"land or naval forces"* of the United States—nor were they "militia, in time of war or public danger, in actual service." The Constitution, therefore, in the article above cited, expressly says: *You shall not hold them to answer* to any of the capital and infamous crimes with which they are charged.

Is not a single, direct, constitutional prohibition, forbidding you to take jurisdiction in these cases, sufficient? If it be not, read the provision of the 3d section of the 3d article. It is as follows: "The trial of all crimes, except in cases of impeachment, shall be by jury."

But lest this should not be enough, in their anxious care to provide against the abuses from which England had recently escaped and which were still fresh in the memories of men,—as the Star Chamber, the High Commission Courts, and their attendant enormities,—the framers of the Constitution further provided, in the 6th amendment, that, "In all criminal prosecutions the accused shall enjoy the right to a speedy and public trial *by an impartial jury* of the State and district wherein the crime shall have been committed."

Now whence, and what, is the authority which overrules these distinct constitutional prohibitions, and empowers you to hold these citizens to answer, *despite the mandates* of the Constitution forbidding you?

Congress has not attempted to grant to you the power; Congress could not grant it. A law to that effect, against the constitutional prohibition, would be merely void. Congress has authorized the suspension of the writ of *habeas corpus,* as the Constitution permits (Art. I, Sec. 99); but the Constitution does not thereby permit the military to try, nor has Congress attempted to deliver over to the military, for *trial, judgment and execution, American citizens,* not in the land or naval forces, or in the militia in actual service, *when accused of crime.* Congress and the President, the lawmaking power, were incompetent to do this, and have not attempted it. Whence, then, comes the dispensation with the constitutional prohibition? Where and whence is the affirmative grant of jurisdiction under which you propose to try, and, if convicted, pass sentence upon, these men, citizens of the United States—not soldiers, not militiamen, but citizens, engaged in the ordinary avocations of life? I am not permitted to know. *Congress* has not in any form attempted to violate or impair the Constitution. They have suspended the writ of *habeas corpus;* this goes to imprisonment— not trial, conviction, or punishment. This is the extreme limit to which the lawmaking power is permitted to go, and it is only in cases of strong necessity that this is permitted. Congress has repealed so much of the 102d section of the Act of September 24, 1789, as required that in all capital cases twelve petit jurors should be summoned from the county in which the offense was committed (Par. 221, Sec. 102, repealed July 16, 1862, page 1164, Sec. 22), but has preserved all other legal provisions made in aid of the Constitution to protect citizens from the oppression of the unregulated and unrestrained Executive power. The accused shall be tried upon an indictment or presentment of a grand jury. If two or more crimes of a like nature be charged, they must be set forth in separate counts. (Act of February 26, 1853, Sec. 117.) You may not compel an accused to answer to a loose story or accusation of several crimes in one count. If the crime charged be treason, which this paper approaches more nearly than anything else, the accused shall

34

have a copy of the indictment, and a list of the jury, and of all the witnesses to be produced on the trial for proving the said indictment (mentioning the names and places of abode of such witnesses and jurors), delivered unto him at least three entire days before he shall be tried for the same; and in other capital offenses shall have such copy of indictment and list of the jury two entire days at least before the trial. (Act of April 30, 1790, Sec. 24, p. 221.)

Against this array of constitutional and legal prohibition and regulation, I know of nothing that can be adduced, except, perhaps, an Executive order authorizing, by direct mandate or by implication, the thing to be done which the Constitution forbids you to do. If you be proceeding in obedience to such Executive mandate, and if that give jurisdiction, still you proceed in a form and manner which the Constitution and law expressly forbid. If my clients be charged with treason or murder (and I conjecture they are charged with murder at least), they must be proved to have been *present, aiding in, or actually committing the overt act, or the alleged murder*. For either of these the punishment or conviction is death. The Judge-Advocate has been unable, in the cases of Arnold and Mudd, to present any evidence *remotely approaching* that prescribed by the Constitution and the laws as the condition of conviction; and yet I am led to infer that he will claim a conviction of one or both of them on the proof presented. What is the profession, on this and on the other side of the Atlantic, to think of such administration of criminal jurisprudence?—for this, the first of our State trials, will be read with avidity everywhere. I ask the officers of the Government to think of this carefully *now,* lest two or three years hence they may not like to hear it named.

But we may mistake the whole case as it presents itself to the mind of the Judge-Advocate. We are here as counsel for the accused, but are not allowed to know explicitly with what crime, *defined by law,* any one of them is charged, or what we are here to defend. No crime known to the law is legally charged in the paper which is here substituted for an indictment. In this paper three distinct crimes are strongly hinted at in a single charge, to each of which different rules of law and evidence are applicable and different penalties are attached; and I had wished to know, so that I might shape the defense of my clients accordingly, for which alleged or intimated crime any one, or each or all of them, are to be tried. This information has been denied us. The Judge-Advocate puts these parties on trial, and refuses (in the most courteous terms) to advise their counsel on what law or authority he rests his claim to jurisdiction; of what crime he intends to convict each or any of the defendants; in what law the crimes are defined and their punishments prescribed; or on what proof, out of the wild jumble of testimony, he intends to rest his claim to convictions.

But it has been said, and will perhaps be said again, in support of this jurisdiction, that the necessities of war justify it—and *silent leges inter arena*. So said the Roman orator when Rome had become a military despotism, and ceased forever to have liberty, and when she retained law only as the gift or by the permission of the ruling despot. *"The law is silent amid arms."* Yes, it is so in a conquered country, when the victorious general chooses to put the law to silence; for he is an autocrat, and may, if he choose, be a despot. But how extravagant is the pretense that a bold, and spirited, and patriotic people, because they rise in their majesty and send forth conquering armies to rescue the Republic, thereby forfeit all constitutional and legal protection of life, liberty, and property!

Cases have often arisen, in which robber bands, whose vocation is piracy on the high seas, or promiscuous robbery and murder on land—*hostes hitinani generis*—may be lawfully put to the sword without quarter, in battle, or hung on the yard-arm, or otherwise put to death, when captured, according to the necessities of the case, without trial or other conviction, except the knowledge of the commanding general that they were taken *fiagrante bello,* and that they are pirates or land robbers. A military court may be called, but it is *advisory* merely; the general acts, condemns, and executes. But the *Constitution* of the United States has nothing to do with this. It does not protect pirates or marauders, who are enemies of the human race; or spies, or even enemies taken in battle. It protects, not belligerent enemies, but only citizens and those persons not citizens who in civil life seek and claim its protection, or aliens who

36

are engaged in its military or other service. The power of the commanding general over these classes is restrained only by the *usages of war* among civilized nations. But these defendants are not charged as spies or pirates, or armed and organized marauders, or enemies captured in war, or persons in the land or naval service of the United States. They belong to none of these classes, over whom military discretion or martial law extends, unless they extend over and embrace all the people of the United States.

But if the jurisdiction in this case exists, whether by law or by the power of arms, I regret that a military commission should be charged with the trial of these causes. The crimes are, as far as hinted at and written about in the charge and specifications, all cognizable in our civil courts. Those courts are open, unobstructed, without a single impediment to the full and perfect administration of justice—ready and prompt, as they always are, to perform the high duties which the well-known principles of law under the Constitution devolve on them. What good reason can be given in a case like this, to a people jealous of their rights, for a resort here and now to military trials and military executions? We are at the advent of a new, and I trust a successful, Administration. A taint such as this—namely, the needless violation of the constitutional rights of the citizen—ought not to be permitted to attach to and infect it. The jurisdiction of this

Commission has to be sought dehors the Constitution, and against its express prohibition. It is, therefore, at least of doubtful validity. If that jurisdiction does not exist; if the doubt be resolved against it by our judicial tribunals when the law shall again speak, the form of trial by this unauthorized Commission cannot be pleaded in justification of the seizure of property or the arrest of person, much less the infliction of the death penalty. In that event, however fully the recorded evidence may sustain your findings, however moderate may seem your sentences, however favorable to the accused your rulings on the evidence, your sentence will be held in law no better than the rulings of Judge Lynch's courts in the administration of lynch law. When the party now in power falls,—as in the vicissitudes of this it must one day fall, and all the sooner for a reckless use of its

37

present power,—so it will be viewed by that party which succeeds it. This is to be expected, and, indeed, hoped; but if, unfortunately, this proceeding be then accepted and recorded as a precedent, we may have fastened on us a military despotism. If we concede that the exercise of jurisdiction claimed is now necessary, and for the best possible object, before we consent that it stand as a precedent in our jurisprudence, we should recall to mind the statesmanlike and almost prophetic remarks of Julius Caesar, in the Roman Senate, on the trial of Lentulus and his accomplices in Catiline's conspiracy: *"Abuses often grow from precedents good in principle; but when the power falls into the hands of men less enlightened or less honest, a just and reasonable precedent receives an application contrary to justice and reason."* It is to be remembered that criminal trials involving capital punishment were not then within the competency of the Roman Senate; and neither the Consul nor the Senate, nor both of them, had the right to condemn a Roman citizen without the concurrence of the people.

If you believe you possess the power of life and death over the citizens of the United States in States where the regular tribunals can be safely appealed to, still, for the sake of our common country and its cherished institutions, do not press that power too far. Our judicial tribunals, at some future day, I have no doubt, will be again in the full exercise of their constitutional powers, and may think, as a large proportion of the legal profession now think, that your jurisdiction in these cases is an unwarranted assumption; and they may treat the judgment which you pronounce and the sentence you cause to be executed as your own unauthorized acts.

This assumption of jurisdiction, or this use of a legitimate jurisdiction, not created by law and not known to law or to legal men, has not for its sanction even the plea of *necessity*. It may be convenient. Conviction may be easier and more certain in this military commission than in our constitutional courts.

Inexperienced as most of you are in judicial investigations, you can admit evidence which the courts would reject, and reject what they would admit, and you may convict and sentence on evidence which those courts would hold to be wholly insufficient. Means, too, may be resorted to by detectives, acting under promise or hope of reward, and operating on the fears or the cupidity of witnesses, to obtain and introduce evidence which cannot be detected and exposed in this military trial, but could be readily in the free, but guarded, course of investigation before our regular judicial tribunals. The Judge-Advocate, with whom chiefly rests the fate of these citizens, is learned in the law, but from his position he cannot be an impartial judge, unless he be more than man. He is the *prosecutor* in the most extended sense of the word. As in duty bound, before this Court was called, he received the reports of detectives, pre-examined the witnesses, prepared and officially signed the charges, and as principal counsel for the Government, controlled on the trial the presentation, admission, and rejection of evidence. In our courts of law, a lawyer who has heard his client's story, if transferred from the bar to the bench, may not sit in the trial of the cause, lest the ermine be sullied through the partiality of counsel.

There is no mere theoretical objection—for the union of prosecutor and judge works practical injustice to the accused. The Judge-Advocate controls the admission and rejection of evidence — knows what will aid and what will injure the case of the prosecution, and inclines favorably to the one and unfavorably to the other. The defense is met with a bias of feeling and opinion on the part of the judge who controls the proceedings of the court, and on whom, in great measure, the fate of the accused depends, which morals and law alike reject. Let it not be supposed I censure or reflect on any one, for I do not. The wrong suffered by the parties accused has its root in the vice of this system of trial, which I have endeavored to expose.

Because our Chief, so venerated and beloved (and no one venerated and loved him more than I), has fallen by the hand of a ruthless assassin, it ought not to follow that the Constitution and law should be violated in punishing men suspected of having compassed his death, or that men not legally found guilty should be sacrificed in vengeance as victims generally because of the crime.

39

There may be a lurking feeling among men which tends to this harshness of retribution, regardless of the innocence of those on whom vengeance may fall. Tending to this feeling, exciting or ministering to it, was the two days' testimony which, without Other apparent point or purpose, detailed the horrors of the Libby Prison; and the evidence that, in 1861, one of my clients took part in the rebellion; and the further testimony (which we showed was utterly fabulous) that another of my clients, in 1863 or 1864, entertained rebel officers or soldiers and corresponded with rebels in Richmond. As if to say: "What matters it how we try, or whether we legally try at all, provided we convict and execute men who have been associated with, or in sympathy with, monsters such as those?" Homer makes Achilles immolate, at the funeral pyre of Patroclus, twelve Trojan captives, simply because they were Trojans, and because Patroclus had fallen by a Trojan hand. If that principle of judicial action be adopted here, it were surely not too much to sacrifice to the manes of one so beloved and honored as our late Chief Magistrate a little lot of rebel sympathizers, because, like the assassin, some of them, at some time, participated in the rebellion, or gave aid and comfort to rebels. If this course of reasoning do not develop the object of that strange testimony, I know not how to read it. Indeed, a position taken by the learned Assistant Judge-Advocate, in discussing my objection to the part of that evidence which relates to my clients, goes to this — and even beyond it—namely, that participation in the rebellion was participation in the assassination, and that the rebellion itself formed part of the conspiracy for which these men are on trial here.

ARGUMENT OF GENERAL EWING ON THE LAW

AND THE EVIDENCE IN THE CASE OF DR. SAMUEL A. MUDD

May it please the Court: If it be determined to take jurisdiction here it then becomes a question vitally important to some of these parties—a question of life and death—whether you will punish only offenses created and declared by law, or whether you will make and declare the past acts of the accused to be crimes, which acts the law never heretofore declared criminal; attach to them the penalty of death, or such penalty as may seem meet to you; adapt the evidence to the crime and the crime to the evidence, and thus convict and punish. This, I greatly fear, may be the purpose, especially since the Judge-Advocate said, in reply to my inquiries, that he would expect to convict "under the common law of war." This is a term unknown to our language—a *quiddity—wholly* undefined and incapable of definition. It is, in short, just what the Judge-Advocate chooses to make of it. It may create a fictitious crime, and attach to it arbitrary and extreme punishment, and who shall gainsay it? The laws of war—namely, our Articles of War—and the habitual practice and mode of proceeding under them, are familiar to us all; but I know nothing, and never heard or read of a common law of war, as a code or system under which military courts or commissions in this country can take and exercise jurisdiction not given them by express legal enactment or constitutional grant. But I still hope the law is to govern, and if it does, I feel that my clients are still safe.

I will now proceed to show you, that on the part of one of my clients—Dr. Mudd—no crime known to the law, and for which it is pretended to prosecute, can possibly have been committed. Though not distinctly informed as to the offense for which the Judge-Advocate claims conviction, I am safe in saying, that the testimony does not point to treason, and if he is being tried for treason, the proceedings for that crime are widely departed from. The prosecution appears to have been instituted and conducted under the proclamation of the Secretary of War, of April 20, 1865. This makes it a crime, punishable with death, to harbor or screen Booth, Atzerodt, or Herold, or to aid or to assist them to escape. It makes it a crime to do a particular act, and punishes that crime with death. I suppose we must take this proclamation as law. Perhaps it is part of what the Judge-Advocate means when he speaks of the "common law of war." If this be so, my clients are still safe, if we be allowed to construe it as laws are construed by courts of justice. But I will show, first, that Dr. Mudd is not, and cannot possibly be, guilty of any offense known to the law.

1. *Not of treason.*—*The* overt act attempted to be alleged is the murder of the President. The proof is conclusive, that at the time the tragedy was enacted Dr. Mudd was at his residence in the country, thirty miles from the place of the crime. Those who committed it are shown to have acted for themselves, not as the instruments of Dr. Mudd. He, therefore, cannot be charged, according to law and upon the evidence, with the commission of this overt act. There are not two witnesses to prove that he did commit it, but abundant evidence to show negatively that he did not.

Chief Justice Marshall, in delivering an opinion of the Court in Burr's case, says: "Those only who perform a part, and who are leagued in the conspiracy, are declared to be traitors. To complete the definition both circumstances must concur. They must "perform a part" which will furnish the overt act, and they must be leagued with the conspiracy." (4 Cr., 474.)

Now, as to Dr. Mudd, there is no particle of evidence tending to show that he was ever leagued with traitors in their treason; that he had ever, by himself, or by adhering to, and in connection with others, levied war against the United States. It is contended that he joined in compassing the death of the President ("the King's death"). Foster, p. 149, speaking of the treason of compassing the king's death, says: "From what has been said it followeth, that in every indictment for this species of treason, and indeed for levying war and adhering to the king's enemies, an overt act must be alleged and proved."

The only overt act laid in these charges against Mudd is the act of assassination, at which it is claimed he was constructively present and participating. His presence, and participation, or procurement,

42

must be proved by two witnesses, if the charge be treason; and such presence, participation, or procurement, be the overt act.

Chief Justice Marshall, in Burr's case (Dall., 500), says: "Collateral points, say the books, may be proved according to the course of the common law; but is this a collateral point? Is the fact, without which the accused does not participate in the guilt of the assemblage, if they were guilty (or in any way in the guilty act of others), a collateral point? This cannot be. The presence of the party, when presence is necessary, being part of the overt act, must be positively proved by two witnesses. No presumptive evidence, no facts from which presence may be conjectured or inferred, will satisfy the Constitution and the law. If procurement take the place of presence, and become part of the overt act, then no presumptive evidence, no facts from which the procurement may be conjectured or inferred, can satisfy the Constitution and the law. The mind is not to be led to the conclusion that the individual was present by a train of conjectures or inferences, or of reasoning. *The fact itself must be proved by two witnesses,* and must have been committed within the district."

2. Not of murder.—For the law is clear, that, in cases of treason, presence at the commission of the overt act is governed by the same principle as constructive presence in *ordinary felonies,* and has no other latitude, greater or less, except that in proof of treason *two* witnesses are necessary to the overt act, and one only in murder and other felonies. "A person is not constructively present at an overt act of treason, unless he be aiding and abetting at the fact, or ready to do so, if necessary." (4 Cr., 492.) Persons not sufficiently near to give assistance are not principals. And although an act be committed in pursuance of a previous concerted plan, those who are not present, or so near as to be able to afford aid and assistance, at the time when the offense is committed, are not principals, but accessories before the fact. (Wharton, Am. Crim. Law, 112 to 127.)

It is, therefore, perfectly clear, upon the law as enacted by the Legislature and expounded by jurists, that Dr. Mudd is not guilty of participating in the murder of the President; that he was not actually or constructively present when the horrid deed was done, either as a traitor, chargeable with it as an overt act, or a conspirator, connected as a principal felon therewith.

3. The only other crimes defined by law for the alleged commission, of which the Judge-Advocate may, by possibility, claim the conviction of the accused, are:

1st. The crime of *treasonable conspiracy,* which is defined by the law of 21st July, 1861, and made punishable by fine not exceeding $6,000, and imprisonment not exceeding six years. 2nd. The crime of being an *accessory before, or after, the fact* to the crimes of murder, and of assault with intent to kill. That the accused is not guilty of either of these crimes, will be clearly shown in the discussion of the evidence which follows.

4. Admitting the Secretary's proclamation to the law, it, of course, either supersedes or defines the unknown something or nothing which the Judge-Advocate calls "the common law of war." If so, it is a definite, existing thing, and I can defend my clients against it; and it is easy to show that Dr. Mudd is not guilty of violating that proclamation. He did not, *after the date of the proclamation,* see either of the parties named therein—dress the wound of Booth, or point out the way to Herold—and the proclamation relates to *future* acts, not to *past.*

5. But of the *common law of war,* as distinct from the usages of military courts, in carrying out and executing the Articles of War, I know nothing, and, on examining the books, I find nothing. All that is written down in books of law or authority I am, or ought to be, prepared to meet; but it were idle and vain to search for and combat a mere phantom of the imagination, without form and void.

I now pass to the consideration of the evidence, which I think will fully satisfy the Court that Dr. Mudd is not guilty of treasonable conspiracy, or of being an accomplice, before or after the fact in the felonies committed.

The accused has been a practicing physician, residing five miles north of Bryantown, in Charles County, Maryland, on a farm of about five hundred acres, given him by his father. His house is between twenty-seven and thirty miles from Washington, and four or five miles east of the road from Washington to Bryan-town. It is shown by Dr. George Mudd, John L. Turner, John Waters, Joseph Waters, Thomas Davis, John McPherson, Lewellyn Gardiner, and other gentlemen of unimpeached and unquestionable loyalty, who are in full sympathy with the Government, that he is a man of most exemplary character—peaceable, kind, upright, and obedient to the laws. His family being slaveholders, he did not like the anti-slavery measures of the Government, but was always respectful and temperate in discussing them, freely took the oath of allegiance prescribed for voters (Dr. George Mudd), supported a Union candidate against Harris, the secession candidate, for Congress (T. L. Gardiner), and for more than a year past regarded the rebellion a failure. (Dr. George Mudd.) He was never known or reported to have done an act or said a word in aid of the rebellion, or in countenance or support of the enemies of the Government.

An effort was made, over all objections and in violation, I respectfully submit, of the plainest rules of evidence, to blacken his character as a citizen, by showing that he was wont, after the war broke out, to threaten his slaves to send them to Richmond "to build batteries." But it will be seen hereafter, that all that part of the testimony of the same witnesses, which related to the presence of Surratt and of rebel officers at the house of the accused, was utterly false. And Dyer, in presence of whom Eglen says the threat was made to him, swears he was not in the country then, and no such threat was ever made in his presence. The other colored servants of the accused, Charles and Julia Bloyce, and Betty and Frank Washington, say they never heard of such threats having been made; and J. T. Mudd and Dr. George Mudd, and his colored servants,. Charles and Julia Bloyce, and Betty and Frank Washington, describe him as being remarkably easy, unexacting, and kind to all about him—slaves and freemen.

From this brief reference to the evidence of the character of the accused, I pass to a consideration of the testimony adduced to prove his connection with the conspiracy.

45

And, first, as to his *acquaintance with Booth.* J. C. Thompson says, that early in November last Booth went to the house of witness's father-in-law, Dr. William Queen, four or five miles south of Bryantown, and eight or ten from Dr. Mudd's, and presented a letter of introduction from a Mr. Martin, of Montreal, who said he wanted to see the country. It does not appear who Martin was. Booth said his business was to invest in land and to buy horses. He went with Dr. Queen's family to a church next day, in the neighborhood of Bryantown, and was there *casually* introduced, before service, by Thompson, to the accused. After service Booth returned to Queen's house, and stayed until next morning, when he left. While at Queen's he made inquiries of Thompson as to horses for sale, the price of lands, their qualities, the roads to Washington, and to the landings on the Potomac; and Thompson told him that the father of Dr. Samuel Mudd was a large landholder, and might sell part of his land. On Monday morning, after leaving Dr. Queen's, Booth came by the house of the accused, who went with him to the house of George Gardiner, to look at some horses for sale. The accused lives about one quarter of a mile from Gardiner's (Mary Mudd, Thomas L. Gardiner), and on the most direct road to that place from Dr. Queen's, through Bryantown.

(Mary Mudd, Hardy.) There Booth bought the one-eyed saddle-horse which he kept here, and which Payne rode after the attempted assassination of Mr. Seward. Mudd manifested no interest in the purchase, but after it was made Booth directed the horse to be sent to Montgomery's Hotel, in Bryantown, and Booth and the accused rode off together in the direction of the house of the accused, which was also the direction of Bryantown. Witness took the horse to Bryantown next morning, and delivered him in person to Booth there. Witness says the horse was bought on *Monday,* but he thinks the latter part of November; though he says he is "one of the worst hands in the world to keep dates."

Thompson further says, that after Booth's first introduction and visit to Dr. Queen's, "he came there again, and stayed all night, and left very early next morning. I think it was about the middle of December following his first visit there."

There is nothing whatever to show that Mudd saw Booth on this *second* visit, or at any other time, in the country, prior to the assassination; but a great deal of evidence that he never was at Mudd's house, or in his immediate neighborhood, prior to the assassination, except once, and on his first visit. I will refer to the several items of testimony on this point.

1st. Thomas L. Gardiner says he was back and forth at Mudd's house, sometimes every day, and always two or three times a week, and never heard of Booth being there, or in the neighborhood, after the purchase of the horse and before the assassination.

2d. Mary Mudd says she saw Booth one Sunday in November at church, in Dr. Queen's pew, and with his family, and that she heard of his being at the house of her brother, the accused, on that visit, but did not hear that he stayed all night; and that on the same visit he bought the horse of Gardiner. She lives at her father's, on the farm adjoining that of accused, and was at his house two or three times a week, and saw him nearly every day on his visits to his mother, who was an invalid, and whose attending physician he was; and never saw or heard of Booth, except on that one occasion, before the assassination.

3d. Fanny Mudd, sister of the accused, living with her father, testifies to the same effect.

4th. Charles Bloyce was at the house of the accused Saturday and Sunday of each week of last year until Christmas Eve (except six weeks in April and May), and never saw or heard of Booth's being there.

5th. Betty Washington (colored) lived there from Monday after Christmas until now, and never saw or heard of Booth there before the assassination.

6th. Thomas Davis lived there from 9th January last. Same as above. Nor is there any evidence whatever of Booth's having *stayed all night* with the accused on the visit when the horse was bought of Gardiner, or at any other time, except that of Colonel Wells, who says that, after Mudd's arrest, "he said, in answer to another question, that he met Booth some time in November. I think he said he was introduced by Mr. Thompson, a son-in-law of Dr. Queen, to Booth. I think he said the introduction took place at the chapel or church on Sunday morning; that, after the introduction had passed between them, Thompson said, Booth wants to buy farming lands; and they had some little conversation on the subject of lands; and then Booth asked the question, whether there were any desirable horses that could be bought in that neighborhood cheaply; that he mentioned the name of a neighbor of his who had some horses that were good travelers; *and that he remained with him that night, I think, and next morning purchased one of those horses."* Now, it will be recollected that Thompson says Booth stayed at Dr. Queen's on that visit Saturday night and Sunday night, and Thomas L. Gardiner says the horse was bought *Monday morning.* So that, if Colonel Wells is correct in recollecting what Mudd said, then Thompson must be wrong. It is more probable that Thompson is right, as to Booth's having spent Sunday night at Queen's. Thompson's testimony is strengthened, too, by that of Mary Mudd, Fanny Mudd, and Charles Bloyce, who would in all probability, have heard the fact of Booth spending Sunday night at the house of the accused, had he done so; but they did not hear it.*

*As shown by the statement of my mother, Booth did stay one night at my father's home in November, 1864.—ED.

It is here to be observed, that though the accused was not permitted to show, by Booth's declarations *here,* that he was contemplating and negotiating purchases of land in Charles County, yet evidence was admitted as to his declarations made *there* to that effect. Dr. Bowman, of Bryantown, says that Booth negotiated with him, on one of these visits, for the purchase of his farm, and also talked of buying horses. And a few days after witness had negotiated with Booth for the sale of his farm, he met Dr. Mudd, and spoke of the negotiation with Booth, and Mudd said, *"Why, that fellow promised to buy my land."* It is also shown by Dr. Blandford, Dr. Bowman, M. P. Gardiner, and Dyer, that Mudd for a year past wanted to sell his land, and quit farming.

This, then, is all that is shown of any meeting between Mudd and Booth in that country before the assassination—a casual introduction at church on Sunday in November—Booth going next morning to Mudd's, talking of buying his farm, and riding with him a quarter of a mile to a neighbor's to buy a horse, and their going off together toward Mudd's and Bryantown, where the horse was delivered to Booth next morning.

We will now turn to consider the evidence as to the accused's acquaintance with *John H. Surratt.* If he knew Surratt at all, the fact is not shown by, nor inferable from, the evidence. Miss Surratt was educated at Bryantown, before the war, and her family lived at Surrattsville, and kept the hotel there (which is on the road from Dr. Mudd's house to Washington) until they removed, in October last, to a house on H: street, in this city, where they have since resided. (Miss Surratt, Holahan, Weichmann.) Dr. Mudd *probably* had met Surratt at the hotel at Surrattsville, or, before the war, at Bryantown, while his sister was at school; but it is not shown by credible testimony that he knew him at all. Let us examine the evidence on this point.

1st. *Mary Sims,* formerly Dr. Mudd's slave, says that a man whom Dr and Mrs. Mudd called *Surratt* was at Mudd's house from almost every Saturday night until Monday night through the latter part of the *winter,* and through the spring and summer of *last year* until apples and peaches were ripe, when she saw him no more; and that on the last of November she left Dr. Mudd's house. That he *never slept in the house,* but took dinner there six or seven times. That *Andrew Gwynn, Bennett Gwynn,* Captain Perry, Lieutenant Perry and Captain White, of Tennessee, slept with Surratt in the pines near the spring, on bedclothes furnished from Dr. Mudd's house, and that they were supplied by witness and by Dr. Mudd with victuals from the house. That William Mudd, a neighbor, and Rachel Spencer, and Albin Brooke, members of Mudd's household, used to see Surratt there then. She says that the lieutenants and officers had epaulettes on their shoulders, gray breeches with yellow stripes, coat of same color and trimming. Their horses were kept in Dr. Mudd's stable by Milo Sims.

2d. *Milo Sims,* brother of Mary, fourteen years old, formerly slave of Dr. Mudd, left there Friday before last Christmas. Saw *two or three men* there *last summer,* who slept at the spring near Dr. Mudd's house. Bedding taken from the house; meals carried by *Mary Sims,* generally, though they sometimes ate in the house, and they all slept at the spring, except one called John Surratt, who slept once in the house. Don't say how long they stayed. It was in "planting tobacco time." He attended their horses in Dr. Mudd's stable.

3d. Rachel Spencer, slave of Dr. Mudd and cook at his house, left him early in January, 1865; saw five or six men around Dr. Mudd's house *last summer;* slept in the pines near the house, and were furnished with meals from it. Were dressed in black and blue. *W ere there only a week, and never saw them there before or since.* She heard no names of the men except *Andrew Gwynn and Watt Bowie.* That *Albin Brooke* lived at Dr. Mudd's then, and was with these men occasionally.

4th. Elzee Eglen, formerly Dr. Mudd's slave, left him loth August, 1863; saw a party sleeping in the pines, by the spring, near the house, *summer before last.* Knew *Andrew Gwynn,* and he was one of them; did not recollect any other names. *Mary Sims* carried them meals, and *Milo Sims* attended the horses in Dr. Mudd's stable. Some wore gray clothes with brass buttons, but without other marks—some black clothes. Did not say how many there were, nor how long they stayed.

5th. Melvina Washington, formerly Dr. Mudd's slave, left him October, 1863, saw party sleeping in the pines near the house *summer before last;* victuals furnished from the house. Party stayed there *about a week,* and then left. Some were dressed in gray, and some in short jackets with little peaks behind, with black buttons. She saw them seven or eight times during one week, and then they all left, and *she never saw any of them at* any other time *except during that week.* That *Andrew Gwynn's* name was the only one she heard; that *Mary Sims* used to tell her, when the men were there, the names of others, but she had forgotten them.

50

That these five witnesses all refer to the same party of men and the same year is certain, from the fact that Elzee Eglen says that Mary Sims carried the party he describes as being there in the summer of 1863 their victuals, and that Milo Sims kept their horses in the stable, and Melvina Washington says Mary Sims used to tell her the names of the party which she described as being there in 1863; and also from the fact that all of them, except Milo Sims, named *Andrew Gwynn* as being one of the party. I will not waste the time of the Court in pointing out to it in detail the discrepancies in their evidence apparent from the foregoing synopsis of their testimony; and therefore, only calling its attention to the fact that all of these witnesses were living with Dr. Mudd during and after the year 1861 (Dyer), down to the several dates given above, when they respectively left, I will proceed to show from the evidence *what* and *when* the occurrences really were about which they have testified.

1st. Ben Gwynn (named by Mary Sims as one of the party) says:

"Q. Will you state whether during last summer, in company with Captain White, from Tennessee, Captain Perry, Lieutenant Perry, Andrew Gywnn, and George Gwynn, or either of them, you were about Dr. Samuel A. Mudd's house for several days?—A. I was not. I do not know any of the parties named, and I never heard of them, except Andrew Gwynn and George Gwynn.

"Q. Were you with your brothers, Andrew Gwynn and George Gwynn, about Dr. Mudd's house last year?—A. No, sir; I have not been in Dr. Mudd's house since about the first of November, 1861. I have not been on his place, or nearer his place than church, since about the 6th of November, 1861.

"Q. Where did you and the party who were with you near Dr. Mudd's sleep?—A. We slept in the pines near the spring.

"Q. How long were you there?—A. Four or five days. I left my neighborhood, and went down there and stayed around in the neighborhood—part of the time at his place, and part of the time elsewhere. He fed us there—gave us something to eat, and had some bed-clothing brought out of the house. That was all."

He further said, that the party was composed of his brother, Andrew Gwynn, and Jere Dyer, who, on the breaking out of the war, were, like all the people of that section, panic-stricken, and apprehending arrest; that he came up to Washington on the loth of November, gave himself up, and found there were no charges against him, took the oath, and went back home. That John H. Surratt, when this party were there, was at college, and witness never saw him in Charles County then or since. That his brother, *Andrew Gwynn,* went South in the fall of 1861, and was never, to his knowledge, back in that county but once since, and that was last winter some time. He corrected his statement as to *when,* the party was there, and fixed it in August, 1861.

2d. Jere Dyer, brother-in-law of the accused, testifies to the same as Ben. Gwynn. Says he and the two Gwynns were members of companies_ organized by authority of Governor Hicks for home protection in 1860; were present on parade in Washington at the inauguration of a statue, on the 22d of February, 1860. When the war broke out the companies were disbanded, many of the members going South, and many of those who remained in Charles County scattering about from rumors of arrests; that there was a general panic in the county then, and almost everybody was leaving home and "dodging about"; that while he and the two Gwynns slept in the pines these three or four days, Mary Sims carried them victuals from the house, and Milo Sims attended to the horses in Mudd's stables; that they were dressed in citizens' clothing; that Andrew Gwynn went South in the fall of 1861; witness never heard of his being back since; that Surratt was not there then, nor, so far as he knows, since.

3d. William Mudd, a near neighbor of the accused, named by Mary Sims as having seen the party she described, says he saw Benjamin Gwynn there in 1861, but saw none of the others, then or since.

4th. Albin Brooke, referred to by Mary Sims and Rachel Spencer as having seen the party they describe (and by Mary Sims as having seen Surratt especially), says he knows Surratt, having met him in another county once, and knew Benjamin Gwynn and Andrew Gwynn, but that he never saw Surratt with any of the men named by

52

Mary Sims at Dr. Mudd's, nor heard of his having ever been there; never heard of Andrew Gwynn being back from Virginia since 1861. That he lived at Dr. Mudd's from the 1st of January to between the 1st and 15th of September of last year, and was at the stable morning, noon, and night, each day, and was about the spring daily; 'while there never saw any strangers' horses in the stable, nor any signs about the spring of persons sleeping there; but that, while living near Dr. Mudd's, in the summer of 1861, he knew of Ben, and Andrew Gwynn and Dyer sleeping in the pines there.

5th. Mrs. Mary Jane Sims boarded, or was a guest, at Dr. Mudd's all last year, except through March; knew Andrew, Ben, and George Gwynn, and John H. Surratt. Never saw or heard of any of them there, nor of any of them sleeping in the pines.

6th. Frank Washington (colored) lived at Dr. Mudd's all last year; knew Andrew Gwynn by sight.; never saw or heard of him or Surratt (of whom a photograph was shown him), or of any of the men named by Mary Sims, being there, or of any men being there in uniform; at the stable three times daily, and often at the spring, and saw no strange horses in the stable; saw no signs of men sleeping about the spring.

7th. Baptist Washington, carpenter, at work there putting up kitchen, etc., from February till Christmas last year, except the month of August; same as above, except as to knowledge of Andrew Gwynn. (Photograph of Surratt shown him.)

8th. Charles Bloyce (colored), at Dr. Mudd's through every Saturday and Sunday all last year, except from loth April to loth May, same as Frank Washington, except as to knowing Andrew Gwynn.

9th. Julia Ann Bloyce (colored cook), there from early in July to 23d December, 1864; same, substantially, as Frank Washington; knew Ben and Andrew Gwynn. (Photograph of Surratt shown witness.)

10th. Emily Mudd and Fannie Mudd live on adjoining farm to Dr. Mudd, and his father's; at his house almost daily for years; knew of

53

the party in the pines in 1861, composed of Dyer and the two Gwynns; knew Andrew Gwynn well; never heard of his being back from Virginia since 1861, nor of Surratt ever being at Dr. Mudd's, nor of any of the others named by Mary Sims, except the Gwynns, in 1861.

11th. Henry L. Mudd, Jr., brother of the accused, living at his father's; same as above as to Surratt.

None of the five witnesses, whose testimony has been shown false in all essential parts by the evidence of the twelve witnesses for defense, referred to above, said that Surratt was one of the party sleeping in the pines, except Mary and Milo Sims. These two witnesses are shown to have established reputations as liars, by the evidence of Charles Bloyce, Julia Ann Bloyce, and Frank, Baptist, and Betty Washington. So all that testimony for the prosecution, of the "intelligent contrabands," who darkened the counsels of the Court in this case, is cleared away. The only part of it at all admissible under the rules of evidence, or entitled to the consideration of the Court, was that showing Surratt was intimate with Mudd, and often at his house last year and year before; and that, like nearly all the rest of their testimony, has been conclusively shown to be false.

Another witness, who testifies to implicate Mudd as an associate of Surratt, is William A. Evans, who said he saw Mudd some time last winter enter a house on H street, just as Judson Jarboe, of Prince George's County, was going out of it; and that Jarboe was then shaking hands with a young lady, whom witness took to be a daughter of Mrs. Surratt, from her striking likeness to her mother, he having known or seen all the family; and that he stopped a policeman on the street, and asked whose house it was, and he said, "Mrs. Surratt's"; and that he drove up to the pavement, and asked also a lady who lived near by, and she said the same. He said this house was between Eighth and Ninth, or Ninth and Tenth—he was not perfectly certain as to the streets, but *was certain* it was between the Patent Office and the President's. Through an hour's cross-examination, he fought by equivocation, or pleading defect of memory, against fixing any circumstance by which I could learn directly or indirectly the day or the month when it occurred, and, finally, he could only say it was "some time last winter." Although his attention had been so strongly attracted to the house, he first said it was on one side of the street and then on the other; and could not tell whether it had any porch or any portico, nor describe its color, nor whether it had a yard· in front, nor whether it was near the center of the square, nor describe a single house on either side of the same square. He said he knew Dr. Samuel Mudd, having met him first at Bryantown Church, in December, 1850.

Every material thing he did say, which was susceptible of being shown false, has been so shown.

1st. Mrs. Surratt's house is not between the Patent Office and the President's, but next the corner of Sixth. (Weichmann, Holahan, Miss Surratt.)

2d. Miss Surratt, an only daughter, says she never saw or heard of Samuel Mudd being at her mother's house, nor heard his name mentioned in the family, and never met Judson Jarboe there or elsewhere before the assassination.

3d. Miss Fitzpatrick, who boarded at Mrs. Surratt's from the 6th of October last to the assassination, and Holahan, who was there from the first week of February last, never saw either Mudd or Jarboe there, or heard of either being there, or the name of either mentioned in the family.

4th. Weichmann, who boarded there through last winter, never heard of Mudd being at the house.

5th. Judson Jarboe says he never was at Mrs. Sur-ratt's house, or met Dr. Mudd or Miss Surratt in Washington before the assassination.

6th. Mary Mudd says Samuel Mudd was at Frederick College, at Fredericktown, Maryland, in December, 1850, and was not at home during the collegiate year, beginning in September of that year; and Rev. Dr. Stonestreet, who was president of that college until

December of that year, testifies the accused was then entered as a student there, and could not by the rules of the college have gone home.

This witness, Evans, boasted often to the Court that he was a minister of the Gospel, and reluctantly admitted on cross-examination that he was also one of the secret police. In his reckless zeal as a detective, he forgot the ninth commandment, and bore false witness against his neighbor. It is to be hoped his testimony that he is a minister of the Gospel is as false as his material evidence. I feel bound in candor to admit, however, that his conduct on the stand gave an air of plausibility to *one* of his material statements—that for a month past he has "been on the verge of insanity."

I have now presented and considered all the testimony going to show that Mudd ever met Surratt at all, and all that he ever met Booth before the assassination and after the first visit Booth made to Charles County—except the testimony of Weichmann, which I will now consider.

That witness says that about the middle of January last he and Surratt were walking down Seventh street one night, and passed Booth and Mudd walking up the street, and just after they had passed, Mudd called, "Surratt, Surratt." Surratt turned and recognized Mudd as an old acquaintance, and introduced Mudd to witness, and then Mudd introduced Booth to witness and Surratt. That soon after the introduction

Booth invited them all to his room at the National Hotel, where wine and cigars were ordered. That Dr. Mudd, after the wine and cigars came, called Booth into the passage, and they stayed there five to eight minutes, and then both came and called Surratt out, and all three stayed there about as long as Mudd and Surratt had stayed, both interviews together making about ten to twenty minutes. On returning to the room, Dr. Mudd seated himself by witness, and apologized for their private conversation, saying, "that Booth and he had some private business—that Booth wished to purchase his farm." And that, subsequently, Booth also apologized to him, giving the same reason for the private conversation. Booth at one time took the back of an envelope, and made marks on it with a pencil. "I should not consider it writing, but more in the direction of roads or lines." The three were at that time seated round a center-table in the middle of the room. "The room was very large—half the size of this court-room." He was standing when this was done within eight feet of them, and Booth was talking in a low tone, and Surratt and Mudd looking on the paper, but witness heard no word of the conversation. About twenty minutes after the second return from the passage, and after a good deal of general conversation, they all walked round to the Pennsylvania House, where the accused sat with witness on a lounge, and talked about the war, "expressed the opinion that the war would soon be over, and talked like a Union man." Soon after getting there, Booth bid the accused good night, and after Booth left, witness and Surratt followed, at about half-past ten o'clock.

It will be observed that the only men spoken of by this witness as having seen the accused on this occasion are Booth who is dead, and Surratt, who is a fugitive from the country. So there is no one who can be called to confirm or confute his statements, as to the facts of these men being together, or as to the character of the interview. But there was *one fact* about which he said he could not be mistaken, and by means of which his evidence against Mudd is utterly overthrown. That is, he alleges the meeting was about the middle of January, and fixes the time with certainty by three distinct circumstances:

1st. He made a visit to Baltimore about the middle of January, and near the date of this meeting.

2d. He had, *before the meeting,* got a letter, which he received on the 16th *of January.*

3d. It was after the Congressional holidays, and Congress had resumed its session. He recollects this fact of itself, and is confirmed in his recollection by the fact that Booth's room was one a member of Congress had occupied before the holidays, and which was given Booth, as he learned, until the member, who had been delayed beyond the time of the reassembling of Congress, should return. Booth told him this.

In refutation of this evidence, we have proved, beyond all controversy, that Dr. Mudd was not in Washington *from the 23d of December to the 23d of March.*

On the 23d of December he came to Washington with J. T. Mudd, who says they left their horses at the Navy Yard, and went into the city at dark, on the street cars, and registered at the Pennsylvania House. They then went out and got supper at a restaurant, and then went to the Metropolitan Hotel and stayed there together a quarter of an hour, and then to the National, where witness met a friend, and became separated in the crowd from accused. Witness strolled out and went back to the Pennsylvania House, to which accused returned in a few minutes after he got there. He saw and heard no one with the accused, though there *might* have been persons with him in the front part of the room (which was separated from where witness sat by open folding doors) without witness seeing them. Witness and accused then went to bed; were together all next day; were about the market together, and at the store making purchases; were not at the National Hotel, and left the city about one o'clock in the afternoon of the 24th, and returned home together. Witness never saw Booth, except on his visit to Bryantown in November. We have shown by the evidence of Lucas, Montgomery, Julia Bloyce, and Jerry Mudd that accused came here on that visit on a sufficient and legitimate business errand—to purchase a cooking-stove and other articles, which he bought here then.

On the 23d of March, Lewellyn Gardiner said accused again came to Washington with him to attend a sale of condemned horses, but that the sale did not occur at that time. They got to Washington at 4 or 5 P. M., left their horses at Martin's, beyond the Navy Yard, and went about looking at some wagons for sale, and went then to the Island to the house of Henry Clark, where they took tea. They spent the evening at Dr. Allen's playing whist, slept together that night at Clark's, and after breakfast next morning went through the Capitol looking at the paintings in the Rotunda, and returned to Martin's at dinner, and after dinner left and returned home. Accused was not separated from or out of sight of witness five minutes during the whole visit, and did not go to any of the hotels or to the post-office, or see or inquire for Booth. Dr. Allen, Clark, Martin, Thomas Davis, Mary Mudd, Henry Mudd, and Betty Washington confirm witness as to the objects or incidents of the visit.

On the 11th of April, three days before the assassination, while Booth, as appears by the hotel register, was at the National in this city, accused came to Giesboro to attend the sale of Government horses, which he and Lewellyn Gardiner had come on the 23d of March to attend. Though in sight of Washington, he did not come into the city, but took dinner at Martin's, and after dinner left and returned home. On this visit he stayed all night at Blandford's, twelve miles from the city, coming up, but not returning. (Lewellyn Gardiner, Henry L. Mudd, Dr. Blandford, Martin, Davis, Betty Washington, Mary Mudd.)

On the 26th of January he went with his wife to the house of his neighbor, George H. Gardiner, to a party, and stayed till daylight. (Betty Washington, Thomas Davis, Mary Mudd.) Except for one night on the occasion of each of those four visits—two to Washington, one to Giesboro, and one to Gardiner's—accused was not absent from home a night from 23d December until his arrest. (Betty Washington, Thomas Davis, Henry L. Mudd, Mary Mudd, Frank Washington.)

After the evidence for the defense above referred to had been introduced, refuting and completely overwhelming Weichmann's testimony and all inferences as to Dr. Mudd's complicity with Booth which might be drawn from it, a new accuser was introduced against him on the same point in the person of *Marcus P. Norton,* who said that at half-past 10 o'clock, on the morning of the 3d of March, as he was preparing his papers to go to the Supreme Court to argue a motion in a patent case there pending (which motion the record of the Court shows he *did* argue on that day), a stranger abruptly entered his room and as abruptly retired, saying he was looking for Mr. Booth's room; and though witness never saw Dr. Mudd before or since, until the day of his testifying, he says that stranger is the prisoner at the bar. He could not tell any article of the stranger's clothing except a black hat. *Win. A. Evans,* a part of whose evidence we have hereinbefore considered, comes to the support of Norton, by saying that early on the morning of either the 1st, or 2d, or 3d of March (witness is certain it was one of those three days) Dr. Mudd passed witness on the road from Bryantown to Washington, a few miles from the city, driving a two-horse rockaway, and there was a man in with him, but whether a black or a white man witness could not recollect. Fortunately for the accused, the 1st day of March was Ash Wednesday—the first day of Lent,—a religious holiday of note and observance in the community of Catholics among whom he lived. Fortunately for him, too, his sister Mary was taken ill on that day, and required his medical attendance (at her father's house, on the farm adjoining his own, thirty miles from Washington) each day from the zd to the 7th of March, inclusive. By the aid of these two circumstances we have been able to show by Thomas Davis that accused was at work at home on the 28th of February (the day before Ash Wednesday); by Dr. Blandford, Frank Washington, and Betty Washington, that he was there at work at home on the 1st of March; by Mary, Fanny, Emily and Henry L. Mudd, Betty and Frank Washington, and Thomas Davis, that he was there on the zd, 3d, 4th, and 5th of March, at various hours of each day. At or within two hours of the time when Norton says he saw the accused enter the room at the National (10.30 A. M., 3d of March), Mary, Emily, Fanny, and Henry L. Mudd, Frank and Betty Washington, Thomas and John Davis, all testify most emphatically to having seen him at his house, on his farm, or at his father's house adjacent to his own— six hours' ride from Washington! We have shown, too, by Mary Mudd, that the accused has always worn a lead-colored hat whenever she has seen him this year, and that she has seen him almost daily; and by Henry Mudd, Dr. Blandford, and Mary Mudd that neither he nor his father owns a rockaway. Now, Norton either saw the accused enter his room on the morning of the 3d of March or not at all, for his evidence, clinched as to the date by the record of the Supreme Court, excludes the supposition that he *could* have been mistaken *as to the day*. Nor can these eight witnesses for the defense be mistaken as to the day, for the incidents by which they recollect Mudd's presence at home fix the time in their memories exactly. With all this evidence before the Court, it cannot hesitate to hold the *alibi* established beyond all cavil.

The only other item of evidence as to anything done or said by Dr. Mudd, or by anybody, before the assassination, tending in the least to show him implicated in the conspiracy, is the evidence of *Daniel I. Thomas,* who says that several weeks before the assassination he met Mudd at the house of his neighbor, Downing, and there, in the course of conversation, Mudd said (laughingly) that "Lincoln and his whole Cabinet, and every Union man in the State of Maryland, would be killed within six weeks." Witness said he wrote to Colonel John C. Holland, provost marshal of that district, at Ellicott's Mills, before the assassination, advising him of Mudd's statement. But Colonel Holland says he got a letter from witness about that time, and there was not a word of the statement in it, nor a reference to the accused, nor to any statement by anybody about killing anybody. Thomas says he told his brother, Dr. Thomas, of the declaration before the President was killed, but his brother says emphatically he did not tell him until after Mudd's arrest—the boot found at Mudd's house having been named in the same conversation. Thomas says he told Mr. Downing about it before the assassination, but Downing says emphatically he did not tell him a word about it *at any time.* Downing also says that he himself was present every moment of the time Mudd and Thomas were together at his house, and heard every word said by either of them, and Mudd did not make that statement, nor refer to the President, or the Cabinet, or the Union men of Maryland, at all, nor say a word about anybody being killed. He says, however, Mudd, when Thomas was bragging and lying about being a provost marshal, did tell him "he was a jack"—which insult was doubtless an incentive to the invention of the calumny. But it was not the *only* incentive. Thomas knew that if that lie could be palmed off on the Judge-Advocate and the Court for truth, it might lead to Mudd's arrest and conviction as one of the conspirators. He had, on Tuesday, before Mudd's arrest, and before his lie was coined and circulated, been posting hand-bills, containing the order of the War Department offering liberal rewards for any information leading to the arrest of Booth's accomplices, and he then, doubtless, conceived the idea of at once getting reward in money from the Government for his information, and revenge on Mudd for his insult in Downing's house. That he gave that evidence corruptly is shown by Wm. Watson, John R. Richardson, and Benjamin Naylor, who say that Thomas, after testifying against Mudd, went to see them, and said, that *"if Dr. Mudd was convicted upon his testimony, he would then have given, conclusive evidence that he gave the information that led to the detection of the conspirator!"* *"He then, asked Mr. Benjamin J. Naylor if he did not mention to him and Gibbons, before the killing of the President, the language that Dr. Mudd had used. Mr. Naylor said that he had never done it, before or after!"* *"He said his portion of the reward ought to be $10,000— and asked me (Watson) if I would not, as the best loyal man in Prince George's County, give him a certificate of how much he ought to be entitled to."* The testimony of Richards, and of Eli J. Watson, coupled with Thomas's testimony in denial of these statements, fill the record of infamy of this false witness.

To accumulate evidence that Thomas's statement is utterly unreliable, the defense brought over twenty of his neighbors, who testified that he could not be believed on oath—among whom were Naylor, Robey, Richards, Orme, Joseph Waters, John Waters, J. F. Watson, Eli Watson, Smith, Baden, Dickens, Hawkins, Monroe, and others, of undisputed loyalty, nearly all of whom had known him from boyhood. His brother, Dr. Thomas, testifies that he is at times deranged; and Dr. Geo. Mudd says he is mentally and morally insane. And, although Thomas's evidence was the most important in the case against Dr. Mudd, the Judge-Advocate has not seriously attempted to sustain him—has not tried to show that he ever told or hinted at this story to anybody before the assassination—and has not asked one of the scores of witnesses for the prosecution in attendance from Thomas's neighborhood a question as to his reputation for veracity—except Wm. Watson, who said it was decidedly *bad*. A feeble attempt was made to sustain him by endeavoring to show that he was a zealous supporter of the Administration, and that, *therefore,* the general voice of his community was against him. But we showed he was a rebel at the beginning of the war, and an opponent of the Administration at the last election—and then the Judge-Advocate dropped him.

This is all the, evidence of every act or word done or said by anybody, prior to the assassination, tending in the remotest degree to connect Mudd with the conspiracy. It consists, in large part, of the testimony of the five negroes, as to the Confederate officers frequenting Mudd's house last year and the year before—two of them, Milo and Mary Sims, as to Surratt's visiting his house last year—of Evans as to Mudd's going to Surratt's house last winter—of Evans and Norton as to Mudd being here on the 3d of March—of Weichmann as to the interview between Mudd, Booth, and Surratt, about the middle of January—and of Thomas as to Mudd's prediction of the assassination in March. I venture to say that rarely in the annals of criminal trials has the life of an accused been assailed by such an array of false testimony as is exhibited in the evidence of these nine witnesses—and rarely has it been the good fortune of an innocent man, arraigned and on trial for his life, to so confute and overwhelm his accusers. I feel it would be a waste of time and an imputation on the intelligence of the Court to delay it with fuller discussion of the evidence of these witnesses—and feel sure it will cast their testimony from its deliberations, or recollect it only to reflect how foully and mistakenly the accused has been assailed.

Having now discussed all the evidence adduced that calls for discussion, or may by possibility be relied on as showing Mudd's acquaintance with Booth, or connection with the conspiracy, and having, I think, shown that there is no reliable evidence that he ever met Booth before the assassination but once on Sunday, and once the day following, in November last, I will proceed to a consideration of the testimony relied on to show that he knowingly aided the escape of the assassin.

1st. Why did Booth go to Dr. Mudd's and stop there from daybreak till near sundown on his flight? I answer, because he had a broken leg and needed a physician to set it. And as to the *length* of the stay, the wonder is he was able to ride off on horse-back with his broken and swollen limb at all—not that he took ten hours' rest. The Court will observe, from the map in evidence, that Booth, taking Surrattsville in his route to Pope's Creek, opposite Matthias Point, where he crossed the Potomac (Captain Doherty), traveled at least eight or ten miles out of his way to go, after leaving Surrattsville, by Dr. Mudd's. (See Dyer's testimony.) Would he have gone that far out of his route to the Potomac crossing if he had not broken his leg? Or was it part of his plan to break it? Obviously, he could not in advance have planned to escape by crossing the *Patuxent,* nor to evade his pursuers by lying concealed in Charles County, within six hours' ride of Washington. He must, as a sane man, have contemplated and planned escape across the Potomac into Virginia, and thence South or abroad; and it could never have been part either of the plan of abduction, or of that of assassination, to go the circuitous route to a crossing of the Potomac by Bryan-town or Dr. Mudd's. So that the fact of Booth going to the house of the accused, and stopping to get his leg set and to rest, does not necessarily lead to any conclusion unfavorable to the accused.

Booth got there, with Herold, about daybreak. (frank Washington.) He usually wore a mustache (see photograph), but he then wore heavy whiskers, and had his face muffled in a shawl, so as to disguise him. The disguise was kept up all day. (Colonel Wells.) He was taken to a lounge in the hall, and then to a front room up-stairs, where the broken bone was set, where a fee of $25 was paid for the service, and where, it is probable, he slept most of the day. They represented that the leg had been broken by a fall of the horse; that they had come from Bryantown, and were going to Parson Wilmer's. After breakfast accused went to his field to work. Herold, whom Mudd had never met (Colonel Wells), came down to breakfast and dinner with the family, and after dinner he and Mudd went off together to the house of Mudd's father, to get a family carriage to take the wounded man to the house of Parson Wilmer, five miles off, at Piney Chapel. (Lovett, Wells.) Now, can any man suppose for a moment that Mudd, at this time, had the slightest suspicion or intimation of the awful tragedy of the night before? Could he, knowing or suspecting the crime or the criminal, have thus recklessly given himself up to arrest and trial, by publicly aiding the escape of the assassin? Could he have been ready to expose his old father to suspicion by thus borrowing his carriage, which would have been noticed by every man, woman, and child on the road, to carry off the assassin? Impossible! I need nothing more of the Court than its consideration of this fact, to clear the accused of all suspicion of having, up to that time, known or suspected that a crime had been committed by the crippled stranger, whom he was openly and kindly seeking to aid.

But the carriage could not be got, and Mudd and Herold rode off toward Bryantown to get one there. Colonel Wells thinks the accused told him that Herold turned back when getting one and a half miles from the elder Mudd's house, saying he could take his friend off on horseback. Betty Briscoe and Eleanor Bloyce, however, say they saw a man riding toward Bryantown with the accused, who turned back at the bridge at the edge of the town.

Mudd made some purchases of calico and other articles, and heard of the assassination. (Bean.) It was not generally known then among the citizens who was the assassin. (Bean, Roby, Trotter, B. W. Gardiner, M. L. McPherson, John McPherson.) In fact, it was not generally known with certainty at the theater, or in Washington, Friday night, whether Booth was the murderer. (Gobright.) In Bryan-town it was commonly understood that Boyle, a noted desperado of that region, who assassinated Captain Watkins last fall, was one of the assassins. (M'. L. McPherson, Bean, Trotter, Roby.) It was not known that the murderer had been tracked into that neighborhood. (Bean, Dr. George Mudd.) Lieutenant Dana told Dr. George Mudd, Saturday afternoon, that Boyle assassinated Mr. Seward and Booth the President, but that he thought Booth had not then got out of Washington. Even next day (Sunday) it was reported there that it was *Edwin* Booth who killed the President.

65

The accused left Bryantown about four o'clock to return home. *Betty Briscoe* says the same man who had turned back at the bridge stopped in the edge of a branch, which the road crosses a couple of hundred yards from the bridge, until Mudd returned from town, and then they rode off together across the branch, "up the road." But *Booz* says he saw Mudd a couple of hundred yards beyond that crossing leisurely going through the farm Booz lives on, by a near-cut which he usually traveled, *alone;* and that he would himself have probably noticed the man at the crossing; which was in full view of where he was, had he been waiting there; and would have *certainly* noticed him had he been with Mudd traveling the main road, when Mudd turned into the cut-off through the farm—but he saw no one but the accused. *Susan Stewart* also saw Mudd in the by-road returning home alone, and did not see any man going the main road, which was in full view. I call the attention of the Court to the plat by which the branch and these roads are shown, and to the fact that there is no road turning off from the main road between Booz's place and Bryantown, except the side road by Booz's house. If further refutation of the testimony of Betty Briscoe on this point be required, it is found in the evidence of *Primus Johnson,* who saw Herold pass the elder Mudd's in the main road, going toward the house of the accused, and some time after that himself caught a horse in the pasture, and rode toward Bryantown, and met and passed Dr. Mudd coming leisurely from Bryantown, *alone, at Booz's farm;* and that from the time he saw Herold until he met and passed Mudd was full an hour and a half. And in the evidence of *John Acton,* who was on the roadside, three miles from Bryantown when Herold passed, at between three and four o'clock, and who remained there an hour, and Dr. Mudd did not go by in that time. Acton also says that between the time Herold and Mudd went toward Bryantown and the time Herold returned alone was but three-quarters of an hour. From the fact that Herold could not have ridden to the bridge and back in that time (six miles), it seems highly probable that he did not go to the bridge, but turned back about where Colonel Wells thinks Mudd said he did. But however that may be is not important, as it is certain from the evidence of these four

66

witnesses that Herold did not wait at the branch for Mudd's return from Bryantown.

As Mudd rode home, he turned out of his way to see his neighbor, *Hardy* (who lives half-way between the house of the accused and Bryantown), about some rail-timber he had engaged there. The house is not in view of the road, a clump of pine intervening. He told Hardy and Farrell of the news. Hardy says:

"He said to me that *there was terrible news now,* that the President and Mr. Seward and his son had been assassinated the evening before. Something was said in that connection about Boyle (the man who is said to have killed Captain Watkins) assassinating Mr. Seward. I remember that Booth's name was mentioned in the same connection, and I asked him if Booth was the man who had been down there. His reply was that he did not know whether it was that man or one of his brothers; he understood that he had some brothers. That ended the conversation, except that *he said it was one of the most terrible calamities that could have befallen the country at this time.*

"Q. Did you say that it was understood or said that Booth was the assassin of the President?—A. There was some such remark made, but I do not exactly remember the remark."

They both say he seemed heartily sorry for the calamity, and that he said he had just come from Bryantown, and heard the news there. Hardy says he stayed there only about ten minutes, and left just about sundown. Farrell corroborates Hardy as to the conversation, except that he reports nothing as to Boyle's name being mentioned; but he says the conversation was going on when he joined Hardy and Mudd. He says the house is less than a quarter of a mile off the road, and that accused stayed there about fifteen minutes.

Now, I ask the Court, what is there up to this point to indicate that Mudd knew or had any suspicion that the broken-legged man was implicated in the crime? If there is anything in proof showing that fact, I fail to find it. True, he had met Booth twice in November—five months before. Had seen him that dark, cloudy morning, at daybreak, faint with fatigue and suffering, muffled in his shawl and disguised in a heavy beard; had ministered to him in the dim light of a candle, whose rays struggled with the dull beams of the opening day; had seen him, perhaps, sleeping in the darkened chamber, his mustache then shaved off, his beard still on, his effort at concealment still maintained. (Wells.) And here let me remind the Court, that there is nothing in the evidence showing that Booth *spoke a* word—but where either of the men are referred to as saying anything, "the smaller man" was the spokesman. Let it be remembered too that Booth was an actor, accustomed by years of professional practice to disguise his person, his features, and his tones—so that if Mudd had been an intimate associate, instead of a mere casual acquaintance, it would have been easy for Booth to maintain a disguise even when subjected to close scrutiny under circumstances favorable to recognition. If the Court will also consider with what delicacy a physician and a gentleman would naturally refrain from an obtrusive scrutiny of a patient coming to his house under the circumstances, they will appreciate how easy it was for Booth to avoid recognition, and how probable that Mudd had no suspicion who his patient was. Had he recognized Booth before he went to Bryantown, and heard there that name connected with the "terrible calamity," would he have jogged quietly home, stopping to chat with Booz, to look after his rail-timber, to talk of the names of the assassins with his neighbors? Unless the Court start out with the hypothesis of guilt, and substitutes unsupported suspicion for proof,—which I respect them too highly to fear for a moment they will do,— they cannot charge him with a recognition of Booth before he returned home from Bryantown.

Hardy says it was about sundown when Mudd left; Farrell says about five o'clock. He had two miles to ride home. It must have been sundown when he got home, and the men had just gone. Betty Washington says that three or four minutes after Herold (the last of the two) disappeared toward the swamp, Mudd came through the hall to the kitchen, and was then first seen by her after his return from Bryantown. The other servants had not come from the field when the men started—and we are therefore left to that one witness to show that the statement of Simon Gavacan, one of the detectives, who says *"he thinks"* Mudd said he went with them part of the way, is incorrect. It is inconsistent, too, with Mudd's statement to Colonel Wells on the subject, which is as follows: "The Doctor said that as he came back to the house he saw the person that he afterward supposed to be Herold, passing to the left of the house, and toward the barn or the stable; that he did not see the other person at all after he left him at the house, which was about one o'clock, I think." This statement, and that of Betty Washington, last above quoted, coincide with and strengthen each other.

It is true Dr. Mudd did say to all who asked him that he had shown Herold the way to Parson Wilmer's by the short route, but this was in the morning, soon after the parties reached the house, and before the idea of the carriage appears to have been suggested. This is shown by the statement of Colonel Wells, who says that the accused, *in the same conversation in which, he said that Booth and Herold had just gone front the house as he came up,* told him that, "Herold, the younger of them, asked him the direct route to Piney Chapel, Dr. Wilmer's, saying that he was acquainted with Dr. Wilmer." He described the main traveled road, which leads to the right of his house, and was then asked if there was not a shorter or nearer road. He said, "Yes, there is a road across the swamp that is about a mile nearer, I think"; he said it was five miles from his house to Piney Chapel by the direct road and four miles by the marsh, and undertook to give him (as he said) a description by which they could go by the nearer route. He said that the directions were these—they were to pass down by his barn, inclining to the left, and then pass straight forward in a new direction across the marsh, and that on passing across the marsh they would come to a hill; keeping over the hill, they would come in sight of the roof of a barn, and letting down one or two fences they would reach the direct road.

The accused meant, of course, that this inquiry and explanation occurred before his return to the house from Bryantown—and so Colonel Wells understood him, for he so in effect says. The statement of the accused to Dr. Geo. Mudd, the next day after Booth left, is to the same effect. He said, "That these parties stated that

69

they came from Bryantown, and were inquiring the way to the Rev. Dr. Wilmer's"—thus putting their inquiry for the route to Parson Wilmer's in direct connection with their early explanation as to whence they came.

I have no doubt that Gavacan, the detective, recollects an *inference* which he, and perhaps also his associate detective, Williams, drew from Dr. Mudd saying that he had shown Herold the route to Parson Wilmer's, that he showed it as Booth and Herold were leaving. But the inferences of detectives, under the strong stimulus of prospective rewards, are inferences generally of guilt; and that these gentlemen were not free from the weaknesses of their profession, and that they grossly misrepresented Dr. Mudd in other important statements, will presently be shown to the satisfaction of the Court.

Now, if Mudd did not know, when he talked with Hardy about the assassination, and spoke of Booth in connection with it, that the assassin was at his house,—as I think the evidence shows he did not,—then when did he first suspect it? Colonel Wells says his *inference* was, from something the accused said, that he suspected the crippled man to be Booth before he left the premises. The evidence not only shows that when Mudd returned Booth had gone out of sight, but it also shows what fact it was that, added to the undue excitement of the strangers, and to the fact that the crippled man shaved off his mustache, thoroughly aroused his suspicion. It was the fact that *his wife said to hint, after they left, that as the crippled man came down to go his false whiskers became detached from his face.* (Lieut. Lovett.) *When* she told him this, and what he said or proposed to do, *was not* shown by the prosecution, and, by the rules of evidence, *could not be* by the defense. But that was a fact which could not probably have been communicated to Mudd by his wife until Booth had gone.

In the evidence adduced as to Mudd's subsequent conduct and statements, I need only call the attention of the Court to two points, for in it there is nothing else against him.

70

1st. He did not tell on *Tuesday* that the boot was there, far down in the leg of which was found by the officers "J. Wilkes," written in pale ink. I answer, the boot was not found by his wife until several days after the assassin left, and was then found in sweeping under the bed. (Hardy.) We have every reason to suppose it was not found until after Tuesday, for the accused, on Friday, before a question was asked or a word communicated to him, *told of the boot himself, and had it produced,* and said, in presence of his wife, it was found by her after the officers were there before. (Hardy.)

2d. Of the three detectives who went to the house of accused, Tuesday, *Williams* says: Accused denied throughout that two men had been there; yet he says on cross-examination, that accused, in the same conversation, pointed out the route the men had taken toward Wilmer's. Gavacan said he at first denied two men had passed there, and then admitted it. Lloyd says he denied it from beginning to end, on Tuesday. But Lieutenant Lovett, who went with and in command of these detectives, speaking of this interview on Tuesday, says: *"We first asked whether there had been any strangers at his house and he said there were."* The three detectives are manifestly mistaken; either from infirmity of memory, or from some less pardonable cause, they have failed to recollect and truthfully render what Dr. Mudd did say on that subject.

The commentators upon the law of evidence give a caution which it may be well for the Court to observe. They admonish us how easy it is for a corrupt witness to falsify a conversation of a person accused, and as the accused cannot be heard, how difficult, if not impossible, contradiction is. How easy for an honest witness to misunderstand, or in repeating what was said to substitute his own language or inference for the language which was really used, and thus change its whole meaning and import. In no case can the caution be more pertinent than in this. The very frenzy of madness ruled the hour. Reason was swallowed up in patriotic passion, and a feverish and intense excitement prevailed most unfavorable to a calm, correct hearing and faithful repetition of what was said, especially by the suspected. Again, and again, and again the accused was catechised by detectives, each of whom was viewing with the other as to which should make the most important discoveries, and each making the examination with a preconceived opinion of guilt, and with an eager desire, if not determination, to find in what might be said the proofs of guilt. Again, the witnesses against the accused have testified under the strong stimulus of promised reward for information leading to arrests and followed by convictions. (See order of Secretary of War.) At any time and in any community an advertisement of rewards to informers would be likely to be responded to—at a time, and on an occasion like this, it would be a miracle if it failed of effect. In view of these considerations, the Court cannot be too vigilant in its scrutiny of the evidence of these detectives, or too circumspect in determining the influence to be given to it.

No more effective refutation of this statement, that Mudd denied on Tuesday that two strangers had been at his house, can be given, than to ask how came Lieutenant Lovett and the detectives at Dr. Mudd's? They did not scent out the track for themselves. They were at Bryantown on Saturday and were at fault, and had they been let alone would probably have remained at fault, and not have gone to Dr. Mudd's. By whom and when was the information given which brought them there? The next morning after the startling news of the assassination reached him, the accused went to Dr. George Mudd, a man of spotless integrity and veracity, and of loyalty unswerving through all the perilous and distressing scenes of the border war, and fully informed him of all that had occurred—the arrival of the two strangers, the time and circumstances under which they came, what he had done for them, the suspicions he entertained, when they departed, and what route they had taken; and requested him, on his behalf and in his name, to communicate this information to the military authorities on his return that day to Bryantown. Dr. George Mudd did make the communication as requested, on Monday morning, to Lieutenant Dana, and further informed him of Dr. Samuel Mudd's desire to be sent for, for any further information which it might be in his power to give. In consequence of this, *and of this alone,* Lieutenant Lovett and the detectives did, *on Tuesday, go* to the house of the accused,

72

accompanied by Dr. George Mudd, who prefaced his introduction by informing the accused that, in accordance with his request, he had brought Lieutenant Lovett and the detectives to confer with him in reference to the strangers who had been at his house Saturday. Of these facts there is no doubt or dispute. They stand too prominently upon the record to be ignored or evaded. But for this information the detectives would not have been at the house of the accused at all. They came at his request, and when they came it is absurd and idle to say that he denied, almost in the presence of Dr. George Mudd, who had been his messenger, and was then in the house, that the two strangers had been there. On the contrary, the evidence shows he imparted all he knew, and pointed out the route which the strangers took when they left—but which Lieutenant Lovett and the detectives did not at once pursue, because they chose to consider his statement uncandid, and intended to put them upon a false scent. Indeed, so accurate was the description given by the accused to Lieutenant Lovett, Tuesday, of the persons who had been at his house, that *the Lieutenant says he was satisfied, from Mudd's description, they were Booth and Herold.*

It was in great part by reason of Dr. Mudd's having delayed from Saturday night until Sunday noon to send to the authorities at Bryantown information as to the suspected persons who had been at his house, that he was arrested and charged as a conspirator; and yet I assert this record shows *he* moved more promptly in communicating his information than *they* did in acting on it. His message was communicated to Lieutenant Dana Monday morning. *Tuesday,* Lieutenant Lovett and the detectives came, and that officer got such information from Dr. Mudd as convinced him the suspected persons were Booth and Herold, and yet it was not until Colonel Wells came, on *Saturday,* that an energetic effort was made to find the route of the assassin. On that day Dr. Mudd himself went with that officer, and followed the tracks on the route indicated beyond the marsh into a piece of ploughed ground, where the tracks were lost. But Colonel Wells had got the general direction, and it was in consequence of the information sent by the accused to the

73

authorities the day after Booth left his house that he was tracked to the Potomac.

But the evidence does not show that Dr. Mudd delayed at all in communicating his information, for it does not' show *when* his wife told him of the false whiskers of the crippled man. But, admit she told him on Saturday evening, as soon as the men left. It was four miles to Bryantown, and his wife may have feared to be left alone that night. Boyle, who haunted that neighborhood, was understood by Dr. Mudd to have been one of the assassins (Hardy), and may not his or his wife's fears of the vengeance of that desperado have prevented him communicating his suspicions *direct and in person* to the officer at Bryan-town? He told Dr. George Mudd next day, when asking him to go to the authorities with the information, to caution them not to let it be publicly known that *he* had volunteered the statement, lest he might be assassinated in revenge for having done it.

Having thus presented and discussed somewhat in detail the testimony in this case, I now ask the indulgence of the Court while I briefly review some of its leading features.

Booth and Mudd met first in November last at church, near Bryantown, casually, and but for a few minutes. Their conversation was in presence of many others, including men of unquestioned loyalty. Next morning, Booth left Dr. Queen's, rode by Mudd's, talked of buying his farm, got him to show him over to Gardiner's, a quarter of a mile off, where he bought a horse, Mudd manifesting no interest in the purchase. They rode away together toward Mudd's house, and toward Bryantown, where Gardiner found Booth next morning at the village hotel. Booth was again at Dr. Queen's in the middle of December. But the evidence shows that he did not go into Mudd's neighborhood, or seek or see him. So far as we dare speak from the evidence—and we should dare speak from nothing else— that is all the intercourse between Mudd and Booth in that neighborhood before the assassination.

What was there in that to attract attention or excite remark toward Mudd more than to Dr. Queen or Mr. Gardiner, or any other

74

gentleman in Charles County, to whom Booth had been introduced, and with whom he had conversed. All that is shown to have passed between them was perfectly natural and harmless, and nothing is to be presumed which was not shown. True, they might have talked of and plotted assassination; *but did* they? Is there, in the intercourse which had thus far occurred, any incident from which such a deduction could be drawn, or which would justify a suspicion that any such thing was thought of or hinted at? Nor did they ever meet again *anywhere* before the assassination, unless the testimony of Weichmann is to be accepted as true, which, upon this point, at least is quite unworthy of credence. He swears to having met Dr. Mudd and Booth in the City of Washington, about the middle of January—certainly after the holidays. But it is in proof by many witnesses, who cannot be mistaken, have not been impeached, and who unquestionably stated the truth, that Dr. Mudd was from home but one night from the 23d of December to the 23d of March, and that night at a party in his own neighborhood. If this be so, and there is no reason to doubt it, then Weichmann's statement cannot be true. The mildest thing that can be said of him, as of Norton, is, that he was mistaken in the man. That which was attempted to be shown by this contradicted witness (Weichmann) was, that Dr. Mudd and Booth, who were almost strangers to each other, met Surratt, to whom Booth was unknown, at the National Hotel, and within half an hour after the meeting plotted the assassination of the President, his Cabinet, the Vice-President, and General Grant—all this in Washington, and in the presence of a man whom one of the supposed conspirators knew to be an employee of the War Department, and had reason to believe was a Government detective! It is monstrous to believe any such thing occurred. It outrages all that we have learned of the philosophy of human nature, all that we know of the motives and principles of human actions. And yet, if Mudd was not then and there inducted into the plot, he never was. He never saw Booth again until after the assassination, and never saw any of the other conspirators at all. Twice, then, and twice only—unless the Court shall accept the testimony of Weichmann against the clear proofs of an *alibi,* and then only three times—he and Booth had met. None of these meetings occurred later than the 15th of January. They are shown to have been *accidental* and *brief.* The parties had but little conversation, and portions of that little have been repeated to the Court. So far as it has been disclosed, it was as innocent as the prattle of children, and not a word was breathed that can be tortured into criminality—not a word or an act that betokens malign purposes. Against how many scores of loyal persons, even in this community, may stronger evidence be adduced than against Mudd, if the mere fact of meeting and conversing with Booth is to be accepted as evidence of guilt? Booth was a guest at the National Hotel—intelligent, agreeable, of attractive manner, with no known blemish on his character as a man or a citizen. He had the *entree* of the drawing-rooms, and mingled freely with the throngs that assembled there. His society, so far from being shunned, was courted; and the fairest ladies of the land, the daughters of distinguished statesmen and patriots, deemed it no disparagement to them to accept his escort and attentions. It is not extravagant to say, that hundreds of true, Union-loving, loyal people in this and other cities, were on terms of cordial and intimate association with him. And why should they not have been? He was under no suspicion. *They* did not shun him. Why should Mudd? And why shall what was innocent in them be held proof of guilt in him? Let it be remembered in this connection, that Dr. Mudd's house was searched and his papers seized; that Surratt's house was seized and searched; that all the effects of Booth, Atzerodt, Arnold, Herold, Spangler, and Mrs. Surratt, that could be found, were seized and examined; and that among them all not a letter, a note, a memorandum, not the scrape of a pen by any person or in any form, has been found implicating Dr. Mudd. Let it further be remembered, that all these persons have been subjected to repeated examinations, under appalling circumstances, by various officials of the Government, eager to catch the faintest intimation of Mudd's complicity, and that not one of them has mentioned or hinted at his name. Let it also be remembered, that anonymous letters have been picked up in railroad-cars, found in pigeon-holes at hotels, rescued from the waves, and that the continent has been traversed and the ocean vexed in search of proofs of the conspiracy, its instigators, leaders, and abettors, and that in all this written and oral testimony there is not a word making the remotest allusion to Dr. Mudd. The probabilities are as a thousand to one that he never knew, or heard, or imagined, of a purpose, much less plotted in a conspiracy, either to capture or to assassinate the President. There is not only a failure to show his connection affirmatively, but, if the rules of law be reversed, and guilt presumed until innocence be shown, then, I say, he has carried his proofs in negation of complicity to a point as near demonstration as it is possible for circumstantial evidence to reach. I once more concede that (if the Court accept Weichmann's statement) it is possible he may have talked treason and plotted assassination with Booth and Surratt, but it is indefinitely removed from the probable; and neither liberty nor life is to be forfeited upon either probabilities or possibilities. I cannot bring myself to fear that this Commission will sanction what, in my judgment, would be so shocking and indefensible a conclusion.

If he and Booth had, at the alleged meeting in January, confederated for the perpetration of one of the most stupendous and startling crimes in the annals of human depravity, who can doubt that frequent meetings and consultations would thereafter have occurred, and that they would have increased in frequency as the time for the consummation of the atrocious plot approached? Yet, though within six hours' ride of each other, they had no meetings, no consultations, no intercourse, no communication, no concert, but were in total ignorance of each other's movements and purposes. Mudd was here the 23d of March, but he was not here for the purpose of seeing Booth, nor did he see him. He made no inquiry for him; did not call at his hotel; saw none of his associates; did not speak of him; did not, so far as appears, even think of him. On the ith of April, only three days before the frightful tragedy was enacted, Mudd was at Giesboro, in sight of Washington. Booth was then at the National Hotel; and if Mudd was leagued with him, that was the time of all others, from the conception to the consummation of the deed, when he would have seen and conferred with him. If Mudd was a conspirator, he knew of Booth's presence here then; yet he did not come to the city—did not inquire for Booth, see him, hold communication with him, learn whether he was in Washington or Boston, Nassau or London. Three days only before the frightful tragedy—three days before the world was astonished by its enactment! Imagine, if you can—if he was a conspirator—what a tumult of thought and emotion must have agitated him then—what doubts and misgivings—what faltering and rallying of resolution—what invocations to "stop up the access and passage to remorse"—and then ask your own hearts and judgments if it is natural, or possible, that, at such a moment and under such circumstances, he could quietly have transacted the business that brought him to Giesboro, then turn his back upon Washington, indifferent to the failure or success of the events with which his own life, the happiness of his family, and all that was dear to him on earth, were bound up? If a conspirator, he knew what had been, and what was to be, done. He knew that the hour for the bloody business was at hand, and that everything depended upon the secrecy and success of its execution. Yet he was indifferent. He sought no interview with his supposed confederates—gave them no counsel or assistance—took no precautions for security—gave no signs of agitation or concern—but, in sight of the place and the agents selected for the enactment of the horrible deeds, turned his back upon them all, with an indifference that bordered upon idiocy, quietly trafficked at Giesboro, and returned to the seclusion of his family and farm. You know, gentlemen, that this is impossible. You know that it could not have happened without outraging every law of human nature and human action. You know that at such an hour his soul would have been shaken with the maddest storm and tempest of passion, and that no mere business affair on earth could have seduced his thought for a moment from the savage slaughter he had in hand. It would have engrossed all his thoughts, and shaped all his actions. No one can, in the strong light of the evidence, believe he *was* a conspirator.'

I then confidently conclude that Dr. Mudd cannot be convicted as a principal in the felony. He did not participate in its commission, and was more than thirty miles distant from the scene when it ,was

78

committed. He cannot be convicted as an accessory before the fact, for the evidence fails to show that he had any knowledge or suspicion of an intention to commit it. If, then, he is to be held responsible at all, it is an accessory after the fact. Does the evidence implicate him in that character? What is an accessory after the fact?

An accessory after the fact is when a person, knowing a felony to have been committed, receives, relieves, comforts, or assists him whom he knows to be the felon. He must know that the felon is guilty to make him an accessory. (I Chit. Crim. Law, 264.)

Any assistance given to him to hinder *his being apprehended,* tried, or punished, is sufficient to convict the offender—as lending him a horse to escape his pursuers; but the assistance or support must be given in order to favor an illegal escape. (I Chit. Crim. Law, 265.) If a man receives, harbors, or otherwise assists to elude justice, *one whom he knows to be guilty of felony,* he becomes thereby an accessory after the fact in the felony. (r Bishop's Crim. Law, 487.) Obviously, a man to be an accessory after the fact *must be aware of the guilt of his principal;* and, therefore, one cannot become an accessory by helping to escape a prisoner convicted of felony, *unless he has notice of the conviction, or at least of the felony committed. (1* Bishop's Crim. Law, 488.) The charge against an accessory consists of two parts—first, of the felonious situation of the principal; and, secondly, of the guilty knowledge and conduct of the accessory. It will thus be seen that *knowledge of the crime committed, and of the guilt of the principal who is aided,* and aid and assistance *after acquiring that knowledge,* are all necessary to charge one as accessory after the fact.

Now, let us apply the facts to the law, and see whether Dr. Mudd falls within: the rule. On the morning after the assassination, about daybreak, Booth arrived at his house. He did not find the Doctor on watch for him, as a guilty accomplice, expecting his arrival, would have been, but he and all his household were in profound sleep. Booth came with a broken leg, and his companion, Herold, reported that it had happened by the fall of his horse, and that they had come from Bryantown, and were going to Parson Wilmer's. The Doctor rose from his bed, assisted Booth into the house, laid him upon a sofa, took him up stairs to a bed, set the fractured bone, sent him a razor to shave himself, permitted him to remain there to sleep and rest, and had a pair of rude crutches improvised for his use. For all this he received the ordinary compensation for services rendered to strangers. He then went to his field to work. After dinner, while the day was still dark, and Booth still resting disguised in his chamber, Mudd left the house with Herold. Even though he had known of the assassination, and that his patient was the assassin, none of these acts of assistance would have made him an accessory after the fact. *"If a person supply a felon with food, or other necessaries for his sustenance, or professionally attend him sick or wounded, though he know him to be a felon, these acts will not be sufficient to make a party an accessory after the fact."* (Wharton's American Criminal Law, p. 73.) But he did not know, and had no reason to suspect, that his patient was a fugitive murderer. The most zealous advocate would not venture to assert that the evidence warrants such conclusion; much less will it be assumed by one acting under the solemn responsibilities of judge. Down, then, to the time Mudd left home with Herold, after dinner, the evidence affords no pretext for asserting he was an accessory after the fact.

But if he was not then an accessory, he never was. It is shown that Herold turned back on the way to Bryantown, and when Mudd returned he and Booth had gone. And the evidence does not show that he suspected them of having been guilty of any wrong, until his wife told him, after they had gone, that the whiskers of the crippled man fell off as he came down stairs to go. True, Booth was guilty, and Mudd had shown his companion the route to Wilmer's; which was the only thing done by Mudd, from first to last, that could have implicated him, *even had he from the first known the crime and the criminal.* But when he did that, he did not know either; for he did not know the crime until he went to Bryantown, nor have even the least suspicion of the criminal, until after Booth had gone. I have read you the law—the *scienter* must be shown. Things not appearing and not existing stand before the law in the same category; and the guilty knowledge not appearing in evidence, in the eye of the law it does not exist. In this case it is not only not shown, but is negatived by the evidence. The conclusion most unfavorable to Mudd which the evidence can possibly justify is, that, having had his suspicions thoroughly aroused Saturday night, he delayed until Sunday noon to communicate them to the authorities. *"If A knows B hath committed a felony, but doth not discover it, this doth not make A an accessory after the fact."* (1st Hale's Pleas of the Crown, 618.) *"Merely suffering a felon to escape will not charge the party so doing—such amounting to a mere omission."* (Whar. Am. Crim. Law, 73.)

Can, then, Dr. Mudd be convicted as a conspirator, or an accessory before or after the fact, in the assassination? If this tribunal is to be governed in its findings by the just and time-honored rules of law, he cannot; if by some edict higher than constitutions and laws, I know not what to anticipate or how to defend him. With confidence in the integrity of purpose of the Court and its legal advisers, I now leave the case to them.

PRISON LIFE AT FORT JEFFERSON IN 1865

A few days after my father left Washington for the Dry Tortugas, my mother received this letter from Sister Mary Rose, a former teacher, and a cousin, and a sister of Dr. George D. Mudd:

From our Monastery of Frederick, July 19, 1865. My own dearest Frank:

I need not, my very dear child, assure you how bitterly and sincerely I have grieved with you and for you in these past days of our affliction and anguish.

And how ardently too I have sought God for grace and strength to sustain and support you and *our loved ones* while the storm passed by. You know me too well, darling, to doubt of my tender sympathy for you even in smaller trials, and if I have been silent for a while may not my very silence have told you that I have been too sad, too sick at heart, even to write?

Our poor dear Sam! What a siege of suffering he has gone through and for an act of charity. How wonderful and hidden are the ways of God! And it is not for us to question these mysterious ways of His providence. It is our part only to join our hands in humble submission, deeming ourselves happy even to be thought worthy to suffer for His Holy Name's Sake.

Yes, believe me, my heart has been with you and the rest of our dear afflicted friends, and although the cross for me has been very, very heavy, gladly, had it been possible, would I have borne a greater portion to have relieved you and others. But 1 trust now the end is near, and that our *dear one* will soon again rejoin his own happy family, which I am sure will then be even happier than ever.

I have had kind letters from each of my brothers regarding Sam and they have grieved for him as for an own brother; indeed, my heart has been touched even to tears to see their solicitude and tender devotion for him. George's last gave me much consolation.

"The Government," he says, "in all its endeavors has been unable to prove anything against our own dear friend and relative, Sam.

The Military Court, however, will be harsh with him I fear; but even so, no matter, we will have everything prepared to obtain his speedy release and return to his interesting and lovely family," etc. Alice Burch said she would tell you the rest.

Please give kind and tender love to dear ones, and believe me, Your cousin,

SISTER MARY ROSE

Not knowing where my father had been sent, my mother wrote to General Ewing and enclosed a letter for him. General Ewing at the time was away, and before his return my mother had received a letter from my father, which was mailed at Charleston. As soon as General Ewing returned, he answered her letter in the following terms:

Washington, July 31, 1865.

Dear Madam:

I was absent with my family when your letter of the 11th of July was received, enclosing letter addressed to your husband, and only returned a few days ago. I have sent your letter to the Secretary of War with a request that he will cause it to be sent to wherever the Doctor now is. I do not know where he has been sent, but it will be known soon I guess. If he has gone to the Tortugas, nothing can be done in his case until the Supreme Court sits, which will be next December.

Your affidavit, with the affidavits of Doctor Bland-ford, Sylvester Mudd, and Mr. Dyer, were laid before the President accompanied with a letter from me to him showing the relation of the facts stated in your affidavit to the other evidence. He read the papers, and informed me that the sentence would not be changed by him as at present advised. So there is no hope for the Doctor's release, except from the courts or from Congress.

I regret very greatly on your account, as well as his, that my hopes of his speedy release are frustrated, or likely to be, by the removal of your husband beyond the jurisdiction of an established State Court,

83

and that the President will not give to your evidence the weight it deserves. You should seek comfort, however, in the reflection that the vindictive and energetic effort to take his life failed, and that he will be returned to you before many months in spite of all that can be done by the Administration to keep him imprisoned. If he is sent to the Tortugas, the place is better for his health than almost any other. The island is dry, and the climate good. Rely on it, wherever he has gone his sanguine temperament will buoy him up, and preserve his health and strength. You doubtless saw in the account of their trip to Fort Monroe, that the Doctor was in excellent spirits.

With very best wishes for you and your family,

I am,

Very truly your friend,

THOMAS EWING, JR.

A letter of Mr. R. T. Merrick, advisory counsel for the defense, written to Dr. J. H. Bland-ford, my father's brother-in-law:

Washington City, August 12, 1865. J. H. Blandford, Esq.

Dear Sir: Yours of the 8th instant, with the enclosed letters, were received a few days since, on my return from the country. On reflection, I think it better not to enclose the letters, but will leave them with the young man in my office, in an envelope addressed to you, and should I not be in when you call, you can, therefore, get them.

After reading and carefully considering the letters, I have concluded that their publication *could do no good,* and might do harm. Let this cruel and unfortunate affair rest quiet for the present. It will wake with greater vigor when the time comes to arouse it.

When *the* time does come, I will let Mrs. Mudd know. When you are in the city call and see me, and we will exchange views in regard to the subject.

Present my kindest regards to Mrs. Mudd when you see her. She must exercise patience and fortitude in her afflictions, and abide the day of her deliverance.

Very truly yours, etc.,

R. T. MERRICK, Atty.

The following letter explains itself. It gives credence to rumors never authenticated. The result was that my father was put in chains and subjected to most rigorous restraint:

Louisville, Ky., August 17, 1865, 9 A. M. Hon. T. T. Echert,

Actg. Asst. Sec of War:

I have important papers. I think the commanding officer at the Dry Tortugas should be put on his guard 8 against an attempt to rescue the State prisoners in his charge.

A company is organizing in New Orleans for that purpose. I have all the facts from a reliable source.

(Signed) L. C. BAKER,

Br. Gen'l Pro. Mar. War Dept.

A true copy:

A. G. Office, Aug. 17, 1865.

E. D. TOWNSZND, Asst. Adj.-Gen.

The second letter my mother received from her husband, after being taken from Washington to the Tortugas. The one written her by him, and mailed from Charleston, was lost.

Fort Jefferson, Dry Tortugus, Florida, August 24, 1865. My Dearest Frank:

To-day one month ago we arrived here. Time passes very slowly and seems longer than that period—years gone by, apparently no longer. What do you think? I have received no letter or news whatever from home since being here. One or two of those who came down with me have received letters, containing no news, and do not advert to the possibility or the subject of release.

You know, my dear Frank, that that subject is the all-absorbing one of my mind. Frank must be sick—the little children are sick—some may be dead, or some other misfortune has happened, are questions frequently revolving in my mind and heart, and the dear ones at home are unwilling to break the cruel intelligence to me.

My dear Frank, were it not for you and those at home, I could pass the balance of my days here perfectly content or satisfied. Without you and the children, what is life for me—a blank, a void. Then, my dear Frank, if you have any regard for me, which you know I have never doubted, let me hear from you and often. I have written to you by every mail that has left this place, and surely some have been received. I wrote to you aboard the boat before arriving here. Mail, sometimes, arrives here in five days from New York.

This place continues to be unusually healthy, and the only fear manifested is that disease may be propagated by the arrival of vessels and steamers from infected ports. At this time there is a vessel lying at quarantine with all hands aboard sick with fever of some description,—several have died, and there is not one well enough to nurse the sick,—no volunteers from among the prisoners going to them, so the chances of life are small.

I am now in the hospital. I have little or no labor to perform, but my fare is not much improved. My principal diet is coffee, butter and bread three times a day. We have had a mess or two of Irish potatoes and onions, but as a general thing vegetables don't last many days in this climate before decomposition takes place. Pork and beef are poisonous to me; and molasses when I am able to buy it, and occasionally (fresh) fish, when Providence favored, are the only articles of diet used. I am enjoying very good health, considering the circumstances.

Sweet, dearest Frank, write to me soon on the receipt of my letter. I am afraid letters have been intercepted from either you or myself. If I don't hear from you soon, I am afraid I will become alike

86

indifferent and careless. I have written to Jere, Ewing, Stone, Ma and Papa some several letters—others, one or two, and not one syllable have I received.

I am afraid when the silence is broken, the news will be so great as to endanger the safety of the boat. My dear Frank, I have nothing to interest you—several hundred prisoners have been released and gone home recently to their families.

My anxiety increases upon the arrival of every boat and mail, and I envy the departing homeward bound. Give my love to all—kiss the children and believe me, truly and sincerely,

Your husband,

S. A. MUDD.

Shortly after receiving the following letter from General Ewing, my mother went to Washington to see the President. President Johnson told her that if Judge Holt would sign papers for my father's release, he (President Johnson) would. Then my mother left the White House for Judge Holt's office. There she told him what the President had said; his brow darkened, and he simply remarked, "Mrs. Mudd, I am sorry, I can do nothing for you."

Washington, August 31, 1865.

My dear Madam:

I have received yours of the 28th instant, and next day one from the Doctor written in excellent spirits. He is doing a great deal better than he would have done at Albany, and is evidently bearing himself with Christian and manly fortitude. I will write him an encouraging letter, and will not neglect to seize the best occasion to attempt his release by legal means.

I think the next time you are here you had better call to see Judge Holt, who has spoken to me twice of you highly, and asked about you and your children. I think you have made some impression on the old gentleman. In all these matters, his opinion will guide the action of the President.

When Mr. and Mrs. Browning return from Illinois, which will be about the 20th of September, I will show him your letter. He feels a deep interest in the Doctor, and a conviction of his entire innocence.

Do not worry too much. You and the Doctor are both young, and will yet live a long and happy life together.

In haste,

Sincerely your friend,

THOMAS EWING, JR.

This letter is explained in that of August 12 to Dr. J. H. Blandford:

Washington City, September 1, 1865. My dear Mrs. Mudd:

About three weeks since I received a letter from Dr. J. H. Blandford requesting me to examine two letters from your husband to you,, and determine whether it would be expedient to publish any portion of them.

I replied to Dr. Blandford, telling him that I thought it would be inexpedient to publish anything at this time, and asking him to call at my office, when in town, and get your letters. I have since heard nothing from him.

Lest my letter to him may not have reached its destination, I now write you. I have your letters, and will take care of them, subject to your order.

I regret that I have no news for you, and hope that you are waiting the coming of a better day with fortitude and patience.

With great respect,

Your true friend,

R. T. MERRICK.

The following order was issued upon the information contained in the letter of L. C. Baker, brigadier-general, dated August 17, 1865:

Hd. Qrs. Dist of Florida,

88

2d Separate Brigade D. F., Tallahassee, Sept. 3, 1865. To The Comd'g. Officer,

Sub. District of Key West.

Sir: Official information has been received at these Headquarters from Washington that a plot exists to release the prisoners at Fort Jefferson. You will take the proper precautions to prevent any uprising of the prisoners, and in case you find this information to be correct take measures to ferret out the leaders and place them in irons.

By command of Brig.-Gen. Newton,

A. C. PRETZ,

1st Lt and A. A. A. G.

Fort Jefferson, Dry Tortugas, Florida,

September 5, 1865.

My dear Frank:

A transport has just arrived and will take off at least a hundred prisoners, thereby thinning our ranks considerably. I am so credulous or hopeful as to expect my release upon the arrival of every steamer, and, not receiving, feel disappointed.

I have received but one letter since being cast upon this desolate, barren isle, and that was from your loving self, dated August 9. I have written between thirty and forty letters to various ones. I have written at least half a dozen to General Ewing, and Stone three or four. Jere and others as many each. I am truly anxious to know whether they intend to keep me here this Administration—I want to know the public opinion.

I have had several opportunities to make my escape, but knowing, or believing, it would show guilt, I have resolved to remain peaceable and quiet, and allow the Government the full exercise of its power, justice and clemency. Should I take French leave, it would amount to expatriation, which I don't feel disposed to do at present.

When you write, do not fail to enlighten and advise me upon all these points. I am with you, my dear Frank, whatever may be your resolve—my only desire for life is the assistance I may be capable of affording to you, our dear little ones, Pa, Ma and family. Were it not for these considerations, apart from the odium, I could remain here in contentment the balance of my days.

When you write, send me newspaper extracts or clippings that may be favorable or otherwise toward us, or to me. When you are reading over the papers, and see anything likely to interest, cut it out and enclose in your letters. At the same time, don't fail to mention all new developments that have arisen since our trial, whether any more arrests have been made, and all particulars concerning.

I want to know whether Ewing is doing anything, and whether any other influence has been brought to bear. I feel considerable disappointment in not hearing from either Stone or Ewing. I wrote to Ewing at the same time I wrote to you on the boat bound to this abominable place. He could judge well, from that first letter, that I made no such admissions or confessions as reported by the various Northern newspaper reports. I have lost all confidence in the veracity and honesty of the Northern people, and if I could honorably leave the country for a foreign land, I believe our condition would be bettered. There was never before a more persistent effort to criminate and to blast one's character and fortune than was resorted to in my case. What could not be effected by fair means, was done by foul—and villainy, and all for the almighty dollar. I saw no love and no patriotism. Had these virtues existed, I should have had a reward (although not asked nor expected) instead of the treatment received.

My dear Frank, I have nothing to mention worthy of interest. I am well in body. I am often cast down by depressing thoughts about you and all near and dear to me. I sometimes in my dreary walks look homeward, and feel an involuntary gloom and despondency to come over me. The thought often arises, or the question is asked within myself, "Shall I ever see home again, or those fond ones left behind?" God alone knows and can answer.

Good-by, my dearest Frank and all. Kiss the children and write soon and often,

S. A. MUDD.

My father unfortunately, on the 25th of September, 1865, endeavored to effect his escape. He stated after his release that he intended, had his effort been successful, to reach some point where the writ of *habeas corpus* was in force, surrender himself to the proper authorities, and then have the writ sued out in his behalf. The disastrous result of his unsuccessful attempt is shown in the order and report that follow:

Headquarters Port Jefferson, PIa.,

September 26, 1865.

Captain H. A. Harris,

80th U. S. C. I., Pro. Mar.

Capt: By direction of the Major Commanding, you will see that Dr. Sam'l A. Mudd is placed at "hard labor." Let him be detailed in the Engineer Dept to wheel sand. And hereafter, when any boat arrives, he will be put in the dungeon and kept there until it departs, and in future no favors of any kind will be shown him.

Very respectfully, your obdt servt,

H. S. MANNING,

2nd L,ieut 80th U. S. C. I., Post Adj't.

Headquarters Port Jefferson, Pla., September 27th, 1865.

Captain E. C. Woodruff,

Actg. Ass't. Adj't Gen'l.

Dep't of Florida.

Sir, I have the honor to report, that, on the 25th ins't. Dr. Samuel A. Mudd, one of the Conspirators, sentenced to this place for life, made an attempt to escape.

Since he has been in confinement here, he has been employed in the Prison Hospital, as Nurse and Acting Steward. When he came here, it was noticed that he immediately adopted the same clothing as worn by other prisoners. Although he had good clothes of his own. On the day he attempted to escape he put on one of the suits he brought with him and in some way got outside the Fort to the Wharf, where the U. S. Transport, Thos. A. Scott, was lying. He went on board that boat and, (with the assistance rendered him by one of the Crew, Henry Kelly), secreted himself under some plank in the lower hold. After a short search he was found and I put him in irons, into one of the dungeons. I also ordered the arrest of the man Kelly, and put him in close confinement.

Dr. Mudd's statement is that Kelly promised to assist him but had not done so. While Kelly denies knowing him or ever having seen him. Enclosed I forward the deposition of Jas. Healy, Coal passer on the steamer, which clearly proves that Kelly has told a falsehood. He has the appearance of being a hard case, and his reputation on the boat was bad.

I am very respectfully

Your obedient serv't.,

GEO. E. WENTWORTH, Major 82nd U. S. C. Inf'ty., Commanding Post.

The above is a literal copy.

ATTEMPTED ESCAPE, AS TOLD BY MY FATHER

Letter from my father to his brother--in-law, Mr. Jere Dyer:

Fort Jefferson, Tortugas Island, F'la.,

September 30, 1865.

My dear Jere:

I wrote to you and Frank by the last steamer, but at the same time intended to arrive before it. Providence was against me. I was too well known and was apprehended five or ten minutes after being aboard the steamer. They were so much rejoiced at finding me, they did not care to look much farther; the consequence was, the boat went off and carried away four other prisoners, who no doubt will make good their escape. I suppose this attempt of mine to escape will furnish the dealers in newspapers matter for comment, and a renewal of the calumnious charges against me. Could the world know to what a degraded condition the prisoners of this place have been reduced recently, they, instead of censure, would give me credit for making the attempt. This place is now wholly guarded by negro troops with the exception of a few white officers. I was told by members of the 161st N. Y. V. Reg., that so soon as they departed, the prisoners would be denied many of their former privileges, and life would be very insecure in their hands. This has already proved true; a parcel of new rules and regulations have already been made and are being enforced, which sensibly decreases our former liberties.

For attempting to make my escape, I was put in the guard-house, with chains on hands and feet, and closely confined for two days. An order then came from the Major for me to be put to hard labor, wheeling sand. I was placed under a boss, who put me to cleaning old bricks. I worked hard all day, and came very near finishing one brick. The order also directs the Provost Marshal to have me closely confined on the arrival of every steamer and until she departs. I know not how long this state of things will continue. I have arrived at that state of mind at which I feel indifferent to what treatment I am subjected. The 161st N. Y. Regiment were very kind and generous to me, and I was as much induced by them to make the attempt to take French leave as my own inclination and judgment dictated. I am now thrown out of my former position, chief of dispensary, and not likely to be reinstated. I know not what degree of degradation they may have in store for me. I was forced, under the penalty of being shot, to inform on one of the crew who promised to secrete me aboard. They have him still in close confinement, and will likely try him before court martial for the offense. I have written a note to the Major and have seen the Provost Marshal, and have taken upon myself the whole blame and responsibility of the affair, yet they pay little or no attention, and the young fellow is still kept in close confinement.

I don't regret the loss of my position. Take away the honor attached, the labor was more confining than any other place or avocation on the island. At the same time it relieved me of the disagreeable necessity of witnessing men starve for the nutriment essential for a sick man, when it could be had with no trouble and but a little expense. Four prisoners have died during the short time I have been here; the last one died the morning I made my attempt to escape. Not a single soldier or citizen laborer has died or suffered with any serious sickness; thereby showing something wrong, something unfair, and a distinction made between the two classes of individuals. Every case of acute dysentery or diarrhea among the prisoners, either dies in the onset or lingers on and terminates in the chronic, which eventually kills.

We have a disease here which is termed bone fever, or mild yellow fever, which has attacked at least three-fourths of the inmates of the Fort. It lasts generally but two or three days; during the time, the patient imagines every bone will break from the enormous pain he suffers in his limbs. None has died with it.

I have not been a day sick or unwell, owing no doubt to the fact of my thoughts being concentrated upon home, my dear Frank, and the children. Little did I think I would ever become the veriest slave and lose the control of my own actions, but such, unfortunately, is

94

too true, and God, I suppose, only knows whether these misfortunes will terminate with my frail existence, or that after being broken down with cares and afflictions of every kind, I be returned to my family a burden, more than a help and consoler. My only hope now is with you and the influence you can bring to bear. To be relieved from my present situation, I would be willing to live in poverty the balance of my days with Heaven my only hope of reward. If money be necessary, sell everything that I possess, and what might be allotted by poor Papa from his already exhausted means.

I feel that I am able now, and have resolution to make a decent living in any section of the world in which I am thrown by the Grace and Providence of the Almighty.

It strikes me that the Hon. Reverdy Johnson, Montgomery Blair, and many others whose principles and opinions are growing daily more popular—their influence could be easily brought to bear in my behalf. You fail to give me any idea of what was being done or any reasons for me to hope for relief by any certain time. You may have omitted this for prudential reasons. I have been too careless in my language among the evil disposed. They have never failed to misinterpret my language and meaning, and to omit everything having a tendency to exonerate me.

Knowing this, I shall be the keeper or guardian of my own thoughts and words for the future. I never knew how corrupt the world was before being visited by my recent calamities and troubles. They have shamefully lied and detracted everything I have said or done—a privilege for the future they shall never have.

No doubt they will get up a great sensation in regard to my attempted escape. Some thirty or forty have made their escape, or attempts to do so, since I have been here, and there never was anything thought of them. Since my unlucky attempt, everything seems to have been put in commotion, and most unfounded suspicions, rumors, etc., started.

My only object for leaving at the time I attempted, was to avoid the greater degradation, and insecurity of life, and at the same time be united again with my precious little family. I don't perceive why there is so much odium attached, as the authorities, by their harsh and cruel treatment, endeavor to make believe.

I will soon be returned to some duty more compatible with my qualifications. In the mean time, assure Frank and all that I am well and hearty, and as determined as ever. Write soon. Give my unbounded love to all at home, and believe me most truly and devotedly, Yours, etc.,

S. A. MUDD.

Oct. 1st. —I am constrained before mailing this, to acquaint you with the following: The young man Kelly, and Smith who was locked up with him, and bound with chains and thrown in a place they denominate the dungeon, on my account, freed themselves from their chains, broke out the iron-grated window, let themselves down from the window by the chains with which they were bound, stole a boat, and made good their escape last night.

Smith was one of the most outrageous thieves that ever walked. You would marvel to hear him tell of his wonderful feats and thefts. Kelly promised to secrete me aboard the steamer, and to save my life. I was necessitated to inform on him. He was brought to the same room in which I was locked. He excused me, and said that the Commandant was a fool to think that they could hold him upon this island, which has proved too true. The authorities are no doubt much disappointed and chagrined at this unexpected occu rence. I feel much relieved.

Yours as ever, etc.,

SAM.

Fort Jefferson, Dry Tortugas, Fla.,

October 5, 1865.

My dear Jere:

A vessel is about leaving port. I take advantage of it to drop you a few hasty lines. I forgot to mention, in the letters previously written, to inform you that none of the drafts, that I drew upon you, will be presented for payment. I was fortunate in being able to borrow twenty-five dollars; the check, so soon as I can obtain the money, will go to liquidate it. I shall endeavor to be as economical as possible, knowing to what straits my family has been already reduced. The only need I have for money is to purchase a few vegetables, and supply myself with tobacco. The only article of clothing I need is shirts. The Government furnishes flannel shirts, which I find very pleasant in damp weather, but very disagreeable and warm in dry sunshine.

If the friends of Arnold and O'Laughlin should send a box of clothing to them, you may put in a couple of brown linen, or check linen, shirts and a couple pairs cotton drawers. You may not bother yourself to this extent if you anticipate an early release. My clothing is sufficient to come home in. I will need no more money before the first of December, or latter part of November. It generally takes a letter ten or twelve days to reach this place, so anticipate the period, and send me twenty-five dollars in greenbacks. Address your letters to me, and not in care of any one, and I will get them without fail. Write me soon and let me know whether my attempted escape caused much comment in the Northern papers. I fear it will have the effect to again agitate the question. I had written so often and desired information and council, that I became truly impatient and vexed. I expected to hear something from Ewing or Stone, but not a word have I received from either. I received a letter a few days ago which gave me more consolation and hope than any yet come to hand, from Henry. Had I received such a letter earlier I would have been content, and would never have acted as I did. I would have succeeded, only for meeting a party aboard, who knew me, before I could arrive at my hiding-place. I was informed on almost immediately, and was taken in custody by the guard. I regret only one thing, being necessitated to inform on the party who had promised to befriend me. It was all done by the mere slip of the tongue, and without reflection; but perhaps it was all providential. He is now free, having made good his escape with a notorious thief with whom he was locked up. I understand, after escaping from the dungeon, in which they were confined, they robbed the sutler of fifty dollars in money, as much clothing as they needed, and a plenty of eatables in the way of canned fruits, preserves, meats, etc. Six prisoners made good their escape on the same boat upon which I was so unfortunate. It seems they were too much elated to look farther after my apprehension.

I am taking my present hardship as a joke. I am not put back in the least. I will soon assume my former position, or one equally respectable. The only thing connected with my present attitude is the name, and not the reality. I have no labor to perform, yet I am compelled to answer roll-call, and to sleep in the guard-house at night. This will not last longer than this week. Write soon, give me all the news, and continue to send me papers. I have received several from you, Frank, and some have been sent from New York by unknown parties, which afforded me considerable recreation. Give my love to all at home, and send this, after reading, to Frank, so that she may know that I am well, etc. I am sorry Tom is going to leave so early. I am under the greatest obligations to him for interest and kindness manifested. I am in hopes my release won't be long deferred, when I shall be able to see you all.

The following pointed and manly letter from Hon. Charles A. Eldredge, Representative in Congress from the Fourth Congressional District of Wisconsin, to Judge-Advocate Holt, speaks for itself:

[From the *Ohio Crisis*, October 11, 1865.]

Fond du Lac, September 25, 1865. Judge-Advocate-General Holt.

My Dear Sir: The following circular letter addressed to me has been duly received, to wit:

"WAR DEPARTMENT, "BUREAU or MILITARY JUSTICE, "Washington, September 12, 1865. "By direction of the Secretary of War a number of copies of the argument of Hon. John A. Bingham in the case of the assassin conspirators, and also a number of copies of the opinion of Attorney-General Speed, are sent enclosed in envelopes to you, in order that they may be well distributed throughout your district. It is especially desirable that the legal profession should be furnished with the information which these documents contain.

"J. HOLT, Advocate-General."

The copies of the argument and opinion which you desire "may be well distributed" in my district, are also received. The importance of it to yourself and the Secretary of War may or may not justify the large expense consequent upon the publication and distribution. The people of my district will not, I presume, mind the expense in these times of light taxation. But I trust you will pardon me the suggestion that black and horrible as is the crime in the consideration of all good men, of the assassination of President Lincoln, neither the blackness of that crime nor the arguments and opinions of those learned gentlemen, will prevent my constituents, and when the history thereof comes to be written, posterity generally, from branding military trials of civilians as infamous violations of the Constitution and laws.

Do not, I pray you, flatter yourself that you and the Secretary of War can, by the circulation of these documents at your own or the people's expense, convince your countrymen that arrests without warrant, imprisonment without trial, sentences without conviction, trial without indictment or jury, and the worse than mockery of your victims in military trials, are anything but crimes—gross outrages of the people's rights and liberties, and violations of the people's Constitution. Respectfully,

CHARLES A. ELDREDGE.

The documents forwarded Mr. Eldredge for distribution, intended as a defense of military commissions for the trial of citizens, were printed at the expense of the people, and were forwarded by mail free of postage.

Fort Jefferson, Dry Tortugas, Florida,

October 18, 1865.

My dearest Frank:

You will no doubt, ere this reaches you, see some mention in the newspapers of my effort to get away. I learn from a friend a pretty lengthy account has been sent on for publication. My dear Frank, it is bad enough to be a prisoner in the hands of white men, your equals under the Constitution, but to be lorded over by a set of ignorant, prejudiced and irresponsible beings of the unbleached humanity, was more than I could submit to, when I had every reason to believe my chances of escape almost certain, and would be crowned with success. Connected with this inspiring hope, and an early union with you and our precious little children, the higher-minded and unprejudiced mind would rather give me credit than blame for the attempt. Why should I be expected to act more honorable than my persecutors, who sent me here? Have they not, from the beginning to the present, endeavored to degrade and humiliate by previously unknown and unheard of tortures and cruelties even in an uncivilized community, to lower us, the victims of injustice, beneath the dignity of the brute creation?

My darling wife, when I am capable of beholding with a serene eye the mild and beneficent sway of the Fathers of the Republic, and the former prestige of the American Flag, the shield, the protection of the citizen, be he at home or in a foreign land, vindicated, then I shall calmly and patiently submit. I am resolved henceforth to yield my opinion, and bear up against all the indignities and hardships they can heap upon me, to the better judgment of my advisers, to God, and the justice of my cause.

You need have no further apprehension regarding my conduct. I have not had a cross word with an individual, soldier or prisoner, since I have been closeted upon this island of woe and misery. I have striven to the utmost of my ability to render myself and those around me comfortable, visiting the sick, and saving my scanty means to the last dime. So for the future, make yourself easy, and rest assured that I will be guilty of no act that will ever have the tendency to compromise my cause. I think hard of my lawyers; they know how ignorant I am of law, and they should have extended all the necessary advice and counsel, which I repeatedly asked for. No mortal mind can appreciate the feelings of one who has been so foully dealt with, and separated suddenly and violently from family and all near and dear, and banished hundreds of miles away,—no opportunities afforded of being visited, and but imperfect and irregular mail facilities, for no fault, and for having done my duty to God and man. To bear patiently under such circumstances requires more than human strength. I trust my present good resolutions will be supported by grace from above, through the prayerful mediation of you and all.

I fear, my dear Frank, you may be in need of money, etc. I enclose in this some medical bills. Try to collect them. You may think and say, "What is the use of all this, Sam will be home time enough to attend to it himself," but take my advice, and do not rely too much on hopes. Make sure of this means; pay off hirelings, and purchase all necessary family supplies for yourself and children. Make provision always for a more unpropitious day. The time may be close at hand when you may be reduced to an even worse condition than at present. I perceive a betrayal of your anticipations and hopes by the kind offer to send me clothing, money and other articles. If my release is to be so speedy, there will be no necessity for them. I can come home in anything. I have learned to disregard the mocks and jeers of this cold and uncharitable world. If it was no fault of my own, I would take a delight in walking the streets of New York on my way home on my knees; but if Providence favors me with a speedy release, I will return by way of New Orleans and through the South.

On the 12th, three more prisoners made good their escape, taking a boat just from under the eyes of the guard in open daylight, about 12 o'clock, and succeeded in getting some eight or nine miles before the loss of the boat was discovered, when they observed it was useless to pursue. These cases never will be known to the public; but cases in which party interests are involved, will find no opportunity of escaping.

Since my effort to get away, eleven have made good their escape, all of whom were sentenced for a long period of years. Do not view my act with dishonor. I am a prisoner under guard, not under a parole, and under no obligations to remain if I can successfully evade and free myself. You will, when you write, inform me whether the act has, or will have, any injurious tendency, also send me the comments of the press, should there be any. When you see any article in the papers to which you wish to direct my attention, mark it around with a lead pencil or pen. You may rely upon my remaining perfectly quiet and content, until I receive a hint from you to act to the contrary. I am for the shortest road home, no matter how difficult. My letters for the future will not be so lengthy. I will write every opportunity, but we fear, owing to a recent change in the government of the Post, will be denied many of our former privileges.

Arnold was clerk in the Provost Marshal's office, and without any cause assigned, has been ordered to hard labor. We will endeavor to deport ourselves as always, as true gentlemen and as men conscious of innocence, and of the gross wrongs and injuries inflicted. Be assured and satisfied that the ills we now suffer proceed from no act of mine, or ours. I am compelled to sleep now in the guard-house, but I am presumed to be doing hard work. It is of little importance as regards labor. Those assigned to active duty are generally the healthiest, which is more than a compensation for the change.

My heart almost bleeds sometimes when I think of you and our dear little children, and the many pleasant hours we used to enjoy together. I feel they will be too large for me to handle when I shall be a free man again, and be able to return to you. My love and devotion appears to increase with every day. With • the change from the white to the colored regiment, many of our former privileges have been denied; yet we are determined not to give them the least cause to complain, and for the future I am determined not to leave or make an attempt without the proper authority. I would not have thought of such a thing, were it not for a change in the government of the Post.

Give my love to all, Ma, Pa, and all the family, and tell them, to write. I am consoled by every letter. I don't wish you to write anything that may have a tendency (if made public) to be detrimental to my cause. Letters are no doubt read by for that purpose, and notes taken of them, and then suffered to proceed. The last letter I received, was dated September 22, and mailed from Baltimore October 8. Exercise prudence. I don't expect you will be able to do much until after the trial of Wintz, Davis & Co.

Good-by, my sweet, precious wife and dear little ones. God bless you all.

Yours, etc.,

S. M.

Port Jefferson, Tortugas, Florida,

October 23, 1865.

My dearest Wife:

I wrote you on the 10th and 11th. Since then orders have been promulgated to look into all correspondence leaving the Post, as well as those arriving, so for the future you need not trouble yourself to be lengthy or make public your domestic affairs. I am , very well, although at present confined to a small damp room with Arnold, O'Loughlin, Spangler, and a Colonel Grenfel, formerly an English Officer, but recently of the Confederate Army. What has led to this treatment, we are at a loss to account. We have all deported ourselves as gentlemen, and as Christians. Do not let this trouble you, I have already borne worse, and I am in hopes, through the mercies of God, to live through these hardships and be a consolation to you and my dear little family. We are now guarded by a negro regiment. Good-by. Pray for me, and give my love to all.

Your devoted husband,

SAMUEL MUDD.

The following letter from my uncle, Mr. Jere Dyer, to my mother, gives some idea of the efforts that were being made to secure my father's release:

Baltimore, November 6, 1865. Dear Frank:

103

Your truly welcome letter did not reach me until this morning, and ex-Governor Ford of Ohio did not leave here until Wednesday. He promised to call to see me before leaving, but failed to do so. He sent a gentleman to see me to apologize for not calling, and also to tell me he met with every success. He had several interviews with Webster, who was in Congress last winter, but is now Collector of this port, having recently been appointed by the President, and he is decidedly in favor of his release. He has promised the Governor his influence, and also told his messenger that everything was working to his entire satisfaction, and he was quite sanguine of success. God grant it; but still, my dear child, be not too sanguine, for you know everything in this life is very uncertain. We, too, have our part to perform, namely: send our petitions to Him who is mightier than man. He may not at first hear us as speedily as we wish, but He has promised that whatever we ask in His name, will be granted. He will not refuse much longer, and will soon return him to you.

I am sorry to hear you have another case of typhoid fever. It seems indeed you have your full share of trouble; but, my child, you must try and be patient, and bear them with Christian resignation, and God will send you your reward.

Poor Cousin Henry—it seems fate is bearing hard on him. How I pity him. He has never known trouble before. Providence truly smiled on him in his younger days, and it does seem hard he should have so many troubles now he is old.

I mailed you Sam's letters last Tuesday. You did not mention having received them. I judge you have not sent to the office. I find they are keeping a pretty close guard over them, but I am satisfied it will not last very long. I suppose they only wanted to try and make him say or do something for them to publish, and try and keep up some excitement against him, but I know he has learned by sad experience to be too much on his guard to give them any further excuse for their villainy and rascality.

I am going to R. I. Brent's office this evening to show him Sam's letters. He is very anxious to see them. Although he is a copper-head, he is a big man, and a warm friend.

Frank, I am always at work whenever there is the slightest chance of doing anything. I try to keep him before all the big men, and make them talk about his case. You know every opinion has its weight, so you must be hopeful, not too sanguine as to any particular time. My own opinion is, from all I can gather, we may reasonably expect him home between this and the first of January. I wrote him a very long letter and mailed it two days before your last one, in which I told him I hoped to see him at the foot of his table on Christmas Day carving that big old gobbler.

Well, I have not had a frolic for a long time, and if it is the will of Heaven it should be so, I hardly think my Heavenly Father would do anything with me for taking two glasses of egg-nog. Do you? Love to all. Your brother,

JERE.

NEGRO TROOPS AT FORT JEFFERSON

RELIEVED IN PART BY WHITE SOLDIERY

Port Jefferson, Tortugas Island, Florida,

November 11, 1865. My dear Jere:

Yesterday, the 10th, four companies of heavy artillery arrived to relieve the detested and abominable negro regiment, and I am in hopes our future treatment will be much milder. It can't be worse. We were placed, without any cause whatever, in heavy leg irons on the 5th of November, marched down to headquarters, then placed under a boss at hard labor cleaning old brick. A tug arrived that day, and it was no doubt to please the crew's gross fancy and exhibit the Major's power, that the cruel act was resorted to. We had been closely confined under guard for more than a fortnight previously. Notwithstanding living in irons, we are closely guarded and not suffered to leave the door for the most trivial thing without having a negro guard with musket and bayonet by our side. At night, our chains are taken off, the door locked, and a sentry placed there on guard. This treatment was not brought about by any fear of escape, or the apprehension of any violence on our part, but is no doubt done to degrade and lessen us in the estimation of our fellow-prisoners and citizens, and to keep down the apparent sympathy of strange arrivals, of which every boat brings many.

I received a letter from you and Fanny* on the 7th, and was much rejoiced to know that your hopes of release were so lively. God grant that your efforts may succeed, and I be delivered from this hell upon earth. Fannie was telling me what papa was doing, which I thought was very improper, knowing that any imprudence is subjected to the inspection of officious officers, who are disposed to place their own wicked construction wherever their personal gain or ambition is likely to be profited. I am afraid papa will find himself in the end the victim of imposition of some of these hostile intermeddlers, although mercy grant the contrary. I have had enough of the humanity and Christian spirit that animates the hand of the saints, to cause me to remember them, and it is but natural I should desire

106

that they should be visited by the same degree of chastisement which they have and are still inflicting upon their fellow-countrymen through motives of patriotism and vindication of the honor and supremacy of the Republic. Every day increases my hate toward the authors of my ruin, and sometimes I can scarcely withhold my angry indignation. The near approach of expected relief I am in hopes will keep me within bounds. Should you be so fortunate as to effect my release, lose no time in forwarding the joyous intelligence. Telegraph it to Tom, and tell him to notify me from New Orleans; also write to Henry Benners, postmaster of this place. You can enclose a letter to his address for me, observing due precautions. I sent you what might be a copy of a letter to Secretary Stanton. I did not write, but scribbled it off so that you and counsel could advise regarding. You can omit and supply as you think the case may require. We are all at this moment in chains. Neither Colonel Grenfel nor myself has been taken out to work the past two or three days, but suffered to remain passively in our quarters. He is quite an intelligent man, tall, straight, and about sixty-one or two years of age. He speaks fluently several languages, and often adds mirth by his witty sarcasm and jest. He has been badly wounded and is now suffering with dropsy, and is allowed no medical treatment whatever, but loaded down with chains, and fed upon the most loathsome food, which treatment in a short time must bring him to an untimely grave. You will confer an act of kindness and mercy by acquainting the English Minister at Washington, Sir V. A. Bruce, of these facts.

Your brother,

SAM.

Application was made on November 20, 1865, by my uncle, Thomas O. Dyer, of New Orleans, to Major-General Sheridan, commanding the Division of the Gulf, for permission to forward to my father certain articles of clothing and luxury. This permission was granted, as will appear by a copy of the order which follows. Up to this time the articles sent my father by his friends had almost invariably failed to reach him; and even afterward many articles, and even sums of money, sent him seem to have been "confiscated."

Headquarters Military Division of the Gulf, Office Provost-Marshal General. New Orleans, November 20, 1865.

Permission is hereby granted to T. o. Dyer to forward this invoice of goods to Samuel A. Mudd, confined at Fort Jefferson, Florida, care of commanding officer there, who will deliver same at his discretion. Q. M. Dept will furnish transportation.

By command of Maj.-Gen. Sheridan,

W. T. SHERMAN,

Brig. Gen'l & P. M. G.

The articles, an invoice of which had been furnished to General Sheridan, were duly sent, and all were received by my father except "2 bottles Bordu Whiskey." These were nevermore heard of. Whether they were cast overboard in transmission, or were intercepted and the contents consumed by some bibulous individual to whom opportunity offered temptation, will perhaps never be known.

Port Jefferson, November 25, 1865. My dearest Wife:

I am as well as circumstances permit. Give my love to all, Pa, Ma, and the family. Tell the children they must be good, learn their lessons, and pray for their disconsolate papa. I am afraid to write more, lest objection be made; and believe me, my dear Frank, your most faithful and devoted husband, confiding in the infinite goodness and mercy of God and the prayerful intercession of many friends, I am in hopes of a speedy release and return to you.

A mail has arrived. The letters and papers have not been distributed, consequently I do not know whether there is anything for me or not. Kiss all the children, etc.

Yours,

SAM.

Dry Tortugas, Fla., December 9, 1865. My dear Jere:

I received your last, dated November 7, 1865, which I assure you has raised my spirits above description. Let me hear from you all, not contraband, at your earliest opportunity.

I received a trunk from dear Tom on the 3d of December, invoiced as containing a quantity of fine clothes, several cans of vegetables, fish, whiskey, etc. The whiskey was not received. I wrote to him acknowledging the receipt. He may not get it, so when you write, inform him.

The negro regiment has been only partially relieved by white troops. Our condition is not much better. We are still in irons, compelled to wash down six bastions of the Fort daily, closely guarded, denied all intercourse with other prisoners, locked up at night, and· a sentry placed at the door. Our fare is something better, and we are allowed to purchase articles of food, etc. I also received twenty-five dollars from Tom. This was placed in the hands of the commander, not to my credit. We are only allowed three dollars per month. I assure you no reasonable cause can be alleged for our present rash and inhuman treatment other than my attempted escape.

I thought I had paid the penalty of my offense when we were paid a visit by Generals Newton and Forsyth, and we are informed by the negro Commandant that it was through their order we were placed in irons. Newton commands this department. *God bless him and his tribe!*

I am well and in hopes of a speedy release from my chains. Good-by, my dearest, brother and friend. Give my love to all and kiss Frank and the children for me,. You need not send me any more money. I will call upon you when I need it. I have enough to bring me home. This note is written far underground.

Your brother,

SAM.

Port Jefferson, Florida, December 12, 1865. My darling Frank:

I received last night yours of the 4th of November, which relieved me of many apprehensions regarding you and our little ones.

I assure you last week has been the most miserable of my imprisonment, on account of the gloom which came over me in consequence of your failing to write at the appointed time. You said nothing in your letter about your previous sickness or indisposition. I, therefore, conclude you have fully recovered. I am truly pleased to see you so hopeful of my speedy release. I can see nothing cheering in what you have communicated, but it may be owing to my want of understanding. It is my impression this flimsy pretense is resorted to to keep up a show of doing something, when in reality nothing is intended to be accomplished. I am pleased to know that you are satisfied; as for myself, nothing short of removal from this place can create an impression of fair dealing on the part of those in authority.

I am sorry to hear of the death of George Garrico and Mr. Bean. Our white population is wonderfully diminishing by death and other causes. The negroes will soon be in the majority, if not already. Should I be released any time shortly, and circumstances permit, I will use all my endeavors to find a more congenial locality. I wrote to you on the 7th, also on the 1st, which I am in hopes you shall have received before this. I sent you on the 7th a couple of large moss-cards, and to-day send you three more, having nothing more suitable at hand. I have some small shell frames for pictures, but cannot send them conveniently by mail. I will try to send them by the next mail if I can arrange a safe box, etc. I was in hopes I would have the pleasure of bringing in person these little curiosities, but fate has decreed otherwise.

Don't bother yourself in regard to my wants; they are all plentifully supplied at this time. I have plenty of money for all my wants, clothing sufficient to last me a year or more.

I am well with the exception of a pretty bad cold, and occasional rheumatic attacks. Give my love to Pa, Ma, and all the family.

SAM.

Fort Jefferson, Dry Tortugas, December 14, 1865.

My darling Wife:

I have received no intelligence from you since the letter dated November 7. In *that* I was led to hope for a speedy reunion. I fear you have been misled and caused cruel disappointment to visit me in this *ungodly* place; a new *pang* to my sufferings.

We have not been visited by a priest up to this time. There is no minister of any denomination here, and no religious observation of Sunday or holidays.

The colored regiment has only been partially relieved. Our fare has much improved since I last wrote, though treatment is the same.

I received a trunk of clothing, cans of vegetables, tobacco and twenty-five dollars from dear Tom on the 3d instant. The clothing is finer than I need, besides I am not situated to wear them. You will please express my thanks and gratitude to Tom when you again write.

Did you deliver the message to Fannie I requested in a former letter, viz: to be more prudent in her writing? The last letter that arrived was not handed me on account of insulting language. She must have been aware that all correspondence is inspected previous to the delivery to prisoners, and language prejudicial to me or herself would be observed, and likely noted. Do caution her for the future, and allow nothing in your power to prevent, to be said or done having a tendency to prolong my misery. I have arrived at that point to which I would accept any terms for an immediate release,— even death I crave to a much longer protraction. So, my darling, try and prevent all language that is not likely to accomplish anything toward my relief. Spare no effort in endeavoring to bring before the Executive my entire innocence. You know well, my darling, could the truth be established, I should receive the thanks and applause of the nation instead of this cruel and unjust treatment.

My dear little Tommy continues still unwell; alas! I fear I shall not be home in time to render him any benefit. I am in hopes I shall be spared this affliction—the loss of one of our dear little children—by a merciful Providence. What I have already undergone is beyond my power of expressing, and nothing but the consciousness of having done no wrong, but a duty, causes me to bear up against my adverse fortune. Written in haste. Write soon. My heart yearns to see you, and the dear little ones.

Good-by, my darling wife, my hope and comfort. Your husband,

SAM.

Fort Jefferson, Dry Tortugas, Florida,

December 20, 1865.

My darling Frank:

I am well, things are *"in static quo."* The weather is very warm—mosquitoes and bed-bugs very numerous and troublesome; coupled with this, I feel much disappointed at not being able to enjoy my Christmas dinner at home, as I have been led to hope.

I have received no letters since yours of the 27th of November and December 5th. Since then I have written—this the third letter to you and one to Fannie. I have received no letter from you containing money, and for the future you need not bother yourself to send me anything, only as I may desire. You and our dear little children will require every dime to sustain you, and no doubt even then will suffer many privations and hardships. When you write, let me know whether you have succeeded in hiring any field hands or a cook for another year. Do all you can to avoid being an incumbrance to others, at the same time be careful to prevent actual want to self and our sweet little children—this thought occasions me more anxiety and suffering than any other. A steamer is coming in—I will await the mail before concluding. The steamer has landed, but brought no mail. How anxious I was that it would bring me the glad tidings of release; but I fear the Almighty thinks it would occasion me too much joy.

My darling Frank, when I read the papers that I now and then receive I can see nothing to inspire me with hope regarding myself, or the restoration of peace and good feeling throughout the States. How much I desire the States to assume their proper relation in the

Union! Should I be released at this time I would be very much bothered to find a place where we could rest happy and content upon the habitable globe—so demoralized have become the people and insecure life, liberty, and prosperity. Nothing is reliable in these times, and God only knows when I shall be suffered to return to you. I will likely be detained longer than you anticipate, to keep up the appearance of justice, or until excitement and agitation is allayed— so, my dearest, do all you can; let not the cares, which now press heavily upon you, lead you to unnecessarily expose your health and strength—con-sider the welfare of our dear little children and my happiness, should Providence speedily favor me.

I am sorry I have nothing entertaining and interesting to relate— such would be a contradiction to this place of woe.

Your devoted husband,

SAM.

The following is a copy of a letter written by my mother to President Johnson:

Bryantown, Md., December 22, 1865.

His Excellency, Andrew Johnson,

President of The United States.

Dear Sir: I hesitate to address you, but love is stronger than fear, timidity must yield. I must petition for him who is very, very dear to me. Mr. President, after many weeks anxious waiting for news from my innocent, suffering husband, Dr. Samuel Mudd, last night's mail brought the sad tidings, he with others, by orders from the War Department, were heavily ironed, and obliged to perform hard work. The plea for this cruel treatment is that the Government is in possession of news of a plot, originating in Havana or New Orleans, for the rescue of the said prisoners. The food furnished is of such miserable quality, he finds it impossible to eat it. Health and strength are failing. To my poor intellect, it seems an ineffectual plan to put down a plot by avenging upon the prisoners the acts of others. I suppose Secretary Stanton knows better. It strikes me very forcibly, your Excellency is ignorant of this order. I saw you in September, and although I felt I was not as kindly treated as others, I looked into your face, and if it is true that "the face is an index to the heart," I read in it a good, kind heart that can sympathize with the sufferings of others. I marked the courteous manner you addressed ladies, particularly the aged. These things encouraged me to pray you to interpose your higher authority. The setting of a leg is no crime that calls for forgiveness. I ask you to release him, and I believe you will do it. I beg you in the name of humanity, by all that is dear to me, in the name of his aged and suffering parents, his wife and four babies, to immediately put a stop to this inhuman treatment. By a stroke of your pen, you can cause these irons to fall and food to be supplied. By a stroke of that same pen, you can give him liberty. Think how much depends upon you. You were elected the Father of this people. Their welfare is your welfare. Then, in the name of God, if you let him die under this treatment, he an American citizen, who has never raised his arm, nor his voice against his country, can these people love you? Forgive me, I speak plainly, but my heart is very sore. You say, "Women are your jewels," you hope for much from their prayers. I do not love you, neither will I ask the Almighty to bless you; but give back my husband to me, and to his parents who are miserable,—the wealth of my love and gratitude will be yours. My prayers shall ascend in union with my little children who are in happy ignorance, daily looking for the return of their "Pa." To Him who has said, "Suffer little children to come unto me," God of mercy I pray you, touch the heart of thy servant, make him give back my husband. Could you look into our household, it would give you a subject for meditation. In the Doctor's childhood home, there is his father, who is old and infirm. When he hears the name of his boy, his lips tremble, but he thinks it is not manly to yield to tears, besides, he has confidence in you. His mother has scarcely left her sick-room since his arrest. "She waits," she says, "to see him"; then like Holy Simeon, "she is willing to die." Pass from this to my little household. I, a wife, drag out life in despondency.

I, who was shielded from every care by him who is now suffering a living death, am miserable and have to battle with this overwhelming trouble. I am the mother of four babies, the oldest, seven years, the youngest, but one. The third, a delicate boy requiring constant care. I have confidence in you and feel you will grant my request.

Very respectfully yours,

MRS. DR. SAMUEL A. MUDD.

Saturday 23d, 1865.

My darling Frank:

The steamer has remained until the present. I send you one or two moss-pictures as• a Christmas gift, being the only thing in my power to transmit. You need not send any person to see me, for at present all intercourse and conversation with outsiders is interdicted, and it would only increase my suffering to be denied the pleasure and satisfaction of some kind friend or familiar face's company.

I am well, but do not enjoy health. We have our Christmas dinner already in prospect, viz: canned roast turkey, sausage, oysters, preserves, fresh peaches, tomatoes, etc.

Wishing from my inmost heart, you a happy, merry and joyful Christmas, I am,

Your faithful, devoted and loving husband,

SAM.

Fort Jefferson, December 25, 1865.

My dear Jere:

To-day being Christmas, I shall endeavor in spirit to eat my dinner with you all, since Providence has decreed the denial of the reality. I can imagine the sight of all my little children, my dearest Frank and yourself, with the usual glass of egg-nog and sweet things, seated around a happy fire with no thought to mar the pleasure and joy of the greatest Christian festival. This was not long since the happiest of my thoughts, but oh! how far from the realization. I hate to contemplate the time that yet intervenes. For the future, do not mislead me to hope for relief by a certain time when there is no certainty. It adds only a new pain to my already languishing life. Do all you can, say nothing when you know nothing can be effected; avoid irritating and offensive language, on all occasions, and with parties whose influence may be of avail, make known the false testimony and unfair measures resorted to in order to effect my conviction. I am very well. Our treatment is the same as when I last wrote.

I received a letter from Fannie dated December 6, mailed the 13th, informing me of your inability to accomplish my release. I have felt considerable disappointment; try for the future to save me this unnecessary anguish. Write often and send me papers. Lose no time in communicating the glad tidings should Providence favor your efforts. Love to all.

Kiss Frank and all my dear little children. Good-by.

SAM.

Fort Jefferson, December 25, 1865. My darling Frank:

I wrote to you on the 20th, and now again on this, that should be to us all a joyful festival, to let you know I am well, and have received through Fannie, the intelligence of our mutual disappointment—the inability to effect the object of my sincerest hopes,'—a speedy reunion. I was much grieved to know that Jere thought it necessary to rent out the farm. I was in hopes you would be able to hire one or two good hands, and cultivate through old Uncle John's management the land yourself, but I know all things will be done for the best, therefore feel satisfied. Bear up, my darling, against all the adversities and calamities which have so suddenly befallen us, with Christian fortitude. I sometimes ask myself the question, "what have I done to bring so much trouble upon myself and family?" The answer is from my inmost heart—"nothing." I am only consoled to know that the greatest saints were the most prosecuted, and the greatest sufferers, although far be it from classing myself with those chosen friends of God. Would to God, darling, it was in my power to afford you some consolation in this, I hope, the darkest hour of our lives. I have endeavored to the best of my ability to lead as spotless and sinless a life as in my power. I have not omitted saying my beads a single day since living on this horrid island. We have not been visited yet by a priest, and I desire much to go to confession and communion and conform to all the requirements of our holy religion, yet I do not know whether I would be allowed this privilege should a minister of our church visit us at this time, since we are yet closely confined under guard and denied all intercourse with outsiders. Our duties are to sweep down the bastions of the Fort every day under a guard. Our condition is the same as when I last wrote. It is alleged my attempted escape has been the cause of our continued harsh treatment, but this can't be so, for none of the rest made the least move, and none of the party was there at the time. When the irons were placed upon us we were told they were only to be kept on while a steamer or vessel was lying at the wharf; but they have been on every day, and taken off at night since the first day they were put on. I am in hopes the day is not far distant when reason and law will take the place of passion, prejudice, and sectional hatred. So far as our conduct is concerned, none have been more quiet and submissive, although certain false statements and representations have been made. My sweet darling wife, good-by. I am truly in hopes you have spent a more agreeable Christmas than myself. God bless you all.

SAMUEL MUDD.

PRISON LIFE IN 1866

Fort Jefferson, Florida, January 1, 1866.

My darling Frank:

To-day being New Year, I have no better means at my command of spending the time appropriately than dropping you a few hasty lines to afford you all the consolation that lies in my power. On the morning of the 28th, Bishop Verot, of Savannah, and the Rev. Father O'Hara arrived here about 6 o'clock. Soon word came that they desired to see me; my chains being taken off, I dressed in my best, and was soon ushered into their presence with my *usual* guard of honor. I found them preparing to say mass, and had the happy fortune of being present during the divine service.

After service I had a short conversation with Bishop Verot and Rev. Wm. O'Hara. I received the contents of the letter formerly addressed to Father O'Hara by Sister Joseph—a cross, a scapular, etc. In the evening I had the pleasure of listening to a very learned and practical lecture from the Bishop. After the discourse, I repaired to my quarters, took my usual supper, said my beads, and enjoyed for a time a promenade up and down my gloomy quarters, when a rap at the door was heard, and my name called. On going to the door, I found our most pious and venerable Bishop had called to bid me good-by; he intended leaving in the morning. I had given the subject of confession my attentive thought during the day, and remarked to the Bishop that I regretted I was not allowed the privilege of confession that evening; he said then, if I desired, he had the permission already accepted, and I had the satisfaction and happiness to confess to the Bishop. The next morning I went to communion. Mass was said by the Bishop, Father O'Hara serving as before. After mass I bade the good and pious old man good-by, and received his blessing. I have not language at my command, my darling, to express the joy and delight I received on the occasion of this unexpected visit. Father O'Hara will remain a week, and I am in hopes I will have the happiness of again communing before he departs; I have made application. I heard mass yesterday. There are many Catholics among the citizen laborers, and we have quite a large congregation, nearly all going to communion. I have now, my darling wife, but one affliction, viz: uneasiness of mind regarding you and our precious little children. Imprisonment, chains and all other accompaniments of prison life, I am used to. I believe I can stand anything, but the thought of your dependent position, the ills and privations consequent, pierce my heart as a dagger, and allow me no enjoyment and repose of mind. I have apprehensions from the idle, roving, and lawless negroes that roam unrestricted through the country. Be careful, my darling, and be ever guarded.

The papers I notice are filled with horrible, most infamous and degraded crimes perpetrated by these outlaws. When you write, inform me what disposition is made of the farm, horses, cows, sheep, etc., and whether any portion of land has been reserved for yourself to cultivate. Will Old John remain with you, or Albin? Consult, my dearest, with Pa and Jere, and try to remain comfortable and free from a dependent position. Give me all particulars that you deem worthy, and that can be written with propriety, for letters are inspected before handed to us. Disappointment produces more pain than the pleasure of hope or release, so my darling when you write again, say nothing illusive, and advise Henry and Fannie to refrain from alluding to what is not certain or reliable. It is all supposition, and I can suppose as well as they. The Court who sent me here, I know well never contemplated the carrying out of the unheard-of sentence, considering the slight foundation for even the suspicion of crime, so, my darling, I do not stand in need of any of these vagueries. Life and everything in this world is uncertain and changeable, and we little know what other trials and crosses Providence may have yet in store for us. I have endeavored to the best of my ability to conform to all the duties required by our holy religion; my conscience is easy, and if death should visit me here (which I pray God to deliver me from), I am in hopes it will not find me unprepared. Live strictly agreeable to the dictates of your conscience and religion, and the trials we have endured may yet rebound to our earthly advantages; if not, I am in hopes we will meet in heaven. I forgot to mention previously I had also the privilege of making the jubilee. The month of December was appointed by the Bishop for the province. Tell Henry and Fannie I will answer their letters by next mail. I fear a copy of a former letter of Fannie's has been sent to the War Department, at least a copy was made of it. The Provost Marshal so informed me. I know not whether it was sent to the War Department. I fear imprudent talk and writing will yet dispose the mind of the President not to listen to your appeals in my behalf. Be careful, my darling child, and refrain as much as possible from expressing any angry indignation toward the ruling powers, or using opprobrious epithets toward my known prosecutors. Such conduct can have only the tendency to protract my stay here by keeping up agitation and excitement, if nothing else. Parties can have but little regard for my welfare, who are ever indulging in idle and injurious expressions. I feel that I should be perfectly satisfied to remain the balance of my days only in your and my little ones' company. My constant prayer is—God be merciful to us and grant me a speedy release, and a safe return to my family. Write often, don't await answer, for months would intervene between the reception of letters.

How much I regretted to learn of the sad accident that occurred to your old home. My heart is often softened by the memory of our happiest days. It was within its hallowed walls that we first indulged in the hope of a blissful future, but alas! to what gloom have we arrived.

Good-by, my darling wife and little children.

Yours devotedly,

SAM.

Fort Jefferson, Florida, January 2, 1866.

My dear Fannie:

The last letter I had the pleasure of receiving from you was dated the 6th of November—the previous letter was withheld on account of its objectionable contents. The offensive matter was read to me, though none of the family news.

I knew, my dear Fannie, you intended no insult to any of the just and proper constituted authorities of the Government in your remarks, but the unworthy servants who scruple not to misconstrue and falsify—having for their chief motives the hope of honor, and the selfish lust and thirst for gain. It would be best for the future, Fannie, since words are of no avail, to abstain from all criticisms—give me only the family and neighborhood news.

There has been no amelioration in our treatment since I last wrote, with the exception that our fare has much improved. Our Commandant is named B. H. Hill, formerly colonel, but now brevet brig.-genl. It was unnecessary to mention what knowledge you had of his disposition toward me—no word or sign of recognition has passed between us or any of his staff officers since he has been in command. Whatever opinions he may have formed concerning me, I did nct wish or desire you to *give* any expression; I prefer leaving all abstruse matters to the solution of time. The opinion of one pro or con can effect but little whilst it is quiescent—it is only when the sympathies of good or evil are aroused, when good or evil is accomplished. Be careful, therefore, in your comments, lest you produce an antagonism, which certainly will not tend to shorten my stay at this woeful place.

I have had the happiness to go to confession and communion—I have given all particulars to dear Frank. Bishop Verot and Father O'Hara visited us on the 28th. When you write to Cousin Ann, tell her I have received the contents of the letter she sent Father O'Hara. The Bishop is a most saintly man, plain and unassuming as an old fiddlestick. Father O'Hara is also a very pious man, and is quite a fine preacher. I feel easy in spiritual matters, but not in the temporal. Frank and the children cause me more uneasiness and suffering than all the miseries of imprisonment. I am truly in hopes she will have the strength to bear up against our present misfortunes and discomforts. When you write tell me if the negroes have committed any outrages in the neighborhood or county. Father O'Hara will be stationed at Key West, and will visit this place once every four or five weeks. You can write to him and make what inquiries you deem necessary regarding our present condition. I don't wish you all to make any more appointments without first and foremost enabling me to comply. You know how slowly the time passes when something pleasant and agreeable is in anticipation: the days and even the hours are counted, preparations and expense are made and incurred, then comes a put off, and finally a smash up—crushed hopes and nasty feelings. This I think is a picture of what has been presented to me. My dear Fannie, I have lost all my sugar teeth, and don't stand in need of sweets—I like something stable and real—no friend to sugar-coated pills.

If you have anything reliable, sufficiently so to allow you to fix a time, I would like much to know it, but where everything is so indefinite and dependent, I much prefer no allusion to the subject. When you write, inform me whether Ewing is interesting himself in my behalf. Be guarded and say nothing in your letters that may be used to my detriment by the evil disposed. Adopt the principle of do much and say little. I was much grieved to hear of the death of Mr. Miles. I am in hopes he is better off than being in this world of strife and degradation. I was also much pained to hear of Pa's loss on Jere's place, the destruction of the dwelling. I am afraid Pa will worry himself too much about his present misfortunes and trials. Try, dear Fannie, to comfort dear Papa and Ma as much as in your power. Excitement, agitation, etc., bring about many bodily disorders and predispose to disease, so do all you can to soothe in trials and tribulations that now press so heavily upon us. Let me know whether Pa has succeeded in hiring any hands fir this year, and what disposition is made of my place, and what Frank contemplates. I have heard nothing of the particulars of your and Frank's visit to Washington—only the fact. You need not tell me, if prudence dictates. Frank has never, in the letters I received from her, made any reference or allusion, and presume her silence was influenced by prudential motives. Tell Henry his three months will have nearly expired by the time this reaches you, and certainly before an answer reaches me. His letter was dated October 30, so the end of the present month will complete the period. All is surmise and speculation. An early release on my part would be a virtual acknowledgment of the injustice of the court martial; therefore, my conclusions are—I will have to remain here some time yet, to keep up appearances. Give my love to dear Ma, Pa, and all.

I will not be able to answer Henry's letter before the next mail. It is impossible for me to answer every letter by the same mail. I have but a few minutes allowed me now for writing, generally by dim candle light, and can't be select in my language, or writing. Tell dear Frank that I either write to her, Jere, or some of you, every mail, and a letter to one must be considered for you all. Likely some of my letters have been held back like yours on account of objectionable contents, for I am confident not one boat has left without my writing to some one of you. Give me all the neighborhood news. You have taken a fancy to your neighbor's wealth, what will be next on the program? Give particulars of all my dear little children and dear Frank. Remember me to all friends, etc., and believe me,

Your most devoted brother,

SAM.

Fort Jefferson, January 22, 1866.

My dearest, my darling Wife:

I will now attempt a description of myself, having exhausted in this and all previous letters all other subjects. I am beginning to realize the saying of the Psalmist—"I have grown old in my youth," etc. Imagine one loaded down with heavy chains, locked up in a wet, damp room, twelve hours out of every twenty-four during working days, and all day on Sundays and holidays. No exercise allowed except in the limited space of a small room, and with irons on. The atmosphere we breathe is highly impregnated with sulphuric hydrogen gas, which you are aware is highly injurious to health as well as disagreeable. The gas is generated by the numerous sinks that empty into that portion of the sea enclosed by the breakwater, and which is immediately under a small port hole—the only admission for air and light we have from the external port. My legs and ankles are swollen and sore, pains in my shoulders and back are frequent. My hair began falling out some time ago, and to save which I shaved it all over clean, and have continued to do so once

123

every week since. It is now beginning to have a little life. My eyesight is beginning to grow very bad, so much so that I, can't read or write by candle-light. During the day, owing to the overpowering light and heat, my eyes are painful and irritated, and can't view any object many seconds without having to close or shade them from the light. With all this, imagine my gait with a bucket and broom, and a guard, walking around from one corner of the Fort to another, sweeping and sanding down the bastions. This has been our treatment for the last three months, coupled with bad diet, bad water, and every inconvenience. The greatest wonder is, that we have borne up so well. The weather

II here since the beginning of the winter has been as warm as summer with you. The inhabitants are nearly always in their shirt sleeves and bare feet. There has been no time yet that a person could not sleep out comfortably in open air, when raining all night. It sounds strange to read of heavy snows and persons freezing to death, in the papers. I am truly in hopes, my darling, you and my precious little ones have not suffered from the want of fuel, and the necessary comforts of life and health. Try, my darling, and do not expose your health—consider the welfare and the duty we owe to our children. Save them, if possible, from being thrown upon this cold and heartless world, uneducated and ignorant of the debt they owe the Supreme Ruler of all. With the picture I have presented, you no doubt think I enjoy no pleasure or comfort. This, my dearest Frank, is not the case. My principal consolation is the knowledge of having no responsibilities immediately, other than the salvation of my own soul. Be assured then that I have done all that laid in my power toward that end. I have already written you concerning the visit of the Bishop of Savannah and Father O'Hara, now stationed at Key West, to this place. I have received no tidings from the letter you sent containing money. I received the contents of the letter forwarded to Father O'Hara. I sent you some time ago a ring, containing a silver set of a cross and four little diamonds in the center, and on each side a heart. Let me know whether you received it or not.

Love to all.

Fort Jefferson, Florida, January 28, 1866.

My darling Wife:

I had the happy consolation on the 26th of receiving four letters, and being relieved from the horrible chains. The letters were, one from Cecie, one from

Jere, and two from your sweet self. I was much rejoiced to know that you were all well, and that our precious little boy was convalescent, or fully recovered. Jere spoke of Pa and Ma's health being yet very bad. I am afraid affliction is the cause. Try, my darling, to cheer and console them all in your power. They are the only friends I have on earth, and the only tie that binds me to the land of my birth. Tell them, my darling, though absent, they are not forgotten, and the truly Christian lessons imparted during my youth, now more than ever, are being appreciated and practiced.

I wrote to you and Henry some days ago. The letter was returned on account of containing some objectionable matter. I have written twelve or fifteen letters to you and home folks since Christmas. I presume they have been forwarded to you, since they were not returned. I have no direct knowledge. Letters are likely delayed on account of having to undergo examination. I have never failed to avail myself of every opportunity to write to you; duty as much as love and pleasure prompts me to do so. Be actuated by similar motives, and, my precious one, I shall be satisfied.

Hoping to hear again shortly from you, and that you may be able to communicate the realization of my brightest dreams, I bid you a sorrowful adieu.

Your devoted husband,

SAM.

President Johnson having received my mother's letter of the 22d of December, 1865, issued an order for better treatment toward my father and his companions in exile. This order having reached those in command, the prisoners were relieved from their chains and given better quarters for a time.

Fort Jefferson, Tortugas Island, February 8, 1866. My dear Jere:

I received your very kind letter of the 26th of January last. I was in hopes ere this, from representations made, that I would be bounding the billows of the wild ocean with home my happy destination. I suppose it is decreed otherwise. I must be resigned. I have nothing new to report other than we have been relieved of our chains, and some interest manifested for our general well-being. Please forward to Frank after reading.

Write soon, remember me kindly to all friends, and believe me,

Most sincerely your brother, etc.,

SAMUEL, A. MUDD.

Port Jefferson, Florida, February 18, 1866.

My darling Frank:

I received yesterday two letters, dated January 25 and February 3, though bringing me nothing definite. I was much consoled to learn you were all in the enjoyment of good health and spirits, and possessed with brave resolutions to bear up bravely against our present adversity. Continue, my darling, upon this happy course, and God, I am in hopes, will crown our efforts.

You (invariably) mention in your letters that the time is but short that I have to remain; afterward you remark, "Should weeks and months pass without receiving a letter," etc. I want you to state in your next what you consider a short time. I am becoming tired of these expressions, because they don't comport with my reckoning. Perhaps you call one, two, or three years short—it seems very short after it is passed, but distressingly long to view in my present position and condition—"in *futuro.*" It generally requires from twelve to fifteen days for a letter to reach me, and about the same time one from you, so you can judge at what time it would take me to get home after my release was known to you—fully six weeks would intervene, not short.

Our chains have been removed, our quarters changed to a healthier locality, and our fare much improved, so I have hopes of a prolongation of the thread of life. Be assured, my darling, nothing will be done willingly on my part to endanger health, or the violation of any rule or order having a tendency to prolong my stay here. You need not bother yourself about sending me money. The clothing sent me, I have no use for, and I can convert them into something to eat, should I require. I have not worn any of the clothing sent me; my occupation not being very clean, it would be the height of nonsense to wear them.

Write soon. Remember me to Cousin Betty, my precious babies, Pa, Ma and family, and Old Uncle John. I will write to Mr. Best by the next mail. Good-by, God bless you and our dear little ones.

Your husband,

SAM.

Baltimore, February 18, 1866.

Dear Frank:

On my way up, I stopped in Washington to see Ford, but learned he was not in the city, so yesterday I went over and had a long interview with him. He told me he had a long interview with the President the day before, and had every assurance he would release Sam at the earliest moment he could consistently do so; the President also remarked to him, he (Sam) was a mere creature of accident, and ought not to have been put there, but in the present state of political excitement he did not think it prudent in him to take any action, as it would be another pretext for the radicals to build capital on. He also stated that the issue between the President and the radicals would be -made in a few days, and if they still persisted in their extreme measures, he would then take a decided stand against them; so, my dear Frank, you will still have to exercise the virtue of patience yet awhile longer.

I have not the least doubt that Sam will be released as soon as Johnson can do so with propriety, and I really think the day is not far distant. These are my own opinions from information derived from different sources, which I will explain to you when I come down, which will be the 8th of March. Let me hear from you as soon as you receive this, and tell me all the news, and tell me how you are getting along.

Your brother,

JERE.

Washington, February 22, 1866.

My dear Madam:

It is not yet time to move in your husband's case. The Supreme Court will try and decide the question as to the jurisdiction of Military Commissions, in a case from Indiana, on the first Monday in March. Let us hear their decision before anything is done.

We are all glad to hear from you, and to know that you are bearing your trials bravely.

Very respectfully yours,

THOMAS EWING.

Fort Jefferson, Florida, February 28, 1866.

My darling Frank:

In all of your letters you seem animated with hopes of an early release. It can't be so, after perceiving the vindictive hate which has followed me to this place.

My attention was called some days ago to some *"ex post facto"* statements made by Captains Dutton and Heichman. I can't divine the motive of the author or the prosecution in appending these affairs and unjust fabrications after my trial, because they do not give me a chance of refutation. To hold me responsible for such, would be equivalent to the denial of all justice, and all that would be necessary to condemn a man would be first to bind and gag him, then allow his enemies to come forward and make their accusations. This is the exact proceeding in my case. In the letter to Jere I wrote in relation to this, fearing he might not receive, I again make mention, and request you to confer with General Ewing or Stone in regard, and let me know what, if any, bearing it has upon my case. It is not my wish to agitate the matter, knowing it will have no tendency to benefit me. All I wish you to do is to speak to my counsel, and act under their wise instructions.

Your ever devoted and loving husband,

SAMUEL MUDD.

My darling Frank:

Mail arrived this morning, being the second without bringing any intelligence from you or friends. You must know my anxiety upon the arrival of every mail, and disappointment when receiving no tidings. The mail will leave this evening. Father O'Hara arrived here this morning, and I learn will return this evening without affording us an opportunity to go to confession; his visit was to the sick. I have no time to say more. Give my love to all. Write soon and pray for a speedy release.

Hoping you and our dear little ones are well, I am most truly and devotedly,

Your husband,

SAMUEL MUDD.

Fort Jefferson, March 13, 1866.

My darling Frank:

Since the reception of the last mail, I have been animated with greater hope of speedy release on account of the firm and decided policy of the President and his endorsement by the people. The President thought, and wisely, that time enough had been given Congress to fully appreciate the public needs; they not acting, every lover of peace and good-will has justified him in taking the initiatory. God grant that his plan may be accepted and acted upon by Congress in the true spirit, and quiet once more be restored throughout the land.

When you write or see Jere again, tell him for me, to go and see Colonel or Judge Turner of the War Department in reference to what statements and language I made use of on my way to this place. I was often in his company. I did explain to him all I knew, which was nothing more than I wrote to Jere on a former occasion.

Hoping the great mystery will soon be cleared up, and an honorable release my portion, I am,

Your loving husband,

SAM.

Fort Jefferson, Florida, March 17, 1866.

My darling Frank:

I know not how to express my indignation concerning the unfairness of the detectives, the Court., and the subsequent action of parties in appending false and injurious statements after my trial, when they know it was not in my power to refute by a legal proceeding, or to make denial without using language deemed improper. You, my darling, are differently situated; you have liberty of action, and for your theme the changes that every fleeting hour makes in your midst and the surrounding world. These you seldom ever advert to, nor do I find the paper well used up in the matter it contains. I, however, my loving one, find no fault, believing you influenced by motives of discretion, and the duties that now press upon you a sufficient cause.

I am now becoming of the opinion that it would have been better for me had I never written a word since being here. I certainly would have been as well off, if not better, for I fear it has caused indignant feelings, and words which are not tolerated at this time, only to a privileged set. Wm. L. Garrison's remarks, which I see quoted in the papers to-day, are as revolutionary as any that animated the rebellion. But enough, I have no news for the future, you must be satisfied with the fact that I am well. It is the only pleasure I have in this lonely place to write to you, and make known many of my sorrows and difficulties, as I have none of joy to relate you.

I think it best for you to leave my case entirely in the hands of my counsel and friends. If you can see Judge Crain, I am confident he would, at the word, lend you his aid in my behalf. I saw his name as chairman of a committee in Baltimore to present certain resolutions to the President. Hastily written,

SAM.

Fort Jefferson, Florida, March 22, 1866.

My darling Frank:

I have just written to Cecie, and am now hastily dropping you these few words to let you know that I am well, and to comply with a precious promise to write every opportunity. I am entirely without news, and I find it impossible to gratify your desire for a long letter without adverting to matter which has no connection with us. Criticism is objected to; therefore, my precious one, accept the will for the deed.

How much I desire to communicate to you something consoling and cheering and free you from the many anxieties and hardships that bother both mind and body, but such unhappily is not in my power. Even the little bird that has strayed away from a more congenial clime, and finds a resting-place here, loses his song, and shows evident marks of despondency. With us all is gloom and monotony, no pleasant change of scenery, or anything new to divert the mind or body. Mail arrives about once in ten or fifteen days, and the papers bring us nothing but stale news, which serves to occupy the mind but a few hours. I am very anxious to hear from you, and when a mail arrives without bringing any intelligence, I feel more heavily my exile.

My darling Frank, I have but one desire, namely: to be with you and see our dear little children properly trained and educated. Fannie writes gloomily of affairs now in your midst, and I fear, unless kind Providence intervenes, great suffering in the community must ensue. God grant that you may be spared, and that I may be allowed soon to contribute my feeble strength toward your support and protection.

Be assured, my sweet Frank, you are the object of all my thought and solicitude upon earth, and my fondest dream is the hour when I shall bid adieu to this land of exile, and fly to the bosom of you, and our precious little family there, never more to part. God speed the time is my daily prayer. Give my love to Pa and all the family, Cousin Betty and Uncle John. Kiss the children for me and believe me most fondly and affectionately,

SAM.

DESCRIPTION OF FORT JEPPERSON

Fort Jefferson, Tortugas, Fla., March 31, 1866.

My darling Frank:

I am just in receipt of yours of March 7, and feel much disturbed at the wretched condition of affairs existing in your midst. Sooner or later the wrath of the Almighty will fall upon these public plunderers and destroyers of the liberty, peace, and happiness of our best citizens.

You spoke of Thomas being implicated or strongly suspected. I am in hopes his day of retribution is nigh. He is no doubt the principal source (fool as he is) of my ruin and present unhappy state. I am truly sorry for poor Padgett and 'Squire George. Negro evidence was brought against me, why can't it be used against Thomas? "It is a bad rule that won't work both ways."

The picture above presents an easterly view of the Fort. No. 1, marked in ink, shows you the location of our quarters. These three marks are loop holes, about four inches wide on the inside and two feet outside—about seven feet above the floor, serving better the purpose of ventilation than agreeable breeze. The door below is the sally port, and is the only entrance to the Fort. No. 2 is the lighthouse; 3, officers' quarters; 4, prisoners' quarters; 5, Logger Head Lighthouse, about three miles distant; No. 6 represents Hog Island, a turtle, and a barrel used to carry water to hogs. Turtles are frequently caught weighing two or three hundred pounds.

In yours of a prior date you remarked that you would in the course of a few weeks visit Washington and Baltimore. By the time this reaches you I expect your tour will have been completed, and if nothing accomplished toward my release, I am in hopes you will have nothing to regret, but, on the contrary, your health and spirits much invigorated by the reaction of both mind and body, which no doubt the observance of Lent, the cares of family, changeable weather, bad colds, etc., has tended to depress. This, together with the advent of stuffed ham, boiled chicken, the springing into life of

133

numerous salads, will brace you up to bear more bravely the vicissitudes of your present condition of life. With us the virtue of necessity is ever our privilege, and on the principle of nature accommodating itself to circumstances, finds me no worse off at the end than in the beginning of Lent. My health continues good, and without the intervention of yellow fever, cholera or some other dread malady, may survive a while longer.

Art often overcomes and subdues nature. A ball can be made to roll up a hill. My disposition is undergoing a change. The virtue of resignation to an adverse and unjust punishment is rapidly dying out within me, and a different spirit supplanting. God knows I try to control these emotions, but it seems almost in vain.

History often reverses itself. Pilate, fearing the displeasure of the multitude, condemned our Lord to death. Is not mine somewhat an analogous case. Owing to the excitement and influence prevailing at the time of my trial, I could excuse much; but since time has elapsed for a sober, dispassionate consideration of the matter, I am becoming vexed at my protracted exile. I suppose it is all human.

I am truly grieved to hear of Mother's bad health— would that I could prescribe something to cure or relieve. I know nothing of her condition or disease, consequently can advise nothing without the risk of doing more evil than good. God grant it may be in my power soon to come to her aid. I must now, my dear Frank, reluctantly conclude by advising your best discretion in the selection of parties to represent my case. I fear those who have been making you such fair promises are influenced principally by selfish motives and have no real personal interest of mine at stake. I leave you and friends judges of the matter; but it strikes me, the party in whom you have been confiding is guilty of child's play, and should no longer be esteemed an adviser and friend. Use more care in writing, and give me all news correct. Let me hear further in relation to these incendiaries.

Your disconsolate husband,

SAMUEL MUDD.

Fort Jefferson, Florida, April 8, 1866. My darling Frank:

I am very well, and the island continues quite healthy. Yellow fever and cholera are reported prevailing at Key West about sixty miles distant; precautions have been taken to prevent its introduction here. I received no letter from you by the last mail. I wrote to you on the 22d and 29th, also to Sissy. Give my love to Pa, Ma, and all the family, Cousin Betty and Mr. Best, and kiss all our precious little children. I have not time to say more.

Hoping we may be spared further afflictions, and our unhappy situation about ended, I am most affectionately and devotedly,

Your husband,

Baltimore, April 9, 1866.

Dear Frank:

This is the first opportunity I have had since my return to write you. I had a long talk with Judge Crain yesterday, and he has promised to get for me the decision of the Supreme Court. It is generally believed that they have decided there was no law for trying civilians or persons not attached to the army by military courts. He has gone to Harford County to attend court, and will not be back before Friday. He promised me when he returned he would go to Washington, and get Reverdy Johnson, as he knew the President was very fond of him, and try to get the President to release Sam; and if he would not do it, he thought he probably could be gotten out through the courts, if the decision of the Supreme court is as represented, which there seems to be no doubt about; but they are keeping it from the people for political reasons. I myself am very sanguine of being able to do something for him in a short time. We will probably have to send a lawyer to Florida to get out a writ, but I hope to be able to accomplish his release without going to any more expense. You may rest assured I will not let the matter rest if I find there is any chance of doing anything for him. When the Judge returns, I will write you and give you all the information I can get.

BROTHER JERE [DYER].

Fort Jefferson, Florida, April 16, 1866.

My darling Frank:

We received papers as late as the 3d instant, and were much delighted to see the veto message of the President upon the Civil Rights Bill and the Proclamation of Peace, restoring the equal rights of all States throughout the South, and the suspension of all military proceedings in civil cases.

I am anxiously awaiting the good news promised in your letter. I was a little indisposed a few days ago, but have fully recovered upon hearing all was well with you. The mail will leave this evening, and my letters have to be examined; unless I am short, it may not meet with approval.

Your husband, etc.,

SAM.

Fort Jefferson, Florida, April 27, 1866.

My darling Frank:

I wrote to you a few days ago in anticipation of a departing mail. To-day I received letters from Fannie, Henry, and Doctor Blandford, and was much grieved to learn that you were all much disturbed at the appearance in the papers of a lying report concerning myself. It seems to be the intention of prejudiced parties not to let the effect of a slander die out without birth being given to another. I have not had a dozen words with a commissioned officer since the present regiment had command of the Post, therefore I could not have been very "querulous." I have not been reticent without a motive. My health has been better than might have been expected. I am not as strong as I might be, for the want of proper exercise. We are under guard all the time, and no exercise allowed except in the performance of duty, which is very light. I can perform all I have to do in a couple of hours. We are confined to our room on Sundays and no exercise allowed. My duty is simply to sweep down the bastions once every day. I am very well, and anxiously awaiting relief from my unjust banishment. Your devoted husband,

136

Fort Jefferson, Florida, May 1, 1866.

My dear Cousin:

We received yesterday the box containing all the articles mentioned, in good condition, for which we are under many obligations of gratitude. Accept my kindest thanks. We are all very well and possessed of the liveliest hopes for a speedy release, through the mercies of a kind Providence. I am entirely without news. I wrote to you early in March, and returned the cards pressed with moss agreeable to request; since then I have received no intelligence from you. I have letters as late as the 12th of April from my family; they were well, and more prosperous than I could reasonably suppose. Don't forget to thank Cousin M. for her kind present of books. I will not have time to write to her by this mail. Enclosed I send you a few moss-cards. I am sorry it is not in my power to send something worthy of your kindness. I shall say to-day a pair of beads for your intention. The weather is exceedingly warm here; two were nearly overcome from the effects of heat yesterday. Up to this time I have heard of no fatal termination in consequence.

Hoping to have the pleasure soon of greeting you in person, I am most truly,

Your cousin, etc.,

SAMUEL-MUDD.

From Carmelite Convent, Baltimore, Md., May, 1866.

Cousin Jere:

After reading this letter, please send it to Frank; it may be later news than she has had. I am glad the things reached them in safety. They were a long time on the way.

SR. JOSEPH.

New Orleans, May 11, 1866.

Dear Sam:

I have sent box containing canned fruits, etc., also enclosed thirty dollars. Anything you need that the authorities will permit, inform me and I will forward to you. Prank and the children are well, also your father's family. I think you may expect relief in a short time. Trusting to hear from you, believe me,

Truly yours,

THOMAS O. DYER.

Dept. General's Office, May io, 1866. The commanding officer at Dry Tortugas will please permit Dr. Mudd to receive this letter with the enclosed thirty dollars.

By order Major General Sheridan,

C. D. McCAPEY,

Capt. & Pro. Mar. Gen'l.

Received of the within thirty dollars, the sum of twenty dollars, to be paid in installments.

P. ROBINSON,

2d Lieut.

Fort Jefferson, Florida, June 2, 1866.

My darling Prank:

I received yours of the 7th to-day, and beyond the fact that Andrew has recovered from his accident, and that you are all well, etc., imparted but little satisfaction. I want no applause, no ovation, on my way home, should Providence vouch the favor. On the contrary, I desire more than ever quiet and contentment in the bosom of my precious little family.

I feel that I have complied with every duty to God, to man and to the Government. My conscience rests easy under all the grossly false and frivolous charges, notwithstanding their approval by an unjust, bigoted, and partisan Court. I scorn the idea, the doctrine that the innocent should suffer to satisfy a bloodthirsty and vindictive people. Was Pilate justified in sanctioning the death of our Saviour to appease the wrath of the multitude, who cried out for his blood? They who contend that the multitude, the mob, must rule, though innocence and justice be trodden under foot, are walking exactly in the footsteps of poor weak old Pilate. Spare me from the many kisses—they bode no good, and the many promised visits deliver me from. These things instead of having the effect you intended, namely: to bear up my spirits, etc., having served only to embitter. You are wrong to tolerate any such sentiment or interpretation—it only coincides with, or confirms, the verdict of the Court, who sentenced me to this hell. I know, my darling, you never intended or thought such an interpretation could be implied. For the future, give me only family, and neighborhood news. You need not say anything upon the subject of my release; for, instead of lessening, it has increased the bitterness of my banishment and close confinement. I should sooner see, than hear talk of it. I would sooner not be told and promised so often, and then not to see it. Your husband,

SAM.

Fort Jefferson, Florida, June 10, 1866.

My darling Frank:

I received yesterday a letter from Cousin Ann, apparently reflecting your opinions, protracting my stay in this hell for several months longer. Thus I am led like an infant beginning to crawl. Phantom-like, at the moment you arrive at the summit of all your expectations, and are about to grasp the coveted prize, it vanishes, or is seen only in the distance. The vagueries which you and others had so implicitly relied upon as certainties, and which were innocently imparted, or intentionally to stimulate hopes, have had their reacting influence. I do not wish to be considered a scold; you know my temperament, that I am naturally nervous and excitable— to such there is perhaps no greater or more painful state of trial than that occasioned by severe and long suspense. When we know precisely what we have to endure, we can usually call to our aid the needed strength, and submission; but a more than ordinary patience and forbearance is necessary to enable us calmly and tranquilly to await the approach of an important period, containing within its fleeting hours the promise to us of life's sweetest joys in doubt —our reunion. One moment hope usurps the misery and promises happiness; we smile, breathe freely, and banish care and anxiety; but an instant more, and some word, look, or even thought changes the whole aspect, clouds take the place of smiles, the heart heaves with apprehension, fear is awakened, and in proportion as we have cherished a confident pleasure or joy, are we plunged into the agony of doubt and disappointment. You are not alone, my darling, in contributing to these emotions; nearly every letter received the past seven or eight months has had the tendency to lead me to expect release at an early day; and that I should now feel indifferent toward the reception of such letters, is only the natural consequence of a nervous sentiment and feeling.

In my last I came to an abrupt close, the mail going off sooner than I expected. I had not time to say all that I intended, and to qualify that which I had written, therefore, have fears you will mistake its purport. You spoke of the sympathy of friends, etc. Their kind wishes can never do me any good so long as I am here caged; on the contrary, I fear you do me harm by the expression of any opinion favorable to the President and his policy. This was hinted at some time ago by a member of Congress, viz: "Even the conspirators were favorable to his (the President's) plan of reconstruction." You will do well, my darling Frank, since you know every word and act is so grossly misconstrued, to cease all utterance upon political subjects and adverting to the sympathy of friends in my regard. I assure you I do not desire it. After all, it may be only flattery, passing away an idle moment, or dissimulation. Acts of indiscretion are often committed by a too-confiding nature. Spurn those who would seek to elevate pride.

My darling Frank, I had promised myself long ere this the possession of more joy and happiness upon our second reunion than realized at the first. We know each other better, thus better able to reciprocate and appreciate our mutual love and affection; besides surrounded by our precious little children, naturally binds us more closely, and will inspire us with every devotion of love and gratitude to promote their welfare. So confident was I at one time, that I did

140

not deem it necessary to write, believing that the arrival of the next steamer would take me rejoicing to your fond embrace.

It is now two months or more since the decision of the Supreme Court was rendered; time, I would say, sufficient to ascertain its application and bestow its benefits, yet hearing nothing definite in relation, leads me to many conjectures. I am well, but you can better imagine than I can express, the animus of a being who has suffered so long the alternations of elevation and depression of spirit. Don't send any more of my letters to outside parties, and have as little to say as possible to the inquiries of others regarding me. Stone and Ewing seem to be doing nothing. I have never received a syllable from one of them.

Try, my darling Frank, to give me as correct an idea of affairs as prudence will permit. Judging from the newspapers, I think matters look quite hopeful, and I can't bring myself to believe that I will be here a month longer. I received a box of eatables and thirty dollars from dear Tom on the 30th of May. This is the third letter I have written to you recently. Father O'Hara paid us a flying visit a few days ago, not in a ministerial capacity; he being called away by the Bishop. We will have no minister here again before November next. He told me he had received a letter from you, and handed me money in compliance with your request; but I was well supplied, and returned him thanks for responding to your ever-solicitous attention in my regard.

Your devoted husband,

SAM MUDD.

Baltimore, June 13, 1866.

Dear Frank:

On my way up last Thursday I stopped in Washington, and had a long talk with Wood, and he requested me to say to you, he had given you his word to do all for Sam in his power, and he never falsified his word. He told me he would give me a letter which he knew would be of great service; he was then very busy, and

141

preferred not writing until he could take the time to write in such a manner as would be satisfactory to himself and us. He promised to try and write it on Sunday, and let me know as soon as he got it ready, but I have not yet heard from him.

Ford [John T. of Ford's Theater] told me yesterday he had engaged Reverdy Johnson* in Spangler's case, and would take action as soon as Congress adjourns; he thought it useless to do anything before, as it would probably do harm. Congress might take some action to defeat him. I am very sanguine, after the adjournment of Congress, we will be able to accomplish Sam's release; and the so much desired event, namely: the adjournment of that august body, will take place about the first of July.

Your brother,

JERE [DYER].

*Reverdy Johnson (1796–1876) was a statesman and jurist from Maryland. He defended notables such as Sandford of the Dred Scott case, Mary Surratt in the Lincoln assassination case, and Maj. Gen. Fitz John Porter at his court-martial.

Fort Jefferson, Florida, June 17, 1866. My darling Frank:

Although your last and Fannie's, received the 13th instant, held out no immediate prospect of release, on the contrary led me to infer you had lost all hopes in previous measures, and parties so confidently relied upon, yet I assure you, though the effect was depressing at first, after due consideration I could but feel grateful to our all-kind Providence for having bestowed upon you so much ambition and cheerfulness to bear up against our sudden change of fortune. I am really proud of your success in farming, and regret my want of language to express due praise. I am afraid my presence would be only an incubus, the long and close confinement, etc., endured rendering me but illy prepared to contend actively with the pursuits which the farm and my profession demand. Since matters have progressed so well, I will be too happy to surrender to you the dictation in all affairs pertaining to the farm. I sometimes try to feel indifferent, and ask myself the question—why should I feel disturbed, my family can take care of themselves?—separation must inevitably come one day, and perhaps it is better now than later. I have had every desire common to a husband and parent to be restored to my family, and feel I have done all consistent with my knowledge of right to be restored, failing in which has but disinclined me to future efforts or hopes. My endeavors are not to be resigned and careless, regardless of every surrounding. You are, my darling, differently situated. You have freedom of action, you have four precious little babes to provide for, to love and be loved, and my daily prayer has been, and for the future will be, that you may be blessed with strength and perseverance to perform agreeably to every duty required by our holy religion.

I can't imagine, after the turn which matters have taken, why a shadow should come over your dream, and render it necessary to put the management of my case into other hands. I almost feel like advising you to take no more counsel, but leave matters *in stain quo,* believing further action now will not hasten, but, on the contrary, cost money needed for the support of you and family. However, being in no situation to advise, I must leave you and our friends to judge what steps are necessary to be taken. I have no news. I wrote to you last on the loth and i3th. I am as well as usual, weak and nervous from the long confinement, otherwise healthy, and not much changed in appearance. Kiss all our darling little children, and, as ever, most fond, and devotedly,

Your husband,

SAM.

Fort Jefferson, Florida, June 21, 1866.

My darling Frank:

Writing is the only pleasure I enjoy, because I imagine myself so many minutes in conversation; yet much is dissipated by its being subject to the criticism and scrutiny of others. My heart yearns to be with you and our precious little children. How much I need your consoling and soothing voice, and the happy and innocent pranks and glee of our dear little ones, to cheer me up. In being separated from you, my dear Frank, I am parted with all that I desire to live for in this world. My restoration, I am afraid, would afford me more pleasure than Divine Providence is willing to accord; this thought gives me uneasiness.

I have nothing new—matters are about the same. My employment is the same, viz: sweeping down the bastions. This does not occupy many minutes to perform, when I can repair at my option to my quarters, which consist of two casemates—being all the time under close guard. My health continues generally good, though I am weak and nervous, which I attribute to the diet, want of exercise and climate, combined with the reception of unfavorable news, and consequent agitation of mind. I have received no letter from you since the one dated June the 1st, from the last week in May up to the present; this is the seventh that I have written to you. I scarcely ever receive any papers, although I have had the benefit of the papers received by my roommates. Write often, and accept the kindest wishes of one that loves you more dearly than life.

Your devoted husband,

SAM.

Fort Jefferson, Florida, June 24, 1866.

My darling Frank

I wrote to you and Henry on the 21st instant, but having written to Jere, I enclose this short epistle in the same envelope. Writing to you is the only source of pleasure I have on this inhospitable island, and I never let an opportunity pass without availing myself of it. The last mail I received no letter from any one—mails arriving so seldom, about once in ten days, making it generally a month between the reception of your letters.

I had made calculations and promised myself the gratification of the only desire of my heart to be with you and our dear little children long before this late period, and you can imagine my sore disappointment when I discovered them to be only castles in the air. I have lost patience and my usual serenity. I have felt like throwing away pen and ink, and foregoing the pleasure of ever writing again—and follow the wise maxim, "Blessed are those who expect nothing, for they shall not be disappointed." I know that you would not knowingly deceive, and am rather disposed to believe you were wilfully imposed upon by those who knew better. I am in hopes you will be more guarded in future, and not suffer your credulity to mislead you again. My darling Frank, I am nearly worn out, the weather is almost suffocating, and millions of mosquitoes, fleas, and bedbugs infest the whole island. We can't rest day or night in peace for the mosquitoes.

The only objection I have to the linen shirts sent me by Cousin Ann, is the fact they are not proof against the penetrating beak of the mosquitoes, and I fear I will have to throw them aside and take to the flannel again. There is a great deal of sickness among the white soldiers; the colored ones stand the climate and diet better. The garrison is composed of one-half black troops. There are about one hundred and seventy prisoners here at this time; out of this number there are not more than thirty whites, the balance are negroes. I have no other news worthy of mention.

Your affectionate husband,

SAMM MUDD.

Fort Jefferson, Florida, June 30, 1866. My darling Frank:

In looking over my daily summary I find that during the present month I have written to you on the following dates, viz: the 3d, 7th, loth, i3th, i7th, 21st, and 24th, besides three or four in the latter part of May. Several mails have arrived without bringing any news from any one. I do not complain, but merely make mention in order that you may know when I last received a letter. I have exhausted in those letters all the language I had at command, expressive of my longing desire to be with you, and bitter disappointment.

Nature does not tolerate an excess in anything without a corresponding reaction. There is a positive and negative to every question and thought—an equilibrium must be kept up, and is essentially necessary to the healthy or natural performance of every material and immaterial act; being lost, destruction either ensues or things fail to be comprehended in their sensible and rational form. I believe I am philosophizing, but all that I wish to be understood is, that suffering is just as natural to follow a sudden fading away of bright hopes, as day, night.

I am now composed, and feel somewhat like my former self, determined and resolute, and will likely remain so until shaken by a repetition of insidious and insinuating intelligence, having only the tendency to confuse, inspire doubt and irregularity of the mind, which many of you so well understand. Try and do not deceive me again; if you know nothing positive, have the resolution to tell me so. I can appreciate your love and anxiety in my regard, and fear you have concealed the true nature of affairs, lest it might cause me pain. How different have I acted toward you. I have never failed to give you, as far as in my power, a true condition of my health, treatment, etc., so that your mind might be prepared even for the worst.

We have received the Baltimore *Weekly Sun* of the 16th and *Gazette* of the 19th. I have seen an extract of Harris's speech made in Congress and some sketches taken from the report of Dr. Craben upon the treatment, etc., of Jeff Davis. If you can obtain these in full, you will much oblige by sending at your earliest opportunity. I expect nothing will be done toward our relief until after the adjournment of Congress. I am in my usual health. I am truly in hopes Ma's health has improved ere this. Tell Tommy and Sammy that Papa had a dream that he was down in the "swamp" and enjoyed a hearty laugh at their race after the little fishes. How much I desire to see you all. Write soon, give me all current news, and believe me most affectionately,

Your husband,

SAM.

Fort Jefferson, Florida, July 20, 1866.

My darling Frank:

Owing to stormy weather, we have not had an arrival of mail for several days. To-day two steamers came into port, one a gunboat, the other a transport, and the mail schooner is just in sight. This is something unusual, and you can't imagine how hopeful I have been the past few minutes. One of the steamers has just come to the wharf bringing some thirty odd additional prisoners from New Orleans and surrounding (Gulf) Military District. The gunboat is anchored out and has just landed a boat crew with four naval officers; they have marched to headquarters, I suppose to confer with the General Commandant. I am inquiring every minute, yet have not heard so much as a rumor. The schooner has just come in, bringing no mail; this throws a gloom over me—it will now be a week or ten days before the next arrival. I have just heard that there are twenty released prisoners, this exciting my envy, and caused the query, "When, oh! when will my time come?"

I suppose the public mind is too much engaged with the affairs of Congress to entertain the subject at present. How anxiously I have been waiting for them to adjourn, and cease unsettling the country. I have now finished giving you all the news that has transpired since I last wrote, which was on the 13th. I wrote Fannie a short note in the same, and sent her some moss-cards. I wrote to Sissy on the 12th. You write so seldom (about twice a month) and give so little news, I find it difficult to say much, or to comply with a former desire of yours, viz: to write long letters. You never think to give me any of the neighborhood news. I desired, in a letter some time ago, to know what disposition was made of John T. Hardy's place, and whether any other farms had changed hands? Beyond births and deaths, you never mention anything. Generally your letters are short, and so careless and indifferently written that I sometimes imagine that you only wish to keep up the forms, and have something to swear by. I have one or two letters which I could neither read nor understand. Words were spelled backwards, and sometimes a whole syllable left out. That which I could not make out, I am not able to state what was wanting. I am partly resolved for the future, to write no letters, only in answer to those I receive. I cannot impart any comfort to you by writing so often, nor relieve myself from misery that ever attends.

147

You must not think I am in a pet or in anger; on the contrary, I feel in better spirits at this moment than for several months past, consequently, better disposed to unload my breast of what has existed for some time. You must not believe me so unreasonable as to expect you always to convey hopeful intelligence; to the reverse, I have desired you to say nothing on the subject of my release, unless you had positive facts, and prudence did not forbid its revelation. My darling Frank, for the future, do not let the subject of my release cause you the slightest uneasiness or trouble. What can't be helped must be borne, contented or otherwise. I can't bring myself to believe my stay will be much longer delayed.

For the want of reading matter, I have the past week overhauled all my correspondence, commencing from the earliest to the latest date after my unfortunate landing at this place. I have been led like a child beginning to walk, with the difference that the child always succeeds in reaching a neighboring chair with a struggle.

My darling Frank, my sweet wife, how anxious I am to see you all. My heart at times almost bursts, and feels as if it would leap from my breast. Knowing this, I am in hopes you will bear up bravely, and remain steadfast for my sake, and for the good of our precious little ones. There is no sacrifice under heaven that I would not make to see and be with you again as in days gone by.

Hoping the time of our cruel separation is close at hand, and that we will be again happy united in bonds of double love and matrimonial accord, I am, my darling Frank,

Your faithful and devoted husband,

SAMUEL MUDD.

GENERAL SHERIDAN INTERVENES

Headquarters Military Division of the Gulf,

New Orleans, July 21, 1866.

My dear Friend:

Your kind note of July 12 has come to hand, and gives me great pleasure to hear from you. I will write to General Foster to subject Dr. Mudd to only such punishment as is warranted by the condition of his sentence.

Should I visit Washington, it will give me great pleasure to pay my respects to you, and to renew to you my bond of love and reverence. I am,

Your obedient servant,

PHIL SHERIDAN,

Major General.

To Rev. N. S. Young,

St. Dominick's Church,

Washington.

St. Dominick's Church, Washington, D. C., July 26th, 1866.

Mr. H. L. Mudd [father of Dr. Saml. A. Mudd]. My dear Friend: I send you this letter from General Phil Sheridan, hoping it may give you all some consolation to learn that your dear son, Dr. Mudd's condition will be ameliorated. I wrote to General Sheridan to obtain for him at least this compassion. I told him that you and the Doctor's family were my particular friends. As soon as you can, let the Dr know the promise General Sheridan has made me; and ask him to inform you if General Foster has executed that promise.

I am sorry that your heart is yet afflicted by the continued bad health of your good wife. You will be resigned, I am sure, under all your great trials. They are intended by our good God to prepare us for a better life and add to our crown of glory. If possible, I shall pay

149

you a visit soon, and once more have the happiness of offering up for you and your good family the Holy Sacrifice of the Altar.

Give my kindest respects and remembrance to each one of your family, and that God may bless you all is the prayer of

Your sincere friend, etc.,

N. S. YOUNG.

Fort Jefferson, Florida, July 26, 1866.

My darling Frank:

I received yours of the 10th this morning. The boat will return to Key West in a short time, so I can't say much. With all my exertions, I have not been able to crawl from my present locality. Yet the mind with hopes, as in a dream, was carried from one period to another, and apparently when in the act of taking my flight to Heaven, and dreading to look back, fearing the fate of the wife of poor old Lot, all vanished as smoke, and the same dread reality existed.

Bright beams begin again to lend their light, and I have been induced to believe, with the visitation of cholera upon the city of "magnificent distances" and crime, a scatteration might be produced, and give our worthy Chief Magistrate a chance to look into my case, and purge it from the foul suspicions placed upon my unsuspecting shoulders, although he will be unable to repair the injury. Every dollar the nation is worth is insufficient to that end.

I am very sorry, my darling Prank, I can't be more entertaining; be not offended with my criticism or resolutions, expressed in the foregoing. I forgot to credit you with the burdens and cares of our darling little children and family, and the distraction that they naturally produce. Write as often as inclination and freedom from the restraint of family will permit. I can't ask more. I can write every day, and it would be an agreeable pastime, but there would be no opportunity of mailing, nor would it be necessary; but I never fail to comply with my promise to write by every mail that leaves this place. If you write often, I will always have a letter to answer, which will be far more agreeable and pleasant.

I shall be content until after Congress adjourns; after that, I shall be anxious, and look for some decided action to be taken by you and my friends; otherwise, I will give up all hopes of ever leaving this place alive, and live only to curse my enemies, as I will merely remark that I perceive not the slightest change in the character of your letters; it is another put off, another child's play—to play and torment and vex me. I will now proceed to give you plainly what I mean by child's play, viz: It was three months before Christmas that I had the happiness of dining with you on that festive day, then you had hired a servant who would remain until the spring (three months longer). I had the duty of supplying her place. Now, my darling Prank, what a splendid dinner! What delicacies, etc.! Don't I enjoy myself? Then how I was favored in finding such a neat, tidy and active servant for you. The spider could no longer spin his silken cords unharmed, etc. The President's proclamation appears in April. May, sweet May would be the consummation of all my earthly joys. I would be treated to green grass, and dipped into some health-restoring fountain. In a word, I would be transplanted to Elysium. Now, do you remember how I floated through the aerial vapors, resting in placid dreams upon the bubbling clouds and visiting the moon? Venus would attend me. The decision of the Supreme Court is made public, this is what has been looked for all the time. I am released from hell and summoned to heaven, but held by terrible Mars. Poor old Achilles, shot in the heel! Un-forgetful mother! why didst thou not turn and dip the other end? Now I have a feast of three months longer. My darling Frank, I have grown weary of these delights; cease, for God's sake, if not for mine, extending the time. The "first of September," "two or three months longer," "be patient," etc., are expressions of yours, and seem only moments in your thoughts of the future; but they excite my calculations, and cause the days, hours, and minutes to be counted, whereas, if you said nothing, since you know nothing, the time might pass by and be forgotten. Don't, my sweet wife, write any more in this loose style. Let me know whether you are sick or well, and the health of all home ones, the neighborhood and farming affairs, etc. I am not so anxious about release, so long as I know you are well and content, but I dislike being treated as a child. I am far less desirous about release now than I was some time ago. Fifteen months of the most brutal and degrading imprisonment has done its work. I am broken down and good for nothing. You spoke of turning gray—I am nearly bald.

In reading the papers, I perceive nothing clearer than the near approach of anarchy. I feel sorry for 13 you and our dear little children, but for myself my enemies have done all the harm they can do me, and death would only free me from a greater misery. I hope they may meet with the chastisement their crimes deserve, in this world, as a warning to future generations. The inspired volume reminds us of Retributive Justice, and those need fear who have perjured, calumniated and endeavored to reform the divine laws, and remodel His works.

I have my usual health. We have three sentries within ten feet of our door that cry out the hours of the night at the pitch of their voices, which awakens us and destroys all sleep. This is a recent change and an aggravation. I have no news. The mail we received to-day is the only mail we have received of this month's news. I received Mr. Harris's speech, and two *Sun* papers from you. You need not bother yourself in sending the *Sun,* as we get it regularly; one of our members being a subscriber; also the *Gazette.* Comments from other papers, you can send.

Give my love to all home ones, present my kindest thanks to Mr. Best for his true devotion to self and family. Your devoted husband,

SAM.

Fort Jefferson, Florida, August 6, 1866.

My darling Frank:

I wrote to you last on the 26th and 30th of July. Mails arrive quite seldom now, owing, I understand, to quarantine regulations. One of the mail boats arrived here this morning, although bringing no mail. She will leave this evening at 6 o'clock. To relieve you of fear in my regard, I post these few hasty lines to acquaint you with the fact that I am in possession of my usual health and spirits. I am more afflicted when I think of you and our dear little children, knowing how dependent you must be, and how incapable you are to provide for self and family without the intervention of kind friends. Your burdens and responsibilities will increase daily, and you must sum up all your resolution and courage to brave misfortune. Instruct and educate the children as well as you can; be gentle, kind and positive, enforce obedience and respect now whilst they are young, and when they grow older they will not give you trouble and cause shame. You can promise yourself nothing certain in this world, therefore do not act on the idea that I will soon be home, and that it will be unnecessary for you to observe duties that it would be my place to attend to. Should I be favored with an immediate release, I fear I shall lack the strength, for a considerable time, to perform the least labor.

In appearance I have not much changed. I am told I am growing fat, and seem a picture of health; appearances deceive, and my legs have to work terribly to get the body along. Begin now, my darling Frank, to act as if you expected nothing, only what was to be accomplished through your own exertions, and you will not suffer the pain of disappointment, nor lack the energy when it is most needed. Give my love to all, write soon, and believe me as ever,

Your fond and affectionate husband,

SAM.

Fort Jefferson, Florida, August 9, 1866.

My darling Frank:

The papers give full accounts of the proceedings of the National Convention, and the President's proclamation restoring all the States to all their former privileges, which with the promise contained in your letter relieves me of all doubt regarding a much longer separation. I now hail with delight the thought of soon being in the fond embrace of you and our little ones, sharing with you, to the extent of my ability, the blessings and privations of life in this miserable world.

We are still under close guard. There is a sheriff at Key West. Should you get out a writ, it may be well to know the fact; but according to the learned counsel in the recent *habeas corpus* case at Charleston, we are in the hands of the President, and you will have to bring action against him. I am sorry to involve expense, which I know you cannot meet without the intervention of kind friends. Steamers pass here almost daily on their way to New Orleans, and other points on the Gulf, and it would be attended with but little delay to one of those to stop and take us off. By acting with the friends of my roommates, it would make the expense much lighter. A message could be sent per telegraph to New Orleans giving direction and instructions to competent parties, thus excluding the necessity of sending a party down from home. This will be my last letter. Give my love to all.

Your affectionate husband,

SAM.

Fort Jefferson, Florida, August 13, 1866.

My precious Wife:

I received yours of the 10th and 28th of July od the 10th. I was sorry to hear of our little Tommy's indisposition. I am in hopes it will soon pass away, and be my fortune to realize your expectations. You spoke of the murder of Mr. Lyles, and the papers mention the robbery of Mr. Posey. Owing to their proximity to you, I have suffered some alarm, knowing your timid nature and unprotected and helpless condition. Such crimes, and far more brutal, are of daily occurrence, and when far away hardly excite our horrors; so soon does the mind become familiar by their daily narration through the press. I think it advisable for the citizens to take measures of precaution, by appointing suitable officers in every district to inquire into the condition and purpose of every suspicious party. These atrocities are only the fruit of the late unnatural strife, and we can only blame the fanatical majority of Congress for their long continuance. Congress by its action has rather favored than imposed the needed restraints upon these horrid enormities.

I rejoice to see the noble response of the people in behalf of the President's policy, the influence of which response, I am led to believe, will soon induce him to exert his constitutional prerogative and issue a proclamation of amnesty restoring to all the States their original rights and privileges. Much, though, depends upon the harmony of the Philadelphia Convention which meets to-morrow. The cholera prevailing there will, I fear, prevent a full attendance.

You seem to manifest some uneasiness on my account, apprehending the injurious effects of the heat upon my feeble constitution. In this regard I must remark that the climate being more moist and equable, is not liable to the evil and depressing effects, as with you. Heat in the sun here is very great, yet rarely attended with "sun stroke"; no fatal case from this cause having occurred since I have been here. Whenever there is a breeze, which is generally the case,. it is always pleasant. A strict eye is kept to the cleanliness of the place, and being remote from the main land, we have no fears of any infectious or epidemic disease. Unsuitable diet, beef, pork, etc., are more frequent causes of disorders and disease than locality or climate. We stand in need of a vegetable and fruit diet, of which this place is woefully deficient. My strength and general health have improved within the past week or two. With suitable diet and proper exercise, I feel that I would soon be my former self again. Allow yourself no unnecessary uneasiness. I have more fear concerning habits contracted by an unavoidable indolence than I have of speedy dissolution by organic or infectious disease. Mails arrive now very seldom, being seventeen days between the last two. Give my love to dear Ma, Pa, and the family.

I wrote to Jere some days ago and enclosed a note to you. We have money enough to supply our wants for some time to come, so give yourself no uneasiness on this point. I am truly delighted to know that your crops are looking well, and promise a fruitful yield. In Fannie's last she spoke rather discouragingly of the prospects of the crops.

Kiss all our dear little children, and wishing you a pleasant and successful trip to Washington, I am, my darling Frank, as ever,

Your devoted husband,

SAM.

Fort Jefferson, Florida, August 18, 1866.

My dearest Cousin:

I received your last a week or two ago. Being like yourself, without anything likely to interest, I delayed writing until the present, hoping for something to turn up, whereby I might be furnished with a theme; but the same old monotony continues to exist, etc. The fear that you may think your kind letters are not properly reciprocated, prompts me at least to an acknowledgment. Instead of a lack of appreciation, I value your letters more than all the rest of my correspondents, because you do not appear to disguise the true nature of affairs, and lead me contrary to the expectations of my friends—thereby, causing the time to pass more observed, suspense more painful, and in the end, the blight of disappointment.

You asked me if I did not feel honored at seeing my name so often mentioned and commented upon in the "public prints." I assure you, so far from exciting my pride, it creates in my heart only feelings of indignation. The greatest honor they can show me is to release me; until this is consummated, I shall consider their time, ink, and paper thrown away, and all they can say as empty. I am truly in hopes that what has been said will be the means of directing *public opinion* to the great wrong perpetrated upon my personal rights as an American citizen, and that the outrage will not be suffered much longer to continue.

We were visited the first week in July last by Father Clauriel (a little Frenchman) from Savannah, Ga. I had the consolation of going to confession, and receiving holy communion on the 8th.

My health is much better now than some two or three weeks ago. I attribute the change to the kindness of the officials in giving us a plank floor to our sleeping quarters. Up to a late period we were upon a dirty floor, which was very wet and damp all the time. After every rain, our quarters leak terribly, and it's not unusual to dip up from the floor ten and twelve large buckets of water daily. We have a hole dug in the floor and little trenches cut, so as to concentrate the aqueous secretion, which facilitates the dipping up process and freeing the room from noxious miasma.

Having nothing more worthy at my command, I send you a small collection of moss-cards---ten small and one large intended for a wreath. I regret my bad taste, manipulation, and paper. Should I be so fortunate as to have an early release, I shall endeavor to procure a large assortment of shells, etc., considered curiosities with you, which I will present you with, should you desire them. They cost us nothing here, and if you wish them, let me know in your next, and if any particular variety.

Present my kindest regards to Sister M. and the rest of the saintly members of your association.

Hoping a continuation of your prayerful supplication, and to hear again from you soon, I am most truly and sincerely,

Your cousin, etc.,

SAMUEL A. MUDD.

To Sr. Joseph. [Carmelite Convent, Baltimore, Md.]

Fort Jefferson, Florida, August 20, 1866.

My darling Frank:

I am now feeling perfectly well, and improved in health and flesh, which I attribute to the laying of a plank floor in our quarters. My hair has also taken new life, and in a short time will have a thick suit, even where it was most thin. I am entirely without news of importance. The mails arrive now about once in three weeks, and in the interim nearly every one becomes cross and peevish. The mail boats, I understand, are not allowed to enter the port of Havana from this place without undergoing quarantine regulation, which causes the delay. The health of the Post remains remarkably good, no epidemic or infectious disease having made its appearance. The principal disorders arise, I think, from the use of stale and salt diet.

We never use it, consequently remain exempt. I have not touched a piece of salt beef or pork for nine or ten months.

Don't let this letter cause you uneasiness; for the future confide in none but the most honest and reliable. You need not reply to it, if prudence forbids. I fear injury to my cause has resulted from matters being made too public. You do wrong also, I fear, in communicating with Cousin Ann, and in mentioning the names of parties. Very often they do not like to be known, and often take offense. Be guarded, my darling child, how you act in the future. Use discretion, and don't depend too much on your own judgment. My soul is tired of this place beyond expression—do nothing that may tend to prolong my exile. How anxiously I am waiting for the arrival of the promised release! Act immediately. I don't see that anything can be gained by delay, for the courts, in the course of time, are bound to release us. Let me have at least an honest exposition of my case before the President.

Give my love to Pa, Ma, and all the family, and accept the most endearing sentiments of the heart of your afflicted and distressed husband,

SAM.

Fort Jefferson, August 22, 1866.

My darling Frank:

I wrote to you on the 20th, 13th, and 20th, opportunity presenting. I again avail myself of this only pleasure, indulging with you a short pen and ink confab. By the time this reaches you, the first of September will be at hand, and with it the promise of a speedy "homeward bound," as fast as steam and sail can bring me, your long-lost and desolate exiled; or will he be again doomed to disappointment? I can't bring myself to believe those in authority will much longer disregard every principle of justice and fair dealing to satisfy vulgar thirst for vengeance. The Government certainly is aware by this time of the unprecedented number of false and perjured witnesses, and by no action being taken to bring these scoundrels to account, an invitation is indirectly given to these and every plotter against the lives and liberty of their fellow-men to continue, and come forward with their mendacious yarns for monied and party consideration. I am firmly convinced, by circumstances, that men were bought to give false testimony. Those in authority, in their zeal to find out the originators, actors, and accomplices, offered enormous rewards for evidence, and the apprehension and conviction of the parties. This alone was a sufficient inducement to the unscrupulous, who were adroit enough to frame a plausible tale, to make "merchandise" of the most sacred right and duty of man, his oath. For God's sake lose no time in bringing this subject before the President. No matter how he decides (pro or con), I shall be happy to have the sanction of his authority.

The report of the Judiciary Committee favors the trial of Davis upon the false and frivolous charges which were adduced upon our trial in connection with the assassination. With equal justice might every distiller of whiskey be arraigned and tried for all the crimes committed by its abuse, and every man be at the mercy of an enemy capable of writing him a fictitious letter. I have read nearly all the charges made by this committee against Davis, and I can't see for my life the least shadow of evidence to connect him with the infamous deed—which circumstances alone are sufficient to refute, independent of the unreliability of the testimony. Arnold's letter, upon which they built the conspiracy, shows conclusively that up to a late period in March, 1865, Booth had no connection with the Richmond authorities, or their Canadian agents. This letter and his statement, which the Government has never made public, is worth all the evidence brought forward by the prosecution, so far as showing the motive and intention of the parties. I believe sincerely there are parties at the head of the different departments of the Government who delight in human affliction and suffering, especially when they can by any pretext prosper their own, or their party's cause. I cannot view the conduct of Judge Holt otherwise; his attempt through a parcel of false and perjured statements, to bring public opinion to bear upon my case, after the trial was over, and when I had no power to rebut, shows his animus and is unpardonable for one occupying his position. I am ignorant of the laws, but certainly this act does not appear to me like justice. It is hard to suffer without the consciousness of having committed the least wrong, and with full knowledge of the foul and unfair means resorted to bring it about. I am almost driven to desperation when I reflect upon the outrages I have already endured and continue to suffer. You will please impart the subject of this letter to my counsel and friends that they may determine and act immediately.

I am feeling quite strong again. We have, through the kindness of officials, a plank floor placed in our quarters, which renders it a thousand times more comfortable. Before, we were on the ground, and half of the room continually wet from leakage through the ceiling. Yesterday a negro accidentally fell overboard, and was drowned. There were a large number present, and no effort was made to save him. How tired I am of this life, and how anxious I am to see you and our precious little children, and home ones. When you write, do not disguise the truth. Let me know the worst and hope for the best. Answer this soon.

Give my love to all, and believe me as ever,

Your devoted husband,

SAM MUDD.

Fort Jefferson, Florida, August 23, 1866.

My darling Prank:

I have just this moment received yours of the 7th and Fannie's of the 2d. I am happy to know that you are all living and have thus far escaped greater afflictions than mere indisposition on the part of our dear little pets. It grieves me to hear of Ma's continued bad health. Your letter differs on this point essentially from Fannie's. God grant she may be spared many years yet is my constant prayer.

I am sorry you were not able to communicate more gladdening tidings after your visit to Washington. I suppose it was too early after adjournment, and the parties whom you mentioned preferred awaiting the action of the Philadelphia Convention, which met on the 14 instant, to obtain anything decisive. I regret to see so much subserviency on the part of our public men, without ideas or mind of their own, but mere weathercocks of public opinion. They seem to throw law and justice entirely out of the question, and are afraid to act only upon what may be public sentiment. So much afraid are they that their acts, though strictly in conformity to every principle of justice, may be used to the detriment of party, they hesitate and postpone action until warranted by circumstances to believe that no injury can result to their political ambition.

Fannie sent me the letters of Father Young and General Sheridan. You will present my thanks to Father Young for having through his solicitation, succeeded in calling the attention and influence of General Sheridan to the grievances under which we suffer.

We have been under close guard both day and night since November last, and no word or act of ours could escape the scrutiny of the sentinel. We can't move five steps from our door without permission of the sergeant of the guard, and followed by the sentry. When we are at work or walking, we can't move faster than the guard is disposed to walk himself, so you see all running, fast walking, wrestling, etc., is excluded. This is now our principal grievance, which has been brought about by no word or act of ours. All the rest of the prisoners, except those confined to the guardhouse, are allowed the freedom of the island; we ask no more. The only amelioration we have received recently is the rendering our quarters more comfortable by a plank floor instead of the former dirt, wet and damp. I do not complain of the labor, it is comparatively nothing, but being under guard is a continual confinement, or a check to all free exercise.

By this morning's mail I learn the four recently arrived prisoners from Charleston will be transferred to Fort Delaware, thereby placing them under the operation of the writ of *habeas corpus*. I think it would be better on the part of the Government to release them at once, than place them where they can effect it with a little trouble and expense. Nature provides for all its wants, and on that principle alone can I explain the peculiarity of my appetite. All articles of meat, salt and fresh, are repulsive. I can't bear the sight of them. My diet consists principally of molasses, when we can get it, butter, canned tomatoes, beans, etc. The bread we get is usually very good, though at times is very bad. Having little or no duty to perform, and no exercise, but little and the lightest diet is required to satisfy the wants of nature. Gross, heavy diet would, in this climate, and under existing circumstances, be highly injurious. I am told by all that I am growing fat, yet I do not consume in a day as much as one of our little children at one meal. With the exception of bread and coffee, we subsist ourselves entirely by making little work boxes, picture frames, which we shell and inlay with different kinds of colors of wood. These command a ready sale to visitors, and soldiers of the garrison. Should my stay be protracted beyond September, you can write to Tom to send me a box, as everything is very high at the post sutler's. I am very well and hopeful.

Yours,

SAM.

Fort Jefferson, Florida, August 31, 1866.

My darling Frank:

The last letters received were Vannie's of the 2d and yours of the 7th of August. I am very well. No news worthy of interest. The mail leaves in a short time, so I have no time to say more. I wrote to you last on the 22d and 23d of August, and made known to you then all that was desirable on my part. I have no further request to make, but hope sincerely this may be the last tidings you may have from me in the shape of a letter from this place. The Fort has been unusually healthy thus far. Remember me to Mr. Best, and tell him not to expose himself, in securing the crops, unnecessarily.

Give my love to all, and pray for your disconsolate husband,

S. A. MUDD.

Fort Jefferson, Florida, September 3d, 1866.

My dear Tom:

162

I have been truly anxious to hear from you for some time. I have been led to believe the whole South exterminated, or reduced to abject slavery, until news of the recent riot reached us. I am grieved at the occurrence, the loss of valuable lives, but proud to know there is manhood enough left among the people to rebuke the oppression of the interventionists.

The mail will leave in a few minutes, so I have barely time to tell that I am well and continue to hope for an early release. Why don't you write to me sometimes? You do not say in any of your short notes with whom you are engaged in business, or speak concerning any of our old relations and friends. Write occasionally and send me papers that may contain matters of interest. The last intelligence I had from home was from Frank dated August 7. Jere seldom writes, and when he does, never gives any neighborhood news, consequently I am ignorant of what is transpiring outside of this miserable place.

Write soon and give all news. Remember me to all relatives and friends, and believe me most truly,

Your brother, etc.,

SAM.

Fort Jefferson, October 11, 1866. My darling Frank:

Yours of the 14th of September, also a box and thirty dollars from Tom has been received.

I regret to hear of your troubles and our afflicted little children. You ask counsel upon the subject of my release (this is done, I suppose, to make delay plausible). You know that I am unable to give advice, being unacquainted with the difficulties and circumstances.

Fearing my silence might be misconstrued, you see I have again written, though contrary to previous resolves. I am well. Give my love to all, kiss our darling little ones, and answer,

Your devoted husband,

163

SAMUEL M.

Fort Jefferson, Florida, October 14, 1866.

My darling Frank:

I received to-day yours of September 24 expressing some fears as to the statement in some paper regarding me. I received word also from the General, informing me of the reception of a letter from you, inquiring into the truth of the matter. I am sorry you should have been misled by so apparent a fabrication. I am very well and my health much better than some time ago.

Parties who are given to lying and suborning perjury to sustain their own wicked preconceived ideas, can easily invent a malicious newspaper report. For the future, give yourself no uneasiness concerning what may be said by newspapers. I wrote to you on the 9th and 24th of September and the 1 ith of October. These letters will reach you, though containing no denial (as I was not aware of the lie), and it will be evident that no such outrage has taken place.

Tell Jere to try and find out from whence this infamous report originated. I can scarcely credit the idea that it came from this place, although I do not know the animus of those around me, having had no conversation nor disposition, since I have been so falsely and inhumanly represented and treated.

Yours,

SAM.

Fort Jefferson, October 28, 1866.

My dear Jere:

Except by indirect allusion of others, it has been a long time since I have heard from you. Time has already falsified the predictions which they gave upon your authority, and it has seemed to me "you picked the stones for others to throw"—but enough, I must be short. The time intervening between this and the assembling of next Congress is growing quite short, and the indications are that there will be a stormy time between the President and the majority.

Should matters be prolonged until that period, I shall give up all hope, for the excitement consequent will be plead an excuse for further delay and continuing the outrage, against me, of all law, justice and humanity. Neither the President nor Congress will assume the responsibility to release, and I shall be here a living sacrifice to the damnable ends of party.

I saw something in the papers some time ago intimating that a memorial was being gotten up by my friends, and would be presented to the President, on his return from the West, for my release. A considerable time has elapsed since, and I have not heard a single word in reference. I am truly desirous of knowing something definite in regard to my future fate, or what may be the pleasure of the Government.

An order came by the last mail to send on the names of all those who have been here six months, except the state prisoners (meaning us), and those who are here upon the charge of murder, arson, and rape. We are the only prisoners that are styled state prisoners. Why is this? Let me know in your next.

Hoping you will not let this (only) auspicious moment mentioned above pass disregarded, and that you will let me hear from you immediately upon the receipt of this, I am,

Most truly your brother,

SAMUEL M.

Fort Jefferson, October 30, 1866.

My darling Frank:

I wrote you last on the 25th, also by the same mail to Cecie and Cousin Ann. I wrote yesterday to Jere,

14 and made known to him all my desires. You had better in future consult him in reference to all domestic affairs, and act agreeably to his judgment. I have but little means of ascertaining the many difficulties and embarrassments under which you have to contend, therefore, incompetent to form an opinion.

I view actions more than I do words. What concerns me most, seems nobody's business, and I am fast losing all forbearance under the cruel and unwarranted oppression to which I am subjected, the result of a tyrannical and unjustifiable usurpation. I have been over eighteen months languishing in prison for no crime against God or man that I am cognizant of, and I think it high time the friends of humanity and law, particularly my own personal friends and relations, were coming to the rescue. I don't believe any good will come of the party or nation that will tolerate such injustice; sooner or later they will meet with the same judgment and chastisement they mete to others.

For the future try not to deceive me by representations from others. The six weeks and the two months have passed, and I am still here a victim to the folly of the nation. Do not let me lose confidence in you, do not throw stones which others have picked.

Jere was kind enough to give you this information perhaps for your own satisfaction. He told Cousin Ann the same, yet he has not written one word in regard to me. Does not this look contradictory, and that he intended to deceive me through you and others?

The Court refuses to try Davis agreeably to appointment, and it is quite uncertain whether they will meet at the regular term in November; if so, their judgment upon the trial of civilians by court martial will continue to remain unfiled, also upon the test oath question. I am unable to surmise, having had no information from any of my friends, and only such news as I have been able to glean from a lying and infamous press.

Let me know at your earliest convenience what has been done favorable, or otherwise. Let me know the whole truth, if prudent, otherwise it will not be necessary to mention the subject. I would rather be in complete ignorance than have the reliance of mere conjecture. Write soon and give all neighboring and farming news.

Sincerely hoping this may be my last letter, and that our present afflictions are near at an end, I bid you a hopeful adieu,

SAM.

PLANS FOR MY FATHER'S RELEASE BY HABEAS CORPUS

Fort Jefferson, Florida, November 3, 1866. My dear Jere:

Colonel Grenfel handed me a letter he received to-day from A. J. Peeler, a lawyer in Tallahassee, Florida, who intends acting in his case immediately. It seems to me, if you have to resort to law for my release, this would be the least expensive and most expeditious medium. He has promised to act for the Colonel free of charge, requiring only the actual expense attendant. With a small amount from each of us interested parties, to pay for trouble, etc., he would no doubt be pleased to undertake our case. The Colonel also received a letter from B. T. Johnson, Richmond, Va., promising to do all in his power toward his release. I have hastily written to acquaint you with the above, thinking the information might be desirable at this time. If you conclude to act through him, you can address, or perhaps telegraph, A. J. Peeler's law office in the South Western Railroad Bank Building, Tallahassee, Florida. I wrote to you a few days ago. Remember me to all kind friends and inquirers. Your brother, etc.,

SAM.

Fort Jefferson, Florida, November 5, 1866.

My darling Frank:

I received on the 13th instant yours of the 19th of October, and Fannie's of the 18th. I am truly sorry to hear that you continue to suffer with your ankle from erysipelas, and that you felt aggravated at the tone of a former letter. Try to be more prudent for the future, and see that you are entirely well before you venture much exercise. I must confess I wrote too precipitately, and without weighing the effect my language and resolution might have. The truth is, your letters were generally so hopeful and cheerful, always directing my attention to some period when I might, with confidence, expect something to be done toward effecting my release,—which invariably ended in disappointment,—I had become as a child whose brightest anticipations had been raised to the highest pitch, experiencing the sudden ebullitions of dissatisfaction. Time is fast proving how unfounded were your hopes, and how unnecessary it was to communicate the same to me. I am sure I would have been spared many hours of anxiety and watching. My fate is made to rest unjustly upon public opinion, and judging from the tone of the press, and the signs of the times, another delay is not improbable. Then, how foolish it was to lead me on. I am the subject of every political caprice and whim, and cannot expect speedy relief from my present degradation and suffering. I feel no inclination to criticise, but it does not seem to me that the President is consistent with his oft-repeated declarations and earnest solicitations to the people to return to the Constitution of our fathers, and conform to its spirit and requirements. How essential it is to the inculcation of the precept, "to remove the beam from your own eye before attempting the mote in your neighbor's." It is no wish of mine to frustrate the efforts of the President in his attempts at restoration, but I do object most strenuously to be made to suffer for the sake of some political expedient. As I am subject to the pleasure of the President, it seems to me a demand ought and should be made upon him, and that I should not be put to unnecessary expense, being here contrary to law and every instinct of justice. I am told by you and Fannie to be patient. You may as well, under the circumstances, tell the ocean to be calm in a storm. Having to submit to the vilest slavery ever allotted to man, unheard, is sufficient to destroy all humanity, did not the little Christianity I possess come to the rescue. I never before could bring myself to believe that men occupying positions of honor, influence, and power could become so innocently affiliated with liars and scoundrels; yet with the acknowledgment of the fact, no investigation is made in regard to my case, where even the evidence itself against me bears the impress of untruth without any other refutation. I am growing daily more impatient. I feel that I am an American citizen and entitled to the protection which the Constitution and laws guarantee. I must now conclude.

Your fond and devoted husband,

SAM.

November 9, 1866.

Dear Frank:

Knowing your great anxiety to hear from me, I write to let you know I have been in consultation with Mr. Reverdy Johnson and his son-in-law, Mr. Ridgely. Mr. Johnson has promised to superintend and instruct, but could not do the necessary work in getting up the law or preparing papers. I had a long interview with Mr. Ridgely this evening. He says he must have time to examine every point, and consult Mr. Johnson, as it is a case of great importance, not only to the Doctor and his friends, but to the lawyer also who has it in charge. He will see Mr. Johnson to-night, and they will be able to-morrow to give their opinion. He will charge two hundred and fifty dollars ($250) to prepare the papers, go to Washington, and swear out the writ, and if it has to be argued before Judge Chase, will charge two hundred and fifty dollars ($250) more, making five hundred dollars ($500). As soon as I get matters thoroughly arranged, I will write or come down. Before this reaches you, we will have to decide what course to pursue, so keep a brave heart, and, with the blessing of Providence, I trust all will soon be well. Your brother,

JERE.

Baltimore, December 7, 1866.

Dear Frank:

I want day and date of the following questions: Let me know when and where Sam was first arrested, the date he was taken to Washington and where first in prison—was it the old Capitol or Carroll Prison?—by whose order he was first arrested and imprisoned, and by whom held? If you have a copy of the charges served on him, send it to me, not the book of evidence or Ewing's argument,—I have them,—but just the specific charges. Let me know the full name of the officer in charge of Fort Jefferson. I think you have the note from Colonel Wells or Hancock, requesting him to report to Washington. Be particular and give dates as near as possible. I will go to Washington to-morrow, and will probably get

169

part of the information asked of you. We are doing all we can, and will probably have the papers prepared by Thursday, or as soon as we can get the information necessary to base our petition on before the court.

I will be down as soon as I get this matter off hand. I would come instead of writing, but would have to return next day, which would make my visit too short. I will be down on Saturday next if possible. Mr.

Ridgely will have to go to the Law Department for some orders and papers covering the Military Court, and if they find out his object, may put some difficulty in the way.

I received a letter from Sam yesterday, very short and urging something be done in his case. He is very well; letter dated 10th of November. Get Henry to assist you in giving the information asked and any other you may think of. If it is any service, I can use it, if not, it will do no harm.

Hoping you and the children are enjoying good health, I am,

Your brother,

JERE.

Fort Jefferson, Florida, December 7, 1866.

My darling Frank:

I have written to you to-day a long letter, and having nothing more worthy, I send you enclosed two large moss-cards, a cross, and a wreath as a Christmas gift. I am afraid they will be much disfigured by folding and the rough usage of the mails, etc. They were pressed by myself. I devote a great deal of my leisure to pressing moss for the want of a more suitable employment, which acts as a diversion to my thoughts, a pastime and a profit. Tell little Tommy, Papa sent him one to pay for the rosebud received some time ago. I had to cut the paper to make it small enough for the envelope. You can paste a piece around to make it fit in a frame. A likeness can also be put within the wreath. Should these arrive in good condition, and you desire more, let me know, and I will send you more by the same means. Bear up bravely against present adversity, and I am in hopes it will not be long before we are restored to each other by a merciful Providence. I have not much hope of its taking place during the session of Congress. The time for action was permitted to go by.

Your loving husband,

SAM.

Washington, December 17, 1866.

My dear Mrs. Mudd:

The Supreme Court of the United States this morning gave an opinion which must secure the liberation of your husband. I have before spoken to you of the case, and the opinion should have been delivered last winter when the case was decided, but was deferred until the present session. I have been unwilling at any time to say anything to you that might induce hopes which, if disappointed, would only increase your suffering; and preferred to wait until I could myself see the light before I told you there was light, and I am now most happy that I can say to you that I think the case is settled, and your husband must be speedily released from his most unjust confinement.

Deeply sympathizing with you in your long suffering, and congratulating you sincerely upon the prospect of its termination, I remain, with great respect,

Yours truly,

R. T. MERRICK.

Fort Jefferson, Florida, December 30, 1866.

My darling Frank:

We are just in receipt of the box sent by friends of O'Loughlin. The articles all came safely to hand and perfectly sound. They are just in time for New Year's, and are considered quite a treat. I also received yours of December 7, written with your usual hopeful spirit; not hearing anything from those better informed, gives but little consolation. The papers make mention of the decision of the

Supreme Court; this surely must have some effect in loosening the reins of power.

Christmas has passed, and with it the usual dull routine of the military. Nothing occurred to divert our minds from the disagreeable reflection of our present situation, and regrets of the past. I am in hopes you have spent a more cheerful one with our dear little children, alone, hearing their innocent jokes and merry prattle. I know you enjoy a feast that serves to blot out from memory many unpleasant recollections, and drown all other cares for the time being at least; with me reigned the gloomy thought of hopes deferred. In imagination, I am sometimes carried back to scenes of the past, and indulge in a pleasant smile at the little oddities and sayings of you and our dear little ones, to be succeeded in turn by the depressing one of an unhappy reality.

We have made application to the Secretary of War, through General Hill, giving many valid reasons for our removal to some Northern prison. I am in hopes it may prove unnecessary, and that we may be released through the medium of the recent decision of the Supreme Court. God grant it may not be much longer deferred.

I wrote to you November 26th, December 1st, 7th, 12th and 22d.

Your devoted husband,

SAM.

CAPTURE OF JOHN H. SURRAT

Port Jefferson, Florida, January 15, 1867. My darling Frank:

I received on the 12th yours of December 31, also papers as late as January 3, containing the decision of the Supreme Court, which fully covers our case, and the denial of Judge Chase of the writ of *habeas corpus* in my case.

It is vexatious to see how partial the laws are made applicable and administered. Milligan was tried during the existence of active war. His case is declared illegal. We were tried after the war, and peace declared. If the trial of Milligan was wrong, certainly ours was more so, and no necessity can be pleaded in palliation.

The chief point of difference in the Court was as to the powers of Congress, which did not involve in the least the illegality of our trial and conviction. The question upon which they did not coincide seems entirely a constitutional one, from which both the citizen and soldier derive all their rights. I don't understand why application should be made to Judge Chase in preference to any other judge. From the partisan course which he has pursued for the past two years, prejudice alone, I am afraid, would be sufficient to influence him to a denial of the benefit of the laws to those of an opposite opinion.

The "writ" should be served on the Secretary of War or the President, and not upon the Commander of this post. General Hill said to one of the prisoners a few days ago, that if the writ were served on him he would not take the responsibility of acceding to the demand. So you see that, notwithstanding the decision of the Supreme Court, the highest tribunal in the land, I am still a prisoner in the hands of the President and his honorable Secretary of War, serving their pleasure.

The arrival of Surratt will be the advent of a new excitement, and the reiteration of every species of lie and slander which were given currency at our trial and subsequently, and serve as a pretext to continue my unlawful and unjust imprisonment. Be slow to credit the wild, loose newspaper articles.

The weather has been cold and pleasant up to a day or two past. It is now growing warm and uncomfortable. We have a garden in the center of the Fort, the soil or surface of which has been brought from the mainland. It is now luxuriant with all kinds of vegetables that have been planted—beets, peas, tomatoes, beans, radishes, etc. The few trees we have never lose their foliage and the cocoanut, the only tree bearing, always with its peculiar fruit. The flowers that are cultivated are always in bloom. We have one or two little caged song-birds that enliven the island with occasional merry notes.

Your devoted husband,

SAM.

The Surratt referred to by my father in the above letter was John H. Surratt, one of the alleged "conspirators." He was, at the time of the assassination of President Lincoln, a young man who had barely reached his majority. When he learned of the assassination he was in Elmira, New York, where he had been sent by the Secret Service Bureau of the Confederate Government.

The day after the assassination a reward of $25,000 was offered by the United States Government for the capture of Surratt, dead or alive. He escaped into Canada, and was secreted five months in Quebec. From that city he took passage on a steamer for London. Subsequently he made his way to Rome, where he enlisted, under an assumed name, in the Papal Guards. When his identity was discovered he was, by order of Pope Pius IX, arrested and cast into prison. He succeeded in escaping, and after experiencing many vicissitudes, finally reached Alexandria, in Egypt.

Here he was arrested and handed over to the United States authorities. He was brought to Washington, and after much delay was tried before a jury in the Criminal Court of the District of Columbia, his trial lasting sixty-two days. The jury disagreed and were discharged. Surratt was subsequently admitted to bail, but his case was never again brought to trial.

174

Baltimore, January 17, 1867. Mrs. Dr. Mudd.

My dear Madam: Yours of the 6th instant came duly to hand. I have not seen the resolution you spoke of, but do not see how it can affect Dr. Mudd's case. I have never abandoned the hope of yet getting him released, and think I will now make application to the judges of the courts of the District of Columbia.

I think it advisable, however, to wait awhile, but will confer with Mr. Reverdy Johnson on the subject. Very faithfully yours,

ANDREW STERITT RIDGELY.

Fort Jefferson, Florida, January 23, 1867.

My darling Prank:

As the mail will go out in a few minutes, I have but barely time to say I am as well as usual, and desire my remembrance to all. Your letters arrive very seldom. Yours of the 31st of December has been received. The hopes it created were immediately blasted, on perusing the paper received the same day. I am rejoiced, however, to know that something has been done, though fruitless.

It is plain, since the decision of the Court, that I am only held by armed hand, and in spite of law. I could ask nothing more final and complete than the decision in question, yet I am uncertain of the period when its benefits will accrue. I wrote to you on the 15th, and addressed the letter to Jere. He will forward as soon as received.

Hoping to hear something more definite shortly, which will have the tendency to shorten our unhappy separation, I am as ever, truly and affectionately,

Your devoted husband,

SAM.

Fort Jefferson, Florida, February 6, 1867.

My darling Frank:

I wrote to you a few days ago, I believe on the 28th of January.

I am becoming discouraged to continue my frequent correspondence, finding the interval growing so long between your very short epistles. I am also beginning to think there was but little calculation or penetration, on the part of those who had the management Df my case, to have impressed you so erroneously. Matters, I fear, have assumed a more complicated nature in consequence. I am in hopes the sober thought of the people will not sustain the ultra and unconstitutional legislation of Congress.

I am well. The weather again becoming very warm, I fear the return of the distressing symptoms which I enumerated in some of my letters last year. We continue to be under close guard, and allowed but little exercise.

Inquire and let me know whether it would be advisable for us to make application for removal North, through General Hill to the War Department. We have had no priest here in his official capacity since last July. A young priest stopped here on his way to Key West two or three weeks ago. I did not learn his name. He said he would pay us a visit in the course of a few weeks. Good-by,

SAM.

Fort Jefferson, Florida, February 14, 1867.

My darling Frank:

Yours of the 28th of January, and Jere's of the 29th, have come to hand. You and Jere, though instructed by able counsel, seem no better informed than myself, and I have had only access to newspapers. Judging from papers, the old ship of state is adrift, floating without a rudder, without a captain, and they threaten to throw overboard the chief engineer, the President.

The Constitution and the decision of the supreme tribunal of the land seem completely overlooked and passed by unnoticed. They now threaten to impeach the President without the legally required court: all the States. When these bounds are passed, God only knows and can judge the finality of their proceedings.

I fail to perceive and conjecture anything favorable. I cannot yet look forward to any period with certainty. In the mean time, I am making myself as content as circumstances will permit. My health has continued unusually good through the winter up to this time; God grant I may be spared another summer here. I weighed a few days ago one hundred and forty-five, which is only a few pounds short of my usual weight. Put in practice your own preaching,—be patient, be prudent, etc. Under our present hard lot I have an innate feeling that tells me the time of our cruel separation will not be much longer deferred. How much I have desired to be with the children catching snowbirds, and enjoy with you their delight of triumph. We are yet under close guard, and I am afraid I will become so accustomed to this life, I will naturally look for the guard to accompany me on all occasions, when it shall please Providence and the head of the enlightened American nation to release me.

Your disconsolate husband,

SAM.

Fort Jefferson, Florida, February 20, 1867.

My darling Frank:

I did not receive yours of January 6, until yester-day—being considerably over a month on the way. I wrote to you on the 14th and Jere on the 16th. I have nothing new, nor additional requests to make. My health continues about the same—suffering an indisposition occasionally with the change of weather.

You need not bother about sending anything for the future unless I request it. I am well supplied with clothing—other necessaries I will be able to obtain through my own exertions.

I have had my occupation changed to that of the carpenter's shop, which affords me more exercise and a greater diversion to my thoughts. I occupy my time principally in making little boxes, ornamenting them with different colors and varieties of wood.

The mail will close in an hour's time, so I must close by desiring my kindest remembrance to all.

Your faithful and devoted husband,

SAM.

Fort Jefferson, Florida, February 26, 1867. My dear Jere:

When I wrote last, I forgot to name the fact that Fort Jefferson and Key West had been made separate divisions, with the Commander stationed at the latter. General Hill will, therefore, in a short time take up his quarters at that place.

Could you be assured that a "writ" would be accepted, the change renders the accomplishment of matters more easy and expeditious, for all the necessary authorities you need command of are there. Here, there is no civil law or authority, and no means whereby you could command an audience with the Commander should he be disposed not to grant it.

You said in case other measures failed, "you would send a lawyer to Florida." Unless you were confident of the result, I think it would be only loss of time and expense without recompense. I mentioned in a former letter the remark that was made to one of our number, and I suppose it would be applicable to myself, that if a "writ" was served upon him, he (the Commander) would not assume the responsibility of yielding to the demand.

My attention has been called to the legislation going on in Congress, having the tendency to thwart the execution of the plain decision of the Supreme Court upon the test oath; if so, it will be used as a precedent

15 by other courts relative to its judgment upon the legality of trials of civilians by court martial. Please inform me plainly upon all these points, and the bearing they are likely to assume. I am growing weary of perplexities arising from the many constructions of public acts.

The action of Congress seems *ex post facto,* which is clearly unconstitutional; but will it not delay and necessarily cause our cases to be specially brought before the Court to be disposed of, not permitting the recent judgment of the Supreme Court to be a finality?

The mail leaves in a short time, consequently I must close. Your brother,

SAM.

Fort Jefferson, Florida, March 5, 1867.

My darling Frank:

Yours of February 12th reached me this morning, bringing me the desired news of all well and hearty. You gave expression to despondency, and asked for something cheering and consoling from me. How willing this would be accorded were it in my power, even the sacrifice of this miserable life, could it be of benefit to you and our little ones.

By referring me to the newspapers for information regarding my situation, you seem no better acquainted than myself with the difficulties in the way of my release. The altered relation which you apprehend will take place with the marriage of Jere, is very natural. It will be impossible for him to extend his former love, care and attention, and to this extent, my darling Frank, is the principal source of your gloom and anxiety. When I think of your dependent state, the trials, inconveniences, and sufferings you have to endure, my heart bleeds and my soul seems ready to leap from this tenement of clay, and rush to the aid and comfort of you and all; but, alas! how impotent are all my efforts, and how incapable of affording you and our little ones assistance at no distant day,—a hope that would enable me to bear with more resignation the grievous trials to which I have been subjected. I am debarred from all friends and advisers, being yet under close guard, not allowed to hold conversation with any one outside of my immediate roommates. How then is it possible for me to form any idea of the future, or to extend to you any hope of our speedy union? I have naturally looked to you and Jere for information and hope, but in vain, to receive anything satisfactory.

179

Jere has written but seldom, and when he did, I could arrive no nearer the truth than before.

We have received papers up to the 23d instant. They make mention of the arrival of Surratt, and his being surrendered to the civil authorities. I am in hopes his trial will be speedy and impartial, and have the effect to clear away many of the mists that surround the tragic affair and lead to my early release from this place of exile and misery, and our once more happy union. To this end, my darling Frank, are all my fondest anticipations centered. Be patient, be prudent; in a word, be a good child, and let nothing occur that will tend to mar the pleasure and happiness of which we mutually dream, and God, upon whose justice and mercy I rely, will not permit a much longer delay. When you informed me in a previous letter that Jere and M. C. were to be married, I was truly in hopes I would be home in time to wish them in person a joyous union, and more happiness than has fallen to our lot. It now devolves upon you to perform this both pleasing and gloomy duty.

I wrote to Mr. Stone on the 1st of December last and directed the letter to Washington, D. C., thinking he would take his seat in the recent Congress; it was returned to me yesterday. I suppose he takes his seat to-day by the new arrangement. Seek advice and counsel from him and Mr. Ewing and see whether something can't be effected through the Legislative Department, the Judicial and the Executive having failed. General Hill is of the opinion that, as soon as Surratt arrives, the Government would send for us; God grant his prediction may prove true.

Try and find out from Mr. Ridgely when he intends taking further action, and what hopes he has of success. There seems to be no mode of redress except through Congress, and they appear to have shut up the portals of felicity, both human and divine, and thrown away the key. Let me know at what time he thinks he will be able to succeed. You have made many guesses when I would be home, which has only the effect to increase my misery; but try once more and see how near you can approximate the truth. If it is one, two, three or four months, or the same number of years, give me the views of counsel. Cut out of the papers all the proceedings in the trial of Surratt as they appear, and send to me by mail.

Your devoted husband,

SAM.

Baltimore, March 6, 1867.

Dear Frank:

This is the first opportunity I have had of writing you since my return.

I have been to Ridgely's office twice since mv return to see him; the first clay he was in Washington; he is now in New York, but expected back to-morrow. I will see him as soon as he returns and let you know the result of my interview. You may rest assured I will do everything in my power to procure Sam's release.

Ford, the proprietor of the theater, has promised to go with me. He says he is determined to leave nothing undone that can be done to have Spangler released, if it costs him five thousand dollars.

I received a letter from Sam yesterday. He received my letter, but, poor fellow, he can't understand why it is Johnson does not act under the decision of the Supreme Court. He seems to think he ought to do it, even at the risk of being impeached. I wrote to him to-day and will mail his letter with this. I wrote him fully, and explained everything to him as far as I was capable. I would send you his letter with this, but left it up at the house.

Your brother,

Fort Jefferson, Florida, March 11, 1867.

My darling Frank:

General Hill left here on the 8th to take up his quarters permanently at Key West. These two posts having been made a separate district, you can inform Jere of the fact should it be of any importance to him. He said in his last letter that in case other measures failed, he would send a lawyer to Florida. I know not the situation of affairs, but from what I can judge of the legislation of Congress, all measures of redress have been cut off by that body. I wrote to Hon. Reverdy Johnson on the subject on the 8th, and desired his opinion of the matter. I want to be satisfied one way or the other; suspense is wearisome.

I suppose the trial of Surratt will be used now as an excuse for delay in my case, upon the part of the lawyers you have employed. Can't it be arranged to have me tried with him? Let me know what is being done; I want prospects of success when you write; also let me know when the trial of Surratt will conic off. I have written this quite hastily on account of being in time for the outgoing mail.

Your devoted husband,

SAM.

Port Jefferson, Florida, March 25, 1867.

My darling Frank:

I received yours of February 28th a few days ago. I am glad you have resolved on more frequent correspondence. You say you feel "miserable" when you do not hear from me regularly. This might be doubted if the number of your epistles implies anything. At no period have I permitted three weeks to escape without writing, yet with you it has not been unusual. I am but one, you are many. My soul is wrapped up in you all, and yet not divided. If you feel gloomy and uneasy on my account, how much more so must I feel for you, as you are the greatest number, and none of us are exempt from the accidents of life, etc.

I am sorry matters still assume no different shape. You remarked that Mr. Ridgely would repair to Florida as soon as Judge Wayne entered upon his judicial functions in that district. You did not state the time it would take place, but led me to infer it would be shortly by saying you would not await the trial of Surratt, which the newspapers represent as going on now. Try always to be explicit, and never speak of a thing in contemplation without giving some idea of the time.

Should Surratt have a speedy and impartial trial, I have more hopes from its result than from everything else, for I know it is bound to lead to my entire exculpation, and it will be impossible for those in power to hold me against the will of an enlightened public.

I wrote to Mr. Johnson on the 8th of the present month, and directed the letter to Washington. Should

Congress adjourn, he will likely not receive it, as he will return to Baltimore. You will please notify Jere of this fact. The letter I wrote to Stone was returned to me. I believe he was a member of the last Congress. Your husband,

SAM.

Fort Jefferson, Florida, April 5, 1867.

My darling Frank:

Would I could be so hopeful as you express. Viewing the situation of affairs by the public press of the country, the days of the Republic have passed, superseded by the sad reality of a military despotism. I feel often animated in spirit as those brave Cretes who, sooner than surrender victims to their enemies, blew up the castle and perished with their cruel and despotic foes who had pursued them thither. The South is certainly placed under no debt of gratitude.

The post-office at this place has been broken up for some reason not accounted for. Our letters, therefore, will be likely post-marked for the future from Key West. You will, of course, direct your letters to the as formerly.

The mail leaves in a few minutes, consequently can't say much more. The priest from Key West arrived here yesterday. I have not yet spoken to him, but will do so as soon as practicable.

The papers record the death of Judge Turner of the War Department, Bureau of *Military Injustice. I* have no reason to lament the occurrence. It was in his power to refute that unjust and slanderous statement appended to the court martial proceedings with Judge Holt's approval. Since he was so notoriously unjust toward me in suppressing the truth or fabricating a falsehood, it is fair to presume he was guilty of all, or many of the misrepresentations and distortions of fact in regard to myself, Davis, and others. The cause of his death is said to be apoplexy, but more likely poison by his own hands. The fate of a guilty conscience. I am still in my usual health.

Your devoted husband,

SAM.

Fort Jefferson, Florida, April 13, 1867.

My darling Frank:

I wrote to you on the 5th instant, and gave all particulars of health, etc., up to that date. Having nothing additional, and not having received any tidings from any one since, you can't expect a very extended epistle.

I have heard nothing from Jere since his return to Baltimore. I suppose he has nothing cheering to communicate, and concluded not to write.

General Butler has brought something new to light in reference to our trial, Booth's diary, which was never heard of before. "When rogues fall out, honest men get their dues," is fully exemplified in this instance; but the most astonishing part of the matter is my retention here in spite of all these developments of foul play and rascality. It has been intimated there is something more yet unknown to the world; you will please let me know fully when you write again.

I have heard nothing of Surratt's trial having commenced. I fear it will be as predicted. He will be kept in prison until perhaps he dies before any trial be given him,—like Davis,—and the delay be made an excuse to protract my imprisonment.

I went to confession and communion on the 8th. The name of the priest is Father Allard, a French Canadian; speaks English very imperfectly. He is quite young. I am sorry I can't write more interestingly. My health has been unusually good up to the present.

Do not give yourself any uneasiness about my fare, etc. We can supply our few wants by making little boxes, frames, etc., which are in great demand. Today we contributed to the Southern Relief Fair at Key West little articles, which were worth to us over seventy-five dollars. Our work-boxes sell readily at twenty-five and thirty cents apiece.

Your devoted husband,

SAM.

Fort Jefferson, Florida, April 16, 1867.

My dear Tom [T. O. Dyer, New Orleans]:

A favorable opportunity presenting, I avail myself to let you hear more directly from me. I have written you on several occasions, but have never received a reply in acknowledgment, consequently fear you do not get them.

Mr. Waters has kindly consented to take this to you in person and present my best wishes for you and all our kind relatives. Waters has just been released, having been sent here for shooting a negro prisoner, in discharge of his duty while in the Confederate service, and for which the Federal authorities had no right to take cognizance. His case though is only one of the many thousand unlawful acts which they have committed, and still continue, upon a brave and defenseless people. You see, notwithstanding the disclosures made by Butler in Congress a few days ago, and the charge made by Frank Blair of a similar nature, no investigation is made or permitted. My sympathies increase rather than diminish when I consider the unjust, tyrannical, humiliating exactions and measures demanded of a defenseless people. A day of reckoning surely will come, but I fear too late for the present generation to bear witness of an offended God and justice.

The last letter received from Frank was dated March igth. At that time they were all well. Surratt's trial was expected to come off in the present month, and it was believed we would be sent for by the Government, to be tried again in conjunction. We are here yet, and

185

have very little hope of this small boon being offered us. The cause of the Government is too weak to expect to gain any advantage, therefore we expect to remain here so long as the Government is in the hands of its present occupants. I send you a verbal message by the bearer. If you can, prudently, let me hear from you in regard.

Colonel St. Ledger Grenfel is kept in close confinement under guard. A few days ago, being sick, he applied to the doctor of the Post for medical attention, which he was refused, and he was ordered to work. Feeling himself unable to move about, he refused. He was then ordered to carry a ball until further orders, which he likewise refused. He was then tied up for half a day, and still refusing, he was taken to one of the wharves, thrown overboard with a rope attached, and ducked; being able to keep himself above water, a fifty pound weight was attached to his feet. Grenfel is an old man, about sixty. He has never refused to do work which he was able to perform, but they demanded more than he felt able, and he wisely refused. They could not conquer him, and he is doing now that which he never objected doing.

Remember me to all, and believe me most truly yours,

SAM.

Fort Jefferson, Florida, April 25, 1867.

My darling Frank:

I received to-day yours of the loth, also the *Weekly Sun* of the 13th. We used to get the *Gazette,* but T suppose the subscription has run out. I wrote to you last on the iith and 15th of April, and to Cousin Ann on the loth. I wrote to you also on the loth, but the officer, whose duty it is to inspect, had not time to examine, consequently it did not go.

Tell Ma, Pa, and family I do not write because I have nothing to engross their attention, and nothing cheering and hopeful to give them consolation. I could only give them a picture of my woes, without the requisite knowledge to impart for their redress, which would only add to their discomfort, consequently remain silent, acting on the principle, "when ignorance is bliss, 'tis folly to be wise." Again I have been so credulous as to believe something would be done through the instrumentality of the lawyers engaged, that caused me to look anxiously from day to day for the arrival of the steamer that would bear me gladly to you all, and did not think it necessary to write.

I am truly glad to hear you are satisfied with the darkies engaged on the farm. Tell Bap. I say to pay his whole attention to the farm, and do not run about looking up little jobs, and he will succeed well. Should he desire any carpenter work, he will find a plenty on the farm, for which, should it be in my power, I will amply compensate him.

A good corn-house is very much needed, also a barn or pen-house for tobacco. At his leisure he could get out the material for them, and leave it to some competent party to estimate value, and take it from rent or otherwise. General Hill, I understand, will leave in a short time for Washington on a furlough or leave of absence. This Post is now in command of Major Stone. He arrived here this morning from Key West. It has been rumored here for several days that all the prisoners at this place would be taken to Ship Island.

The number of prisoners is now about forty-five, including both black and white. I have not been able to trace this rumor to any reliable source. How much I desire to see and be with you all. It was three weeks between our last letters. Good-by.

Your devoted husband,

SAM.

Fort Jefferson, Florida, May 11, 1867.

My darling Frank:

It will not be in my power to write you at this time as long a letter as I desire. The mail will leave in the course of an hour, so I must hurry to be in time to have it examined previous to mailing. I was too late the last mail, consequently did not get off the letter I had

187

written, so the last letter I wrote to you was dated the 25th of April, the interval being much longer than I generally suffer to pass.

Do not forget to see dear Papa and extend to him whatever comfort you can. Tell him to give himself no uneasiness on my account—not worry himself too much about me and your affairs, etc. I fear he suffers more from mental perplexities, resulting from the condition of the country and domestic affairs. Thank him, my darling Frank, in my name, for his ever kind attention and parental solicitude toward us and the dear little ones, and to consider that whenever I write to you or any of the family, it is as much to himself and Ma. Advise him not to read the newspaper for a little while, and see whether he receives advantage from the abstinence. I received yesterday a package of newspapers from Tom, and a box. I have not yet received the box or invoice of articles, etc.

Hoping this may find you and all the family in the enjoyment of health, etc., I am,

Your loving husband,

SAM.

"SOMEBODY HAD TO SUFFER"

Fort Jefferson, Florida, May 25, 1867. My darling Frank:

The papers mention the release of Davis under bail, without trial. This truly seems strange to me. I feel confident they will not try Surratt, but postpone from time to time until finally released, the Government or the prosecution not appearing against him. Rage has become impotent; the bloodthirsty wretches, feeling no longer security in their demon pursuits, have shrunk away into ignominious nothingness, or are crying under the weight of a guilty conscience. I can't see what Surratt's case has to do with me—it is only an excuse or put off. How strangely justice is administered in this enlightened nineteenth century. None believed a few years ago that a corporal's guard could be mustered throughout the country to carry out the atrocious measures now heaped upon a helpless and defenseless people, but it seems there is never lack of means to the ends of vile purposes. I am afraid I may say too much, and in consequence you may fail to hear from me, so I will postpone all expressions of opinion until I can see it will be of some avail. I am entirely without news of interest.

The report of the committee appointed to inquire into the condition, etc., of the penitentiary of the State, gives a gloomy exhibit of the depravity and increase of crime among the recent "emancipated." Laws made corrective and milder for that class of our population called down upon the State and people the virtuous indignation of the immaculate Congress. It has now in its pride and presumption absorbed all the powers of the Government, Legislative, Judicial and Execu-tive—not governed even by the laws of God, only so far as appears righteous to them. They would dictate to God Almighty himself sooner than acknowledge the error of the position they have assumed. Write soon and often. Give me all the news of the neighborhood and answer all my little queries.

Your husband,

SAM.

Fort Jefferson, Florida, June 3, 1867. My darling Frank:

The month of June, you will perceive by the above date, has been ushered in with all its glory and sunshine, and the promised release of your most disconsolate yet *in futuro*. Mail came on the first. I received no letter, nor the papers which you subscribed for.

I have seen the copy of Booth's diary. I can see no reason for its being withheld from the Court which convicted us; on the contrary, it goes to confirm the statement of those who participated with him, or who were confederates. It shows clearly that I could have had no knowledge of the deed, and would have tended had it been before the Court, to establish my innocence. I shall leave the whole matter with you and friends to be dealt with agreeable to your best judgment.

I am curious to know what offense will be set up by the Government in Surratt's case. I am very much afraid the trial will meet with another postponement so that they can urge a longer continuance of my exile on this account. Our country seems a complete mobocracy instead of a Government of law and order.

The President does not feel warranted in the execution of his plainest duties under the Constitution without first consulting the mob spirit. I am well, though growing exceedingly weary of the continued usurpation. Could I perceive that the Government had the slightest shadow of suspicion against me, I could feel perhaps more resigned; but take the whole evidence and circumstances adduced on trial, and no court of justice, it seems to me, could fail establishing my entire innocence. I remarked this to Judge Turner on my way to this place, when he remarked that somebody had to suffer, and it was just as well that I should as anybody else. This I believe was as good an answer as he could make, but I could not see the justice. I have written very hastily in order to be in time for the outgoing mail.

For God's sake urge action on the part of those entrusted with the care of my case. Davis has been set free, and Surratt, once regarded as his prime agent, seems now without a charge against him, and here am I, having suffered the tortures of the damned, without one word of rebuke to those who have caused all—and without pity, sympathy, or consolation from an enlightened public. Try and give me some definite news in your next.

Hoping this may find you all in health, I am, as ever, fondly and devotedly,

Your husband,

SAM.

BOOTH'S DIARY

"Booth's Diary," referred to by my father in the above letter, was found in a pocket of the clothing Booth wore at the time he was shot and killed by Sergeant Corbett. The "Diary" was offered and read in evidence at the trial of John H. Surratt. It was not put in evidence at the trial of the alleged "conspirators" before the Military Commission, although it was in the possession of Secretary of War Stanton. It is as follows:

"Te amo."

April 13, 14, Friday, the Ides.

Until to-day nothing was ever thought of sacrificing to our country's wrongs. For six months we had worked to capture. But our cause being almost lost, something decisive and great must be done. But its failure was owing to others who did not strike for their country with a heart. I struck boldly, and not as the papers say. I walked with a firm step through a thousand of his friends; was stopped, but pushed on. A colonel was at his side. I shouted *sic semper* before I fired. In jumping, broke my leg. I passed all his pickets. Rode sixty miles that night, with the bone of my leg tearing the flesh at every jump.

I can never repent it though we hated to kill. Our country owed all our troubles to him, and God simply made me the instrument of his punishment.

The country is not

April, 1865, what is was. This forced Union is not what I have loved. I care not what becomes of me. I have no desire to outlive my country. This night (before the deed) I wrote a long article and left it for one of the editors of the *National Intelligencer,* in which I fully set forth our reasons for our proceeding. He or the gov'r—

Friday 21.

After being hunted like a dog through swamps, woods, and last night being chased by gunboats till I was forced to return, wet, cold, and starving, with every man's hand against me, I am here in despair. And why? For doing what Brutus was honored for—what made Tell a hero. And yet I, for striking down a greater tyrant than they ever knew, am looked upon as a common cut-throat. My action was purer than either of theirs. One hoped to be great. The other had not only his country's, but his own wrongs to avenge. I hoped for no gain. I knew no private wrong. I struck for my country and that alone. A country that groaned beneath this tyranny, and prayed for this end, and yet now behold the cold hand they extend to me. God cannot pardon me if I have done wrong. Yet I cannot see my wrong, except in serving a degenerate people. The little, the very little, I left behind to clear my name, the Government will not allow to be printed. So ends all. For my country I have given up all that makes life sweet and holy, brought misery upon my family, and am sure there is no pardon in the Heaven for me, since man condemns me so. I have only heard of what has been done (except what I did myself), and it fills me with horror. God, try and forgive me, and bless my mother. To-night I will once more try the river with the intent to cross. Though I have a greater desire and almost a mind to return to Washington, and in a measure clear my name—which I feel I can do. I do not repent the blow I struck. I may before my God, but not to man. I think I have done well. Though I am abandoned with the curse of Cain upon me, when, if the world knew my heart, that one blow would have made me great, though I did desire no greatness.

To-night I try to escape these blood-hounds once more. Who can read his fate? God's will be done.

I have too great a soul to die like a criminal. o may He, may He spare me that, and let me die bravely i6

I bless the entire world. Have never hated or wronged any one.

This last was not a wrong, unless God deems it so, and it's with Him to damn or bless me. And for this brave boy with me, who often prays (yes, before and since) with a true and sincere heart—was it crime in him? If so, why can he pray the same?

I do not wish to shed a drop of blood, but "I must fight the course!"

END OF DIARY EXCERPT

'Tis all that's left me.

Fort Jefferson, Florida, June 10, 1867.

My darling Frank:

I wrote you on the 3d, more to let you know that I still live and remember, than impart news otherwise of a consoling character— such must be the nature of the present.

The Tortugas is a desolate group of islands unproductive alike of news as well as vegetation. The casual arrival of mail affording but little change from the usual monotony on account of its rather ancient date. We glance hastily over the files of newspapers to see what is said having reference to us and what the progress made toward restoring the States to their former status; this being done, the balance of the paper is read with no more interest than the transactions of centuries past. Within the past week we had three days of storm, cloudy and rainy weather, although lending a short respite to the customary dazzling sun-shine—the dampness being intense, searches up every old rheumatic disposition, penetrates every joint, which more than counteracts the enjoyment. To obviate the evil effects of the dampness I am forced to wear constantly flannel or net shirts; though warm, I find them more tolerable than the effects of the above cause. I attribute my improved health principally to their agency.

I received to-day yours of the 10th of May, and one from Sissy of the 15th. I am rejoiced to know that you all continue well, and the families healthy. Do not lose courage; though my confidence in the honesty of the generality of man is impaired, my increased trust and hope in the Providence and justice of God more than repays. I feel that though men may bury every instinct of humanity and stifle every emotion of conscience, truth and innocence will be declared and made manifest, even if the stones of the earth have to rise up as witnesses. Truth and virtue will ever shine—then, my darling Frank let us be brave and steadfast in all the ways of rectitude, and I feel assured the time that intervenes between our happy reunion, yet though in the unknown future, cannot be much longer delayed.

I must now reluctantly bring my letter to a close, and scribble a few lines to Sissy. The mail will leave this evening, so if I don't hurry, my letter will not be in time for the necessary examination and mailing. My health continues good; occasionally I am depressed by the excessive heat. In weight and flesh I am about the same as when I left home. Give yourself no uneasiness for the future. Were I home at this moment, nothing would tempt me to read a newspaper, for they only tend to engender hate, and make the mind familiar with crime of every description. Kiss our darling little children, train them to obedience and good behavior now whilst young, and when they grow older, we will be spared the blush of shame at their unruly conduct.

Hoping this may be my last from this barren and miserable isle, I am, as ever,

Your fond and devoted husband,

SAMUEL MUDD.

Fort Jefferson, Florida, June 15, 1867.

My darling Frank:

I have received no letter, nor the *Gazette* from Jere which you said you requested. M. C. perhaps occupies all his thoughts for the present.

Should you see Cecie tell her I have no knowledge of being reinstated in any position by General Hill, nor am I conscious of having received any personal kindness or unkindness. We were fed like brutes for more than fourteen months, kept in chains over three months, and up to the time I left, under close guard day and night, and allowed no conversation with any one outside the room. We were informed that the orders for this treatment emanated from the War Department. He did promise to send any application we should make, with a favorable recommendation to the headquarters of his department. So far as I am acquainted, all grievances which came under his personal observation were redressed, but owing to the difficulty of seeing him, much suffering and dissatisfaction ensued.

We made application through his adjutant, Captain Van Reed, on two different occasions a short time after he assumed command, without meeting with any response from the Government, so we concluded to bother him no more, and never, to my knowledge, was the application renewed until he was ordered to report to the Government in person, in answer to a note I had addressed. Had we been ordered out and shot, it would have been much kinder than the treatment we received. We were treated in every respect as the most ferocious wild beasts, for which I blame no one personally.

Your fond and devoted husband,

SAM.

Fort Jefferson, Florida, June 23, 1867.

My darling Frank:

I see by the papers that Surratt's trial has actually commenced, the prosecution endeavoring to obtain a verdict consistent with public opinion, apparently regardless of justice. Public opinion is pretty apt to be right, if not misinformed or prejudiced. If the prosecution will let the truth be known there would be no objection to a verdict consistent with the enlightened public mind; but this seems remote to their intention; "they have given the dog his bad name, and he must suffer, right or wrong." Individual character and honor of the nation are at stake, and it would be a sacrilege for either to suffer by

195

the decision of a petty court and twelve jurymen. I am for the support of both, but not at the expense of justice. Judge Fisher has granted the prayer of the prosecution, and ordered the empaneling of a new jury, which I suppose will be the representatives of the personification of the public opinion, and will have a verdict in accordance.

It has been raining very hard off and on for three or four days, and our casement, clothing, bedding, and wearing apparel became very wet and damp. My health continues better than could be expected under the circumstances. I am occupied in the quartermaster's carpenter shop. I have more annoyance from conflicting orders than from the work I have to perform. I shall bear patiently until the trial of Sur-ratt is over, then if something is not done toward freeing me from this hell, I shall grow very sad and disheartened.

Write often and acquaint me with the principal features of the Surratt trial.

Your fond husband,

SAM.

Fort Jefferson, Florida, June 30, 1867.

My darling Frank:

I received, on the 22d instant, yours of the 10th, bringing the ever glad news of the continued health of yourself and all the family. I wrote to you on the 23d, but owing to some remarks being found objectionable, my letter was returned. It was then too late to write another, the mail leaving immediately after. For the future you must excuse brevity.

Mail arrived here on the 28th bringing New York papers up to the 20th. I have not been able to see them, but understand, with much satisfaction, that the trial of Surratt is progressing, for another excuse for delay will be done away with, and perhaps may shed some light upon the terrible deed for which he is now being tried.

I sent you a cribbage board in a box containing little presents from my roommates to their friends. Let me know whether it has been received. I am sorry I had nothing more worthy at the time. I had a very nice box, which I intended sending to you, but was induced to give it to the Southern Relief Fair at Key West.

I wrote to you on the following dates, viz: April 5th, 13th and 25th, May 4th, 11th, 18th and 25th, June 3d, 10th, 15th (and 23d which did not go) and to-day, 30th.

Our correspondence is carefully inspected, and letters of yours and others may be withheld without my knowledge. I acknowledge the receipt of all that come to hand.

The Fort is now commanded by Major Andrews.

From the slight acquaintance I have had, he seems quite a good man. Nearly all the older officers have been relieved; the present number seem much kinder and better disposed.

Hoping this may find you and our dear little children in the enjoyment of health etc., I bid you a reluctant adieu.

Your loving husband,

SAM.

Fort Jefferson, Florida, July 8, 1867.

My darling Prank:

Mail arrived yesterday bringing me a letter from Cecie, but no news from you or any one at home. I have seen the New York papers up to the 27th. The trial of Surratt seems to progress slowly. I feel impatient to see its conclusion, and hope something may be done to effect our union.

My health and spirit is much improved, likewise the health of the island is excellent—very little sickness and nothing of an epidemic character. I am entirely without news. Write often and give all news correct.

Your devoted husband,

SAM.

Fort Jefferson, Florida, July 14, 1867.

My darling Frank:

The mail boat came last night bringing no mail. How disappointed I feel at not hearing from you. I learn that owing to the quarantine regulations and the withdrawal of several steamers from the line, we will have mail twice a month. I shall, however, write every opportunity, hoping you may possess greater postal facilities.

This Post continues quite healthy, and as far as I have been able to ascertain no fatal epidemic prevails anywhere on the Gulf coast. I wrote to you on the 30th of June, and to you and Cecie on the 7th of July. If you do not hear from me regularly, you must not attribute the cause to my not writing, but to irregularity of the mail and other causes. You must write regularly and acquaint me with all particulars of interest—how affairs are progressing on the farm, in the family, at Pa's, and the immediate neighborhood. I suppose ere this reaches you, the trial of Surratt will have ended, and you will be able to give me some idea of facts in relation, and whether any action is contemplated in regard to what concerns me most—my release. If something is not done immediately, I am afraid my impatience will get the better of me, and I will once more become gloomy and despondent. It has been said there is more law than justice; but as God is above the Devil, I shall ever be inspired with hope.

I was visited yesterday by a Captain Dove—resident of Washington, and brother, he said, of a Dr. Dove residing there. He was aboard of a light-house steamer, and may be inspector of light-houses on the Gulf Coast. He seemed quite friendly and well disposed. He said he was with Lieutenant Thomson during the war, who married Miss Mudd of Washington. He was well acquainted with John Mudd. I have but little desire to make the acquaintance of any one connected with the Government since being visited with such gross wrongs by its unworthy agents. I am entirely without news. My health continues good, and the treatment we receive more humane than formerly.

We have been entirely without vegetables of every description for a considerable time, and the rations are principally salt pork and indifferent bread; we can't complain, since soldiers get the same. We often use "pusly," which grows around the unfrequented portions of the Fort, and think it quite palatable. The weather has not been so hot this summer as last. There are millions of little mosquitoes that are very annoying; bedbugs sometimes get ahead of us.

Remember me to dear Pa, Ma, and family, and to all inquiring friends. Tell our dear little children that Papa often thinks of them and dreams of them, and they must all pray for him to come home speedily and safely. Write me long letters, and give me news about all.

Sincerely trusting this may find you all in the enjoyment of the blessings of health and free from all want, etc., I am, as ever, true and fondly,

Your devoted husband,

SAM MUDD.

Fort Jefferson, Florida, July 27, 1867.

My darling Frank:

I received yours of the 30th of June a day or two ago, and was delighted to know you were all well. The mail arrived this morning bringing us the *Weekly Sun* of the 13th, but no letter. I see mentioned in the papers the box of articles sent by us has safely come to hand. I sent you a cribbage board, the only thing I had on hand at the time. It was quite an extemporaneous getting up; Colonel Hamilton having kindly offered to take any articles we desired to send North, caused us to bundle up what we had on hand at the time and forward with him. The board I sent was not completed—there was a drawer intended for cards and little pegs. I have been principally engaged in such work ever since I have been in the shop. I am still employed there, and am becoming quite proficient in the use of tools, etc. My health continues as usual— good as the majority on the island, which is nothing to brag upon. The climate is very debilitating in itself—the absence of suitable diet makes it more so. The clothing I wear daily is heavier than I wore in

199

extreme cold weather at home. I am thin, but feel no discomfort from it. I had an opportunity some days ago to have my likeness taken, but thought it might occasion some injurious strictures and would not have it done. I am truly in hopes it will not be long before I will be able to present the original, if not the representative.

The subject that action is now made to hinge upon, seems clear, and there is not the least doubt in my mind but that the counsel for the defense of Surratt will be able to establish his innocence beyond the shadow of a doubt, and the wanton butchery of his mother. In case of his acquittal, I cannot see upon what pretext they can hold me; for had Surratt been on the same trial that I was, he would certainly have been hung, though innocent—no amount of evidence in his favor could have saved him.

It should be the duty of all good citizens to bring those infernal perjurers and suborners to the bar of justice, and have meted out to them the punishment their crimes deserve—an example should be made of them. Lose no time in taking action. From the lateness to which the time has been suffered to extend, I am afraid it will be cold weather before I get home, or perhaps never, so long as such damnable influences are made to operate upon those in authority.

Remember me to dear Ma, Pa, and family, and believe me ever devotedly,

Your husband,

Fort Jefferson, Florida, August 9, 1867.

My darling Frank:

Mail has just arrived bringing me yours of the 12th and 22nd of July, also a package of intelligence, though of an older date. The boat will return in a few minutes, so I can barely acknowledge the receipt of these kind favors, and let you know I am well. I have not yet perused the papers, so am unable to make comments. I will write again to-morrow and be more lengthy. I am glad to know you were so prudent as to disregard the letters of DeCue.

Let me be an after consideration. Be economical and provide the best you can with the means at your disposal; this is all the advice I can give off-hand, and without much consideration. This is the first opportunity I have had to write since the 26th of July.

Remember me to all, and believe me ever fondly,

Your husband,

SAM.

Fort Jefferson, Florida, August 10, 1867.

My darling Frank:

I wrote you a hasty note yesterday, but agreeable to promise write again to-day, although I must confess I have nothing worthy to communicate.

You seem desirous to know something about my health, fare, looks, and weight. I thought I had satisfied your curiosity on these points previously. Having nothing to occupy my pen, I again attempt a description. My health is not good, but much better than formerly. Our fare consists principally of salt pork, bread and coffee—fresh beef two or three times in every ten days. We had issued yesterday to us, eight in number, about a peck of Irish potatoes, the first vegetables of any kind since last January, with the exception of corn and beans occasionally.

As regards my looks, being an interested party, I might be inclined to flatter; but to answer your inquiry, I must pass a judgment or opinion no matter how incompetent, therefore, agreeable to the best estimate I am capable of forming, my appearance is about the same as when I left home, with the exception that my hair is considerably thinner, consequently the bald head more perceptible, and no doubt larger in circumference. I have no wrinkles, and wear constantly a mustache and goatee. Owing to the peculiarity of my skin, and not much exposed to the sun, I am paler or fairer than when I left home. I may be a few pounds lighter, perhaps about a hundred and forty-four or five. My manners about the same, impulsive, etc. Generally, have but little to say, but think a great deal. I am very weak, though in appearance strong. This I think is attributable to the climate and the want of free exercise. The rules governing the Fort are very rigid and severe, more barbarous than ages by-gone—refusing to work or obey an order, is punishable with instant death by shooting.

On the 31st of July, one of the prisoners being crazy drunk, noisy, and a little unruly, was shot and killed by one of the sentries. Instead of meeting with rebuke, the soldier was commended for his conduct. The prisoner's name was Winters, alias Lee, belonging to the 17th Infantry. He was a very orderly disposed man, nothing criminal about him. He was sent here for desertion. I don't think Job had greater misfortunes than have been visited upon us. A day of fortune came for him; the question is, how long shall ours be delayed?

Your devoted husband,

Monday Morning, August 12, 1867.

My precious Frank:

The storm which began yesterday still continues, though not quite so furious. A boat is at the wharf and will leave with the mail so soon as it subsides, so I will avail myself to let you hear from me at the latest moment. Exercise a little of that virtue, which has been so often recommended to me, toward Mr. Best and the darkies—patience. Mr. Best is growing quite old, and with bad health it is natural he should be cross and a little childish. Try to bear with him until I get home, should it be my fortune soon.

I look upon the resolution passed in Congress some days ago, appointing a committee to investigate further the assassination, as having the tendency to prolong my stay here, though I am in hopes the trial of Surratt will shed all the light that may be desired, and will end in my speedy return to you. It is useless for me to make any comments. I hope to see its conclusion the next mail, when I am in hopes I shall be better prepared to express myself. Don't lose any time in pressing the matter before the President and others in authority through your lawyers and friends. Give me all particulars in your next concerning the trial. Write a long letter and tell Henry to write to me, and give me all the news. Above all, try not to deceive me; let me know positively what bearing the trial will have upon my case, and when I may expect release from this wretched den. My love to all.

Your fond husband,

SAM.

Fort Jefferson, Florida, August 18, 1867.

My darling Frank:

A boat arrived this morning from Key West bringing no mail. She will return in an hour or two. A man came from aboard, who visited us fifteen minutes after he landed, and who represented himself as a "correspondent of the *New York Herald.*" He seemed anxious to obtain news upon many subjects, but our suspicion being aroused, he proved unsuccessful.

Should you see any representation coming from this point in the *Herald,* in which our names figure, be slow to credit. I send you his card. His name is Doyle, and he wears a detective's appearance. We had but little conversation with him.

Fearing my letter will not have time to pass through the regular channel in time, I must reluctantly bring it to a close by desiring to be remembered to all the loved ones at home, to our darling little children and family. I am in my usual health and in hopes this may find you in the possession of the same.

Write soon and give all news that may be of interest, particularly that which may have a bearing upon my stay or release. Boat is going.

SAM.

Fort Jefferson, Florida, August 25, 1867.

My darling Frank:

I received two letters from you, mailed July 31 and August 12, and one from Sissy, July 31, also several papers which have interested me considerably, so far at least as to know that the long and wearisome trial of Surratt is now over (for a time at least), and the change which has been effected and contemplated in the Cabinet.

The *New York Herald,* so bitter before in its denunciations of everything Southern or Democratic, has now turned around and advocates their principles and advises action upon the part of the President, which it scorned down a few months ago. By straws we know the direction of the wind, and we can conclude from these incidents the allaying of strife, and the return to sober reason and justice. The way seems now clear for our early reunion, if those entrusted in the management of my case be sincere and not actuated by sinister motives. Those who may fear prosecution may desire my detention and may hold out some inducement to the attorney to be tardy. I do not comprehend the conduct of Mr. Reverdy Johnson, and his son-in-law may be influenced by him. I have become so that I mistrust everybody, except our immediate family and connections, until they prove by conduct worthy of confidence. I am in hopes I will promote no unkind fears toward those in whom you have confided, but avert to the fact that you might take advantage of the least suspicion of unfair play. I will be home in October agreeably to calculations I have formed, yet I have so often been led astray, I can feel no confidence in any conclusion I arrive at. I am very well, though the island is becoming sickly. We have had one case of yellow fever here since I last wrote, which proved fatal. It originated here, and was not imported. A general renovation has ensued, which for the future will prevent its recurrence. I have no fears regarding it, which is its greatest preventative. We have a Dr. Smith attending the Post who says he is related to Mr. Wm. B. Hill's family, and seems acquainted with many in that county and the D. C. He seems quite a nice man, and has manifested a kind feeling toward me. Major Stone, who is also in the immediate command, has displayed much energy, and relieved many grievances. Although the laws are rigidly strict governing the Post, we have been specially favored, and been objects of their kindness. We are permitted to purchase from Key West, potatoes etc., which before we were denied.

Remember me as ever to all the dear ones at home, and believe me,

Your devoted husband,

SAM.

August 26, 1867.

My darling Frank:

The mail boat having remained up to the present, and my letter of yesterday not handed in, I take advantage to add a postcript. Since I wrote yesterday, another case of fever has been admitted to the hospital, which from present symptoms, will likely prove fatal.

The weather has been very calm for several days and very warm, causing no doubt the generation of the peculiar poison which gives rise to the disease. Water and everything in the shape of vegetation rapidly undergoes decomposition here. The sea water suffered to stand in a bucket two or three hours becomes very offensive to the smell.

I have read the speeches of Messrs. Brady and Merrick, and am much pleased at their able, learned, and providential success. Reflecting upon the situation of affairs, I know no more auspicious moment to press the matter of my release than the present. The argument of Merrick being sustained by such substantial proof carried conviction to the hearts of those hitherto most prejudiced, and made them familiar with the foulest murder and crimes, under the cover of law, that ever defaced the pages of history. Well may those seek to cover their flight from the scene of their bloody tragedy, by attempting to visit their displeasure on the President. The spectre of ghosts ever haunts their guilty visions, and they gladly seek to find some place of repose.

Your devoted husband,

SAM.

RAVAGES OF YELLOW FEVER

New Orleans, September 1, 1867.

Dear Frank:

I received a letter from Jere last week containing note from Merrick stating Governor Black of Pennsylvania and himself would attend to Sam's case, but he would need one thousand dollars for Governor Black. I wrote to Jere and told him I had five hundred dollars which was at his disposal, and to call on his father for the balance. Let me know if they are doing anything for Sam, or if his "praying friends" can raise five hundred dollars.

We are having a deal of yellow fever. I will write to you soon, and answer questions asked in your letter. Your brother,

T. O. DYER.

Fort Jefferson, Florida, September 3, 1867.

My darling Frank:

I wrote you last on the 28th of August. Since then three more cases of yellow fever have proved fatal, and a number of new cases have been admitted to the hospital. To prevent the spread of the disease, one of the companies has been removed to one of the adjacent islands, and a hospital erected on another, where the patients are carried as soon as taken. One of the officers is now sick with the disease and not expected to recover; quite a panic exists among soldiers and officers. The prisoners, as a rule, seem to feel no alarm. The outbreak of fever ought to furnish a reasonable cause for our removal to a more healthy locality. As it has made its appearance here and in so malignant a form, it will most likely become epidemic or confined here for an indefinite period, for we have no frost here, and the climate does not vary much with the season; besides every soldier and prisoner is provided with a blanket or two, and as his clothes are all woolen, will serve as retentatives of the poison or miasma. It is likely a report will be made by the commanding officer to the War Department concerning the true condition of affairs, and the extent of the epidemic. You can advise with friends, and act as

206

seems most fit. Humanity, apart from every other reason, ought to prompt our removal.

Let me know whether a petition signed by the officers of the Post would be of any avail. I have thought over the matter, and think that under present circumstances, the public mind might justify some ameliorating action upon the part of the President. Write immediately in answer and give all news.

Your fond husband,

SAM.

Fort Jefferson, Florida, September 8, 1867.

My dear Jere:

I wrote to you on the 6th and acquainted you with the true condition of affairs at that time. I spoke of the illness of Dr. Smith and wife. He died last night. Mrs. Smith will likely recover; they leave two nice little children. Nearly every man now on the island is infected with the disease. The hospitals are all full, and the greatest consternation prevails. Dr. White-burst arrived last night from Key West. He will relieve me. The two days I have had the management of the hospital no deaths have occurred, and all have improved that were taken in time. The mail is leaving. Good-by,

SAM.

Fort Jefferson, Florida, September 13, 1867.

My darling Frank:

It is now nearly eleven o'clock at night, and though tired and worn from constant attention upon the sick and dying, having buried two to-day, I cannot refrain from letting you share the gloom which surrounds this seeming God-forsaken isle. Although three-fourths of the garrison have been removed, the epidemic seems to increase with unabated fury. The first three or four days of my attendance in the hospital we were not visited with a single death. Since then the number has largely increased, the most experienced nurses have been seized with the disease. It is impossible to obtain suitable nurses to bestow the attention required, and seven unfortunate beings have been ushered into eternity, without a kind word or ministering angel of religion. Our hospital being insufficient to hold the numbers, a second, then a third, and yesterday a fourth, were provided, and they are all filled. We have scarcely well ones enough to attend the sick and bury the dead. They are not suffered to grow cold before they are hurried off to the grave.

Dr. Whitehurst, who was expelled from the island in the beginning of the war, on account of the sympathies of his wife, is now an incessant laborer from Key West. He is quite an old man, but has endeared himself to all by his Christian, constant, and unremitting attention at all hours, even when duty seemed not to require. I remain up every night until eleven or twelve, and sometimes later. He is up the balance of the night, and there never was greater accord of medical opinion. He did not arrive here for several days after the duties of physician of the Post had devolved upon me by the illness and lamented death of Dr. Smith, and I assure you I felt much gratified when my conduct had met with his approval, being almost without any experience in the treatment of the disease, and having nothing to govern me other than the symptoms which the dread malady presented. By this accident I am once more restored to liberty of the island at all hours, day or night. Every officer of the Post is down with the disease, and but one remains to perform all the duties. He is a newcomer from Baltimore, and recently married. His name is Lieutenant Gordon. Little or no guard duty is performed, and but little difficulty presented to those who might be disposed to escape. I have resigned myself to the fates, and shall no more act upon my own impulse. Not one of the prisoners has as yet died, and those that take the disease pass through it without any apparent suffering.

Mrs. Stone, the wife of the Commandant, is quite sick with the fever. She is a patient of Dr. White-burst. He manifests some anxiety in her regard, and I fear the disease will overcome her and she be numbered among its victims. I am well acquainted with her. No deaths have occurred since yesterday morning. There are three very low, and their cases present a doubtful issue at this time. I am very well, and have no fears of the disease. My manner gives confidence to all around, and has a tendency to revive the flagging spirit. I am bravest in danger. I fear the boat may leave, so shall post right away. Good-by.

Fort Jefferson, Florida, September 16, 1867.

My precious Frank:

The mail has not yet left since the date of the 13th. We have lost only two, both of whom died this morning, one being an officer, Lieutenant Orr. The infection is subsiding, only for the want of victims. I am not very well, though; feel badly, which I attribute to the loss of rest and constant attention to the sick, etc. I received yours of August 23d, day before yesterday, and Fannie's of the 28th. Judging from these letters, matters look less favorable now than before the trial of Surratt. In the name of the Almighty, what can the American idea of law and justice be? I am sick of the words—law, justice. I feel almost like insulting any one who would advise recourse to it. If I am to wait here until the affair is settled by the Court, it may be unnecessary for the want of a subject.

The disease now prevailing here will not likely stop with the change of season, it will no doubt be confined here for an indefinite period, and when I am worn down with exhaustion and fatigue, I will be an easy prey to the infection. Thus far it seems to be the curse of the Almighty. No more honor is shown the deceased, be he officer or soldier, than to the putrid remains of a horse. They are buried to get rid of the stench and infection. We have no commander of the Post now, everything is in the hands of the physician.

Dr. Smith's child, a boy about three years old, has the fever. He is a very intelligent child, and has amused me on several occasions. I fear he will not get over it. Mrs. Smith has recovered from the fever.

A little daughter about seven years old remains exempt, having been sent to a different portion of the Fort. The little boy was very fond of me, and used to turn somersaults for me. I will write again tomorrow. Good-by,

September 17, 1867.

My darling Frank:

The boat left this morning early for Key West for medicine, etc., consequently I could not get this off of the hasty scrawl previously written. Although many deaths have occurred, and no abatement up to the present hour, I feel no alarm, and you must not suffer any uneasiness.

I visited my little pet to-day, and found him, to my great sorrow, almost in the agonies of death. He had the black vomit, and not expected to live many hours. We have also a man in the hospital with the same fatal precursor, and he will not live to see morning. We have saved only one thus far after the appearance of the black vomit. The little boy is a patient of Dr. Whitehurst. I visited him to-day, at his request, in consultation. We have now over a hundred cases of fever in hospital, and the percentage of deaths is unprecedentedly small, taking the average mortality in other places where the disease has prevailed as an epidemic.

Arnold had it, and is now well. I kept him in our room. O'Loughlin has it now, and getting along very well. Should I get it, I will not have any one to attend my case other than Dr. W., who is very old, and is a little slow in his actions and treatment. The disease being quick, has to be treated vigorously from the start. Should I have time, I will endeavor to give to the world my theory and experiences of the disease, as confined to this island. The disease ends its course quick, and has to be taken in time and treated vigorously to get the patient through the first stage in order that a successful termination may be promised. You see I have, for the want of a subject, expended these three small sheets with matter which will likely never be of any concern to you, except so far as relieving your mind of further anxiety and concern on my account. Were our separation to be much longer prolonged, or no hopes of a speedy release, I could willingly resign now to the fate which we must all one day inevitably suffer. The future is unknown, and should I be carried away with this scourge, I have nothing to will you and our dear little children but my undying love and affection. The mail is expected in on the 19th so I will postpone until to-morrow further remarks. It is now twelve o'clock at night, and I have to visit all the patients before retiring, so good night.

September 18, 1867.

My darling Frank:

I have been so engaged to-day that I did not think of getting a pen. It is now 10 o'clock. I am in the dispensary and everything quiet as death, except now and then a new case is brought in for treatment. Two cases have come in since 9 o'clock. They are generally taken sudden and most frequently at night. We have had three deaths to-day. The little son of Mrs. Smith died at 3 o'clock this morning; poor woman, she has lost her husband and son—not being here more than six weeks. A little girl only survives; she will leave by the first boat for the North. Mrs. Smith was telling me yesterday that all her family reside in Montgomery County, Md. A Rev. Mr. Prout is an uncle of hers in Nanjemoy, Charles County, Md. The other two deaths were soldiers. An indescribable gloom pervades the garrison—many are conjecturing who will be the next. Only one officer still reports for duty, and he now shows evident symptoms of the disease; perhaps to-morrow I will chronicle him among the sick.

September 19, 1867, 10 A. M.

My darling Frank:

The boat arrived this morning as anticipated, bringing me yours of September 4. I see nothing encouraging. I see that we are still styled the "assassination conspirators" in the President's amnesty. If it go upon fact, it has no reference, but the name is sufficient—"Give a dog a bad name and you may as well kill him."

We had one death this morning; we will not likely have any more to-day. All the patients now in hospital are doing well. O'Loughlin is improving. I attend him in our room.

September 19, 1867.

My precious Frank:

211

My letters come to hand now unopened, and you need have no fear to make known what action is contemplated. If it is not immediate and bids fair for my release, I would have nothing to do with it, because it will be only loss of time and money, a source of aggravation and mutual anxiety. I would much prefer nothing to be done so long as such infernal scoundrels have the control of the courts and access to the public treasure to suborn perjury. The best thing you can do is to cause our removal to some Northern bastile, where the laws are in force. A sufficient excuse now offers itself—the presence of the epidemic of yellow fever, etc. The mail is being made up by the postmaster, so I must conclude. My undying love to all.

Many of the deaths reported have not occurred here, but on an adjacent island where we have erected a hospital; more than half sent there have died. I claim the credit of having broken up this establishment, and having inaugurated an entirely different System of treatment. Dr. Smith admitted, before his death, that he had never seen a case of it before, and acknowledged his incompetency to treat the malady. He never consulted with me upon the subject, and the fate he suffered may be the consequence. We had several cases in the Baltimore Infirmary during the epidemic that prevailed at Norfolk in 1855. I became acquainted then with the pathology of the disease, but have acted here entirely upon my own theory, and with unprecedented success. I can say with truth that none have died that have been seen in time and had proper attention and nursing. I am universally respected by all the soldiers, and they seem ever ready to shower compliments and favors.

Major Stone has kindly promised to make known my services to the authorities at Washington, but unless they have the magnanimity to release me, their word of praise will be of no consequence. I am very well and feel much better to-day than yesterday. I truly grieve to hear of the unfortunate death of Billy Bowling.

Kiss our dear little children, and as ever,

Your fond and devoted husband,

Fort Jefferson, Florida, September 21, 1867.

My dear Jere:

I wrote yesterday to Frank. The mail will leave at 10 o'clock; it is now eight.

I wrote to you a few days ago, and gave all particulars of the fever then raging here. Since then several have died, among them the little son of Mrs. Dr. Smith; Lieutenant Orr and Mrs. Stone, wife of the Commandant. Arnold had it and is now well. O'Loughlin was taken day before yesterday, and was getting along very well up to late yesterday evening, when, owing to the imprudence of some visitor giving account of the recent deaths, he became excited, sank into a collapse, and with difficulty we could save his life up to the present. He has revived considerably, but is yet in a critical condition. Our attention is unremitted; and assure his friends he shall suffer for nothing. We have now by his side all the delicacies the island can afford.

Mrs. Stone died last night, and was buried this morning. Major Stone will leave at ten for the North to take his little son, an only child. I had a talk with him this morning, and gave my views of the situation. I told him plainly there was no abatement in the disease; that, instead of becoming milder, it was evidently more malignant. I told him in a short time the garrison would be without officers, and it would be death to any unacclimated officer who would be sent here; also that in this climate the disease was likely to continue an indefinite period, owing to the fact that there is not much change of temperature with the season. He promised to see General Grant in person and represent the matter. You can form no idea of the gloom that pervades this God-forsaken place. I have just been called to O'Loughlin; will finish when I return.

O'Loughlin had a convulsion a few minutes ago. My heart almost fails me, but I must say he is dying. God only knows who will be the next. There will be likely two or three more deaths during the day.

Arnold received the box sent by his friends. Why don't you write sometimes? Good-by.

SAM.

Fort Jefferson, Florida, September 23, 1867.

My darling Frank:

I wrote to you day before yesterday. The mail came this morning and will return immediately, so I have to hurry. I received no tidings from any one to-day. I have written to Jere, and have sent some trifling articles to him to be distributed among you all.

O'Loughlin died this morning. We did all that was possible, but our efforts were in vain. We prolonged his suffering life for two days by constant nursing and attention.

I am not feeling so well to-day, my head aches. It may be from sitting up so much, but fear it is the premonitory symptoms of the prevailing epidemic. Five were buried this morning, including O'Loughlin. The hospital is full, and scarcely nurses enough to attend the sick. I have been acting physician and nurse for a considerable time, until I am nearly exhausted. My heart sickens at the prospect which is before me. Were an enemy throwing shot and shell in here a more horrible picture could not be presented—a useless expenditure of life and money. Thousands of dollars worth of property has been destroyed as infected, clothing, etc.

Give my love to all, and believe me, ever fond and devotedly,

Your husband,

SAM.

Fort Jefferson, Florida, September 26, 1867.

My dear Jere:

I send to-day, through the kindness of Captain Hamilton, as a present to you one crabwood cane and an unfinished cribbage board. I have sent a package or two of moss-cards, and some common shells. Tell M. C. to select what may please her fancy, and to send the balance, together with the box, to Frank to be divided between Fannie, Cecie and Ern. There are five crabwood crosses— four were made by poor O'Loughlin, at the request of his sister, for Cousin Ann. Since his death it would be best to send them to his sister. The other I made myself. I intended making several more, but was taken from the shop. I am sorry I have nothing more worthy to send. The fever continues unabated. Lieutenant Gordon, of Baltimore, and Zulinski, a Polander, are now dangerously ill with the fever. There is but one other officer at the Post who is convalescent, and he unfit for duty. My health continues good.

I wrote your name on the stick for you. Should it be removed by any means, you can know it by its being much the largest stick of the bundle. It is very heavy and intended more to look at than for use. I am sorry I have nothing suitable to send to Pa or Ma. When you write give me some idea what you think would please them.

The schooner *Matchless* has just arrived from Key West. Major Stone, on his way North, was taken sick and died there on the 25th. He promised to make known the services I have rendered to the Post. His death will prevent likely any mention of my name in connection with the present epidemic. Unless the patient is attended to immediately, it is almost invariably fatal. Thirty deaths in all from fever have taken place since the middle of August up to the present date. Two companies have been sent to an adjacent island, which thus far has remained quite exempt from the disease; a case now and then occurs among them.

Remember me to all. Write soon and give news of all that is going on. Yours,

SAM.

Fort Jefferson, Florida, September 25, 1867.

My darling Frank:

When I wrote last I mentioned the death of little Harry Smith, son of Dr. Smith, and spoke of the illness of Mrs. Stone. With much sorrow I announce her death; she died on the morning of the 21st.

Major Stone, her husband, became so alarmed (although he idolized her) he did not go to see her buried, but bundled up immediately and started with the intention of going North, taking his little son, an only child, about two years. Before reaching Key West he was seized with the fever, and died there on the morning of the 25th instant. He was very kind toward us, and had promised to make known to the authorities at Washington the service I had rendered the garrison during the recent epidemic, which he thought would have considerable weight in restoring me to liberty, and to my family. Now that he is dead there is no one here whom I can expect to take any interest in my behalf, and the future may not be so propitious with me.

In my last I mentioned the name and good health of Lieutenant Gordon of Baltimore. He has since been swept away by the disease; he was buried yesterday, twelve o'clock noon. He leaves a young wife to bemoan his loss. He was kind and courteous always. I am not acquainted with his wife. They have no children. The disease thus far has destroyed one family, Major Stone and wife, and made desolate three young wives, Mrs. Orr, the wife of Lieutenant Orr; Mrs. Smith, the wife of Dr. Smith; and Mrs. Gordon, the wife of Lieutenant Gordon. I attended Mrs. Smith through the active stage of her disease, and a nobler woman I never met. She left here the evening of the 27th for home, which is in Montgomery County, Md. The child of Major Stone was well when last heard from. Mrs. Orr was a missionary, and luckily left in May last on a visit home (Jefferson Barracks) to spend the summer.

When Dr. Whitehurst arrived, I yielded to his age and experience, and was relieved from further attention upon the officers and their wives, at my own request. My duties were then principally directed in the hospital. All those that have died in the official circle were patients of his and had all the advantages of his experience and knowledge. I feel much relieved that they did not die upon my hands, for likely another charge of murder, etc., would be brought upon my unsuspecting shoulders.

Since you last heard from me twelve deaths have occurred, eight only in hospital, which is a small percentage considering numbers and the facilities of treatment. I believe I understand the disease now thoroughly, and can treat it as successfully as any other disease, if taken in time.

I wrote to Dr. Dent a few days ago, and gave him the mode of treatment pursued with such happy effect, when in time and practicable. Sometimes the poor creatures are struck with delirium from the beginning, and are perfectly wild and unmanageable; some die the same day they are taken, but most live to the third day. More die for the want of proper nursing and care than lack of medical attention. I am up all day until twelve o'clock at night. Dr. Whitehurst comes around between that time and day. I sleep until five or six o'clock in the morning and return at seven. The number in hospital has diminished somewhat recently, but only for the want of victims. Nearly every one in the garrison has had the disease, many a second time. The cases that come in now are of the most malignant form, which shows that the principle of the disease is still active. Colonel Grenfel is quite sick with the disease; he was taken yesterday. I will do all that is possible to save him. He has been acting as nurse upon many of the officers recently.

The mail boat came in late yesterday evening, bringing some medical supplies, but no mail.

A Dr. Thomas has been assigned to this Post as medical director, and will be here to-morrow. Dr. Whitehurst will leave immediately after his arrival, and will take Mrs. Gordon in charge on her way home. She will stop with the Doctor at Key West until a steamer passes northward bound. I shall vacate my position as soon as he leaves. I shall miss him a great deal. He makes no charge for any service rendered, which shows his unselfish spirit, and the motive which actuated him to come to us in our greatest need. There are but two officers left; one is convalescent, and the other is lying at the point of death, but may survive with good nursing. You can't imagine the gloom and indifference which pervades the whole garrison. No more respect is shown the dead, be he officer or soldier, than the putrid remains of a dead dog. The burial party are allowed a drink of whiskey both before and after the burying, which infuses a little more life in them. They move quickly, and in half an hour after a man dies, he is put in a coffin, nailed down, carried to a boat, rowed a mile to an adjacent island, the grave dug, covered up, and the party returned, in the best of humor, for their drinks. Such are life and scenes in Tortugas. But ten men appear at roll-call, and not more than twenty fit for duty in garrison. Two companies have been sent away, which thus far have escaped the disease. They will not return until the infection is declared at an end, which will be some time yet.

My health has been very good up to the present. I sometimes feel a little indisposed, but attribute it to sitting up late and loss of usual rest. You will no doubt see full accounts of the disease here in the papers, so I shall defer until my next, further comments. Try and give me some satisfactory news when you write.

Your husband,

SAM.

10 o'clock at night, September 29, 1867.

My darling Frank:

Lately I have been holding on to the letters I write you until I know definitely when the mail leaves in order that you may hear from me at the latest period. I concluded this hasty scrawl early this morning, fearing the boat would return immediately to Key West. Learning she would not, delayed until to-morrow. I now proceed to give a detail of the day's occurrence. We lost one man to-day about noon. He had the fever, which ended fatally to-day. Lieutenant Zulinski (a Polander), the officer I mentioned in the foregoing as being very ill with the fever, is rapidly sinking. I have not seen him to-day. His nurses represent him in a critical condition. Should he die, it will make five out of six officers, a remarkable fatality. We have admitted six new cases to-day. This is a decline of less than one-half the usual number for many days past, being generally fifteen or sixteen. I am in hopes the boat, which is expected in to-morrow, may bring a mail,

218

and that I may hear you are all equally well as myself, and may disclose something definite and reliable as to my stay here. I do not like to act upon conclusions of my own, but would do so, if matters bid fair to be protracted, and an easy mode of escape offered. I will likely conclude this sheet to-morrow should I have time before the mail goes out; if not, I bid you a reluctant good night and pleasant dreams.

Yours,

SAM.

September 30, 1867, 9 o'clock P. M.

The mail boat did not leave to-day owing to the non-arrival of the one expected from Key West. No deaths have occurred to-day, although there is one not likely to live until morning. I was interrupted a few minutes ago, and told that he was breathing his last, by his nurse. I went to him, and with the application of a pitcher or two of cold water to the head he was relieved of the convulsion, and is now doing as well as can be expected. With good and proper attention he would get over it, but that is impossible here. The nurses are ignorant and careless, and I can't act both the physician and nurse. Lieutenant Zulinski is *in statu quo,* no appreciable change for the better yet observed. Colonel Grenfel is quite sick; his case is doubtful. More were admitted in hospital to-day. The reason is, there are not more than a dozen on the island yet to have it. We will call them up to-morrow, and learn the reason why they did not have the disease. I suggested the idea to the Doctor this evening. I will write again to-morrow. Good-by.

SAM.

MY FATHER STRICKEN DOWN

Fort Jefferson, Florida, October I, 1867. My dear Jere:

To you and the uninformed public this Post may appear very important to be held by our country as a strategic position, offensive and defensive; but to us nothing seems more ridiculous, and the only object for the full garrison is to hold us, now four prisoners, Grenfel, Arnold, Spangler, and Mudd. We conclude therefore, since they do not remove the entire garrison from this infected spot, that they would prefer to sacrifice us with the garrison, sooner than cause our removal to a more salubrious locality. Thus far four valuable officers have yielded up their lives, and misery untold has been entailed upon their distressed families,—not saying anything of the brave men in the ranks who have perished,—to carry out what can only be termed a complimentary sentence in atonement for the life of the Chief Executive of the people, though such sentence is contrary to law and every principle of justice.

By the hand of Providence my fetters have been broken, yet I run not, preferring to share the fate of those around me and to lend what aid in my power to breaking down the burning fever, overcoming the agonizing delirium, and giving all the hope and encouragement possible to the death-stricken victims of the pestilence.

Dr. Whitehurst from Key West, an old man sixty odd years of age, is attending here night and day, doing all that human judgment and skill can effect, without the hope of any other reward than that promised to those who do unto others as they wish to be done by. I have done all that lay in my power, and feel encouraged by the gratitude expressed by those I have relieved. It is high time that the public was made acquainted with the fact, and those in power made to yield to a proper sense of duty and regard for justice, instead of visiting upon helpless victims an unjust and tyrannical punishment. A million and more dollars have already been thrown away to debauch the public morals in the vain hope that they might fix, with some plausible degree of justice, the stigma of the crime of the assassination on innocent victims.

We have, up to the present, lost by the fever at this Post thirty-three in all, counting men, women, and children, which is a small mortality, considering the number attacked with the disease and the inadequate facilities for treatment. I suppose ere this reaches you you will have heard of the death of Lieutenant Gordon of Baltimore. He had been here but a short time, and had been married but two months. Lieutenant Zulinski is lying dangerously ill with the fever. There is but one officer here to perform all the duties, and he only a second lieutenant; all the rest have died. Two companies have been sent to an adjacent island, and thus far have remained quite healthy and free from the fever. The whole garrison could have been removed as well and the epidemic at once cut short; but this did not appear a part of the program, and the pestilential vapors have spread death and destruction. O'Loughlin dead—stain upon the country. I and all labored day and night to save him, but in vain. The vital spark was too weak, and he yielded in quiet submission to the omnipotent hand of Providence.

Your brother,

SAM.

October 14, 1867.

My precious Frank:

I received yours and Fannie's of the 23d of September, on October 11, to which I replied in a very few lines on that day. I sat up in bed to write them, but now I have fully recovered from the fever, with the exception of strength and flesh, which will take some time to restore in this climate under the circumstances we are placed.

Since I have been sick I have had the greatest desire for fruits, apples, peaches, etc. These we barely meet with, except in the very imperfect state of hermetically sealed cans. Although the State abounds in fruits at all seasons, we seldom meet with any. Occasionally a few oranges, bananas, and pineapples come on the boats, but the price is so enormous we can't afford to indulge in a plentiful supply.

We have pretty constantly on hand Irish potatoes, yams, or sweet potatoes, onions, ham and butter, for which we pay the following prices, viz: ham, thirty cents; butter, seventy cents; Irish potatoes, seven dollars per barrel; yams, seven dollars per barrel; onions, eleven dollars per barrel. We have received lately a very fine barrel of potatoes from Mr. Ford, also one from an unknown party, with a splendid ham. I have but little appetite for such things, and indeed doubt very much whether I would enjoy fruits, which I have mentioned, were they brought here. I feel, with the returning seasons, the inclination for the sports and pursuits I have been accustomed to since childhood, and without the same degree of liberty, freedom of speech, etc., but little enjoyment realized.

You mentioned in your letter that Jere said Mr. Black had undertaken my case, and that he felt confident of success. You forgot to name when it would take place, and how it would be accomplished. If the Government refuses the writ of *habeas corpus* to be served or be of any force here, how is he then to proceed? I have already written to you plainly on the subject in anticipation of the next dodge of the political tricksters. It is all done to consume time and rob you and friends of every farthing they can. When the apples are ripe they will fall without human intervention—so with my release. When I am released from here, I shall thank no mortal man for it, but shall look upon it only in the light of every other thing in nature, that it was ordained, could not be otherwise. Jere has given you this to satisfy you. It would have been better had he imparted this information himself than entrusted you with it.

Could I believe the Government would be influenced by my good conduct, I could send to you, signed by every officer and soldier of the Post, the most praiseworthy testimonial in regard to the services recently rendered the garrison during epidemic of yellow fever here. Many have come forward and pressed me to permit them to make some public manifestation of the esteem they hold toward me, but thus far I consider it only a superfluous idea, and of no practical value. It could only serve to excite my vanity, which I am in no mood at this time to gratify. You know I was never ambitious of much preferment, and I have grown less so of late years. One of the

222

officers came to me yesterday in person, and desired me to make known my services to the Government through the men of the garrison. I told him I would await a reply from my friends on the subject. Let me know if anything of the sort will be of service when you write.

Give my love to all and believe me most fondly, Your husband,

SAM.

Fort Jefferson, Florida, October 18, 1867.

My darling Frank:

Sissy spoke of your intended trip to Washington. I can't see what you expect to accomplish, when millions of dollars have been expended and a number of officers' and soldiers' lives sacrificed to hold us here. I can see nothing but the most determined spirit, in spite of every principle of law and justice, to restrain us of our liberty, and the comfort we might be able to afford our distressed families.

I can have no sentiments of good feeling toward those in power, no matter what their politics. Pilate believed in the innocence of Christ, but was he justified in giving him up to the executioners at their cry for his blood? Such is the position, such is the light in which I hold those now in authority. A formal petition to the Government, with preamble enumerating the services I rendered the garrison, has been drawn up and signed by every non-commissioned officer of the Post. The privates will also sign it, but it will require some time to get all their names. This has been done without my knowledge. The officers, two in number, expressed themselves favorable toward the idea, and are confident it will be attended with success. Influenced by their opinion, I have consented. The appeal could be made more through curiosity to know what action the Government will pursue. I will, if I can find time before the boat goes out, send you a copy of what is intended to be forwarded to Washington. If you think proper you can present the copy in person to any one of influence, and see what effect or tendency it may have. Knowing the great prejudice pervading all classes of society toward all the so-called

223

"conspirators," I have but little hope of a favorable result. How anxious I feel concerning your welfare and our dear little children; it is the only pain I suffer. I have grown used to my present confinement, and it no longer occasions me dissatisfaction. I have now all the liberty I could desire here. I have plenty of books, papers, and pen and ink, at my command. I have access to a very choice library of over five hundred volumes. My fare is as good as the island can afford, and I am pressed often to accept presents in the shape of little luxuries from the soldiers, so you see, so far as bodily comforts consist, I am in want of nothing; yet so long as I am separated from you, I shall feel miserable and unhappy.

Sissy mentioned that two of the most able lawyers have been engaged in my case. She did not state when or how things would be proceeded with. This serves only to increase my curiosity and anxiety, and I would much prefer no allusion made, if all can't be told.

We have lost no cases of yellow fever since the 6th inst. We have now only two cases in hospital. There are not over five in the garrison who have escaped the disease, with the exception of negroes. The negroes have been remarkably exempt. They sleep all the time and wake up well. I am as well now as I ever was with the exception of weakness. I am still doing duty in the hospital. I am relieving the post physician of most of the duty. Good-by.

SAM.

Fort Jefferson, Florida, 1867.

My dear Jere:

The mail will leave in a few minutes, so I must be short. I have just finished a few lines to Frank.

There are but three cases of fever now in hospital under active treatment. Dr. Thomas, physician of the post, is down with the fever. He is in a fair way to get well. All the duties of physician of the post are again upon me, which I am beginning to find unpleasant. The soldiers are never tired of lavishing upon me compliments and sentiments of their good-will. They have voluntarily drawn up a preamble and petition, which they wish forwarded through the proper channel, reciting my services during the epidemic of fever here. If you think such an instrument will be of benefit, let me know, and I will forward you immediately the original or a copy, which you and friends can present in person. I have written to you several times within the past month or two, without receiving any reply. I am at a loss to account for your silence. For God's sake try and give me some truthful idea of the situation that I can look to some period in the future with some degree of hope. I have lost all energy and disposition to live under present circumstances. I have preferred not acting under my own impulses, fearing I might frustrate measures you had in contemplation for my relief; therefore, I desire to know the whole truth, *so that some action, of my own, can, be devised.* Give my love to M. C., and remember me to all kind and inquiring friends.

Hoping to hear from you soon, I am,

Very truly,

SAM.

Fort Jefferson, Florida, October 22, 1867.

My darling Frank:

Dr. Thomas, our new post physician, is now quite sick with the fever. The whole duties, as I have already stated, have again devolved upon me, which I am beginning to find unpleasant. The epidemic influence of the fever still continues, but from the fact that all having had an attack of the disease, they are less liable to a second; and abatement is the consequence. We have but one fresh case since I wrote, viz: the Doctor. We have only one in hospital that is dangerously ill; all the rest are convalescent. There are two companies over on an adjacent island, which I believe the commanding officer intends bringing over the first of next month. These have remained exempt from the disease and otherwise healthy. The whole garrison could have been removed as well, but Providence decreed otherwise, and those entrusted with the

225

command at that time have been swept away by the rude hand of the pestilence, in consequence of this necessary precaution being omitted.

I am still possessing my usual health with the exception of strength, which I find very slow in returning after an attack of this fever. My duties, however, are light, and I am able to get along as well as I might expect. There is no news stirring upon this desolate island—everything is lifeless and inactive. The dull spirit of the soldiers, etc., seems to add desolation to the appearance. You can imagine better than I can describe the condition and haggard walk of those who have recently been visited with the fever, and are on the slow march to health.

I send you enclosed the petition gotten up by the officers and soldiers. This is signed only by the noncommissioned officers; the other which is designed to be sent to the President is signed by every officer and soldier in the garrison. I shall await with some curiosity to know what effect it will have. I was in hopes that, long ere this, some measure of relief would have been devised by my very knowing and sympathetic friends, and that I would be happily in your midst.

From all quarters I hear that there is considerable good feeling manifested, and that a pressure is being made by the public for my unconditional and immediate release. I am inclined to doubt, since nothing practical is resorted to. You will please give me all the information on the subject of my release that you deem expedient, in your next. I want to know the time when I may expect the benefits of the action at law contemplated. I look upon law nowadays as equivalent to injustice, something that aggravates and adds insult to injury. I hope times have changed, and the result be otherwise.

The enclosed petition you can make use of in any manner thought advisable by friends. The weather continues very warm, the thermometer standing between 80 and 90 degrees in the shade. We can't expect any abatement in the fever until a change takes place in the atmosphere; it will not be much lower even during the winter. Agreeable to writers on the subject, the disease is capable of extension in all latitudes above forty degrees, so it may continue here indefinitely.

Hoping the time of our unhappy separation is growing short, I am as ever,

Your devoted husband,

SAM.

Following is a copy of the petition gotten up by the garrison at the Tortugas for the release of my father. All names of signers omitted:

It is with sincere pleasure that we acknowledge the great services rendered by Dr. S. A. Mudd (prisoner) during the prevalence of yellow fever at the Fort. When the very worthy surgeon of the Post, Dr. J. Sim Smith, fell one of the first victims of the fatal epidemic, and the greatest dismay and alarm naturally prevailed on all sides, deprived as the garrison was of the assistance of any medical officer, Dr. Mudd, influenced by the most praiseworthy and humane motives, spontaneously and unsolicited came forward to devote all his energies and professional knowledge to the aid of the sick and dying. He inspired the hopeless with courage, and by his constant presence in the midst of danger and infection, regardless of his own life, tranquillized the fearful and desponding. By his prudence and foresight, the hospital upon an adjacent island, to which at first the sick were removed in an open boat, was discontinued. Those attacked with the malady were on the spot put under vigorous treatment. A protracted exposure on the open sea was avoided, and many now strong doubtless owe their lives to the care and treatment they received at his hands. He properly considered the nature and character of the infection and concluded that it could not be eradicated by the mere removal of the sick, entailing, as it did, the loss of valuable time necessary for the application of the proper remedies, exposure of those attacked and adding to the general fear and despondency. The entire different system of treatment and hospital arrangement was resorted to with the happiest effect. Dr. Mudd's treatment and the change which he recommended met with the hearty approval and warm commendation of the regularly appointed surgeons, with whom, in a later stage of the epidemic, he was associated. Many here who have experienced his kind and judicious treatment, can never repay him the debt of obligation they owe him. We do, therefore, in consideration of the invaluable services rendered by him during this calamitous and fatal epidemic, earnestly recommend him to the well-merited clemency of the Government, and solicit his immediate release from here, and restoration to liberty and the bosom of his family.

The original of this petition, it appears, never came into the hands of President Johnson, although mailed to him.

Fort Jefferson, Florida, October 26, 1867.

My dearest Frank:

Mail came day before yesterday, and will leave today. I received yours of October 7, complaining of the non-reception of my letters, when I have let no opportunity escape without writing. I used to feel pleasure when writing to you, but now I am feeling an indisposition and want of motive to actuate me to anything, since I know or feel that improper surveillance is exercised without my knowledge.

I wrote to you a few days ago and sent a copy of a petition gotten up by the soldiers for my release. I have not as yet, for reasons best known to myself, presented the instrument to the officers of the Post. The whole garrison have an unbounded confidence in my opinion, and prefer me to the regularly appointed physicians. There seems an idea among some, however, that by signing the instrument they might detract from the knowledge and intelligence of my associates in medicine, and thereby cause displeasure.

Dr. Thomas, whom I mentioned as being sick with the fever in my last, is still confined to his room, though in a fair way to recover. One fresh case has been admitted to the hospital since last writing. There are now three cases under active treatment, one of whom had the black vomit yesterday, and will most likely die, though his countenance and other symptoms present no such indication.

Your letters up to the present fail to give me the least satisfaction in regard to what is contemplated. Such letters serve only to keep me here longer, for I might devise some measure myself, but fear to act lest

I might frustrate the actions of my friends. I want the whole truth and nothing but the truth, or not a word on the subject, because it seems only to aggravate me. I sometimes feel like swearing out against ever writing again on account of not getting proper answers to my letters, or answers to the questions I ask.

You said in your letter you have had a large number of masses and prayers said for me. Perhaps they have served to keep me alive and in suffering. I think if my stay is to be much longer, you better direct their attention to my speedy and happy death. I have lost all hope in prayer so far as the accomplishment of any worldly good. The good seem only to suffer in this world as a general rule. I must count myself out of this category, but my endeavors are to conform as near as I can to every injunction of the Christian. My health continues good, though weak and emaciated from my recent sickness. I am still performing all the duties of post physician.

I am sorry I have nothing new to impart; the same desolation, isolation and monotony prevail. Remember me to all.

Your fond and devoted husband,

SAMUEL MUDD.

October 27, 1867.

Boat detained on account of night wind.

Since writing the above, I have had an interview with the commanding officer, who informed me he had already made mention of my services to the Department at Washington. He has also the original document gotten up by the soldiers with all their signatures. I don't know what action will be taken in regard to it. He is evidently favorable and will do all he can, consistent with his position, toward my release.

In this connection I give a short extract taken from my father's notes on yellow fever [—NM]:

I will now, as near as I can, by a pen description, give you an idea of the embarrassment I labored under upon assuming the duties as surgeon of the post, that were unexpectedly thrust upon me, and the track followed by the germs or poison, as evidenced by the appearance of disease.

Thus on the 4th of September, seventeen days after the epidemic of yellow fever had broken out, the surgeon, Dr. J. Sim Smith, a gentleman much respected and beloved by the garrison, was himself attacked with the fever, and by his illness, the Post was left without a physician in the midst of a fearful pestilence. The thought had never before entered my mind that this contingency might arise, and consequently I found myself unprepared to decide between the contending emotions of fear and duty that now pressed to gain ascendency. Memory was still alive, for it seemed as yesterday, the dread ordeal through which I had passed. Tried by a court not ordained by the laws of the land, confronted by suborned and most barefaced perjured testimony, deprived of liberty, banished from home, family and friends, bound in chains as the brute and forced at the point of the bayonet to do the most menial service, and withal denied for a time every luxury, and even healthy subsistence, for having exercised a simple act of common humanity in setting the leg of a man for whose insane act I had no sympathy, but which was in the line of my professional calling. It was but natural that resentment and fear should rankle in my heart, and that I should stop to discuss mentally the contending emotions that now rested upon a horrid recollection of the past. Can I be a passive beholder? Shall I withhold the little service I might be capable of rendering the unfortunate soldier who was but a tool in the hands of his exacting officer? Or shall I again subject myself to renewed imputations of assassination? Who can read the motives of men? My motive might be ever so pure and praiseworthy, yet one victim of the disease might be sufficient to start up the cry of poison and murder.

Whilst these disagreeable thoughts were revolving, a fellow-prisoner remarked, saying: "Doctor, the yellow fever is the fairest and squarest thing that I have seen the past four or five years. It makes no distinction in regard to rank, color, or previous condition—every man has his chance, and I would advise you as a friend not to interfere." Another said it was only a little Southern opposition to reconstruction, and thought the matter ought to be reported to Congress in order that a law might be passed lowering the temperature below zero, which would most effectually put an end to its disloyalty.

But I must be more serious; and you will perceive that the time had now arrived in which I could occupy no middle ground. I felt that I had to make a decision, and although the rule of conduct upon which I had determined was not in accord with my natural feelings, yet I had the sanction of my professional and religious teachings and the consciousness of conforming to that holy precept, "Do ye good for evil," which alone distinguishes the man from the brute.

It being our breakfast hour on the morning of the 5th, and thinking it required some condescension on the part of the commanding officer to call upon an humble prisoner to serve in the honorable position of surgeon of the post, I concluded to spare him this disagreeable duty, and instructed Mr. Arnold, a fellow-prisoner and roommate, who was acting clerk at headquarters, to inform Major Stone, then commanding, that should my services be required, I had no fear of, nor objection to, performing whatever aid was in my power toward the relief of the sick. On approaching headquarters, Mr. Arnold met Major Stone coming to my quarters to inquire whether I would consent to attend the sick of the Post until the arrival of a regular surgeon.

When informed that I had offered my services, the Major seemed much pleased and had me forthwith detailed. Fortune favored me, and it so happened that during the intervals, amounting to nearly three weeks, that I had the exclusive care of the sick, not one died.

Time will not permit me further digression. I shall pass over many incidents of interest connected with hospital management, difficulties I had to overcome in breaking up the prior arrangement of sending away the sick in open boats over a rough sea two miles and a half distant, and also in obtaining an opposite order from the commander to send to one of the islands near by as many of the well soldiers as could be spared from the garrison. This latter measure, though I had advised it on the day I took charge of the hospital, was not carried out until the arrival of Dr. D. W. Whitehurst of Key West, Florida; a noble, kind-hearted gentleman, who superseded me on the 9th of September.

The first case of yellow fever at the Dry Tortugas, in the epidemic of which I now speak, occurred on the 18th of August, 1867, in Company K, which was located in the casemates on the south side of the Fort immediately over the unfinished moat, which at low tide gave rise to quite offensive odors. To this circumstance the surgeon of the Post attributed the cause of the disease, and at his request the company was removed and the port holes ordered to be closed, to prevent the supposed deadly miasma from entering the Fort.

Having the honor at this time of being a member of the carpenter's shop, it fell to my lot to aid in the work of barricading against the unseen foe, and it was during this patriotic service the 22d of August, that I made my first note of the epidemic. The places occupied by the beds of the four men, one on the 18th, one on the 10th, and two on the 21st, that had gone to the hospital sick with yellow fever, were all contiguous. The Fort was hexagonal in shape with a bastion at each corner, and the company, after its removal, was placed on the east side, the bastion forming the center with several casemates above and below boarded up separating it from Company L on the north and the prisoners on the south, and in the most eligible position for the spread of the poison, owing to the prevalence of the wind, which from early in April up to this period had blown continuously from the southeast, varying only a few degrees.

There was a lull or temporary suspension of the activity of the poison on the 22d and 23d. For two days the company remained without any new cases, but on the 24th day one man was taken from

232

the same company on stretchers, being unable to walk. The fever then rapidly extended right and left until it reached Company L, which was nearest the point where it arose this second time, and later the prisoners' quarters, which were more remote, were attacked. To show and to prove to you that the germs, or cause, spreads by continuity of matter, and not with the disease, the first two cases that occurred in Company L. and the first two cases among the prisoners, were immediately next the boarded partition that separated them from Company K, where the fever was raging, having followed along the rows of beds, up to this line of division, and then passed through the open spaces between the plank, which were loosely nailed.

There were at this time two hospitals, the Post Hospital within the Fort, and Sand Key Hospital on an adjacent island about two miles and a half distant, which latter was fitted up as soon as the fever began to assume an epidemical form. The sick that occurred during the night and following day were immediately taken to the Post Hospital, and from thence at 4 o'clock P. M. they were carried in boats by the surgeon, on his accustomed visit, to Sandy Key Hospital. Notwithstanding the fact that most of the sick walked from their beds to the Post Hospital, and no effort or pains on the part of the surgeon to isolate the disease were taken, owing to the belief in its miasmatic character, the germs or cause had not up to this time, September 12, Viz: 25 days, reached either of the hospitals, if we may judge from the circumstance that not one of the many nurses, who waited upon the sick day and night and even slept in the same room, were stricken down with the fever.

The disease after extending into Company L, and to the prisoners' quarters, next made its appearance into Company I, located in the inner barracks, a building about three hundred feet long, thirty feet wide, and four stories high on the east side, running north and parallel with the Port, and immediately in front of Company K and Company I, and distant about sixty feet.

I was called into this company on the morning of September 8, and found Sergeant Sheridan and a private that slept in the next bed ill with the fever. Sergeant Sheridan and the first sergeant of Company K were great friends, and when off duty were constantly in each other's quarters. Sheridan generally wore a heavy cloak during the showers of rain that were frequent at this period, and I feel satisfied that the poison was carried by the ferment set up in the cloak, or mechanically, by adhering formites, though it is possible for it to have been wafted across from Company K, the two beds in Company I being near the window facing that company. Then the fever gradually worked its way along through the whole company without a skip in regular succession as they slept.

At the northern extremity of the barracks two rooms were set apart, thirty feet square, as the Post Hospital. On the 7th we were necessitated by the increasing number of sick to provide other hospital quarters, and for convenience four casemates opposite on the ground tier, under Company L, were boarded up as a temporary hospital, with our kitchen and dispensary intermediate. On the 8th our hospital supply of beds and bedding gave out, and on the 9th we were compelled to bring the bed along with the patient into the hospital. Two days after the admission of the infected beds, our nurses began falling sick, three being attacked during the day and night of the 11th of September. Then the three laundresses, families who did the washing for the hospitals and separate quarters on the west side of the port, sixty or seventy yards apart, were all simultaneously attacked upon the first issue of soiled clothing after our hospital became infected.

Then again, upon the breaking up of the Sand Key Hospital, and the return of the nurses to the Fort, they were all speedily stricken down with the fever upon their being placed on similar duty. These nurses had remained free from all disease up to their return to the Fort, although the majority of the cases whom they nursed at Sand Key died with the fever.

But the most remarkable spread of the disease occurred on the night of the 16th of September in Company M, which was quartered in the casemates immediately above the hospital and Company L, and notwithstanding the proximity up to this date, twenty-nine days since the epidemic began, had remained entirely exempt from the fever, owing no doubt to the fact that it laid behind the bastion, which, with the prevailing southeast wind, produced a downward or opposing current. However, on the morning of the above date, about nine o'clock, a small rain cloud, common to that locality, arose to the south of the fort, which came tip rapidly with a heavy wind, lasting about twenty minutes, and which blew directly from the hospital, and Company L, toward Company M, and the night following every man went to bed in his usual health, yet between eleven and one o'clock nearly one-half of the company, or thirty men, were attacked with the most malignant form of the disease—beginning at the point nearest the hospitals and extending thirty beds without missing or skipping a single occupant.

It had been my custom to remain at the hospitals every night until eleven o'clock to see that every patient received the medicine prescribed and was quiet. On this occasion I had not retired more than fifteen minutes before I was sent for by the sergeant of Company M to come to his quarters, that several of his men were sick. Feeling much fatigued, I did not attend the summons, but referred the messenger to Dr. Whitehurst and the steward of the hospital. At one o'clock the sergeant himself came down to my room and begged me for God's sake to get up, that one-half of his company were attacked with the fever, and that he did not know what to do with them, as the hospitals were already full. I went along with the sergeant, and found his statement fully correct, and the wildest alarm and confusion prevailing.

As the hospitals were already crowded, we concluded, for convenience, to enclose the six casemates nearest the regular hospitals, which was speedily executed with canvas, and in less than two hours all moved back and were quiet under comfortable treatment. The next night or two after, the balance of the company, in the order of their beds, were attacked with the disease without an exception.

The disease did not extend among the officers at headquarters until it had at first reached the negro prisoners, several of whom were employed by the officers as servants, and who were in the daily habit of carrying to and fro their blankets. The humble individual who now addresses you was not attacked until the 4th of October, forty-seven days after the beginning of the epidemic, though constantly at the bedside of the sick, and in the midst of the infected hospitals and quarters.

One evening, at our usual supper hour, feeling much depressed and exhausted from the unaccustomed duties I went over to my mess, where I was besieged with many questions concerning the sick, and notwithstanding the solemnity of the occasion, a hearty laugh was frequently indulged at the expense of our ready wit, Edward Spangler.

The debilitating effects of the climate, added to the condition consequent upon the excitement, very much depressed me, and after finishing my bowl of coffee and slice of bread, I fell upon my rude cot to spend a few minutes of repose. The customary sea breeze at this hour had sprung up, and I was shortly lulled into sweet sleep. My faithful and ever solicitous roommate, Edward Spangler, who on former occasions had manifested so much concern when the least indisposition was complained of, seemed to anticipate my every want, was not unguarded at this time. As soon as he found me quiet, he closed the door and turned back several intruders, stating that the Doctor was feeling unwell, and had laid down to rest himself. In the course of an hour, he said, he will be through his nap, when he will return to the hospital, where all who desire can see him. Spangler made money by trafficking with the soldiers, and we are mainly indebted to him for something extra to the crude, unwholesome, and sometimes condemned Government ration that was issued to us. He was not generally select in his epithets toward those whom he disliked, yet if he saw them in suffering, it excited the liveliest sympathy, and he would do anything that laid in his power for their relief. At a later period he, in conjunction with Mr. Arnold, watched over me in my illness as attentively as if their own brother, and I owe my life to the unremitting care which they bestowed. The reader, I am in hopes, will excuse this little degression from the subject—a tribute of thanks is due, and I know

236

no more fitting place to give it expression. I may perhaps be doing injustice by omitting another name equally deserving of my esteem, Michael O'Loughlin. He, unfortunate young man, away from his family and friends, by whom he was most tenderly loved, fell a victim to the pestilence in spite of every effort on our part to save him. He had passed the first stage of the disease and was apparently convalescent, but, contrary to my earnest advice, he got out of bed a short time after I left in the morning, and was walking about the room looking over some periodicals the greater part of the day. In the evening, about five o'clock, a sudden collapse of the vital powers took place, which in thirty-six hours after terminated his life. He seemed all at once conscious of his impending fate, and the first warning I had of his condition was his exclamation, "Doctor, Doctor, you must tell my mother all!" He called then Edward Spangler, who was present, and extending his hand he said, "Good-by, Ned." These were his last words of consciousness. He fell back instantly into a profound stupor and for several minutes seemed lifeless; but by gently changing his position from side to side, and the use of stimulating and cold applications, we succeeded in restoring him to partial strength and recollection. I never met with one more kind and forbearing, possessing a warm friendly disposition and a fine comprehensive intellect. I enjoyed greater ease in conversational intercourse with him than any of my prison associates. He was taken sick whilst my kind friend, Dr. D. W. White-hurst of Key West, Florida, had charge of the Post; from him he received prompt medical attention from the beginning of his illness to his death.

The news had spread around through the garrison of the neat and comfortable appearance of the hospital and the improved condition of the sick, which had the effect to gain for me a reputation, and the confidence of the soldiers—all I could desire to insure success. It was not long before I discovered I could do more with nine cases out of ten by a few consoling and inspiring words, than with all the medicine known to me in the materia medica.

AGAIN IN CHAINS

Fort Jefferson, Florida, December 6, 1867. My dear Frank:

I wrote to you on the 24th and mailed the same on the 29th. I wrote to you and Jere on the 4th of December and addressed the letter to Jere, and requested him to forward to you as soon as read. I did this in order "to kill two birds with one stone"; that is, I wished to acquaint both with what has transpired here, and desire advice in relation.

I mentioned in those letters the arrival of a gentleman here sent by the Butler Congressional Committee to obtain statements in regard to the assassination. I gave him a declaration under oath, which in substance amounted to the fact that I did not know anything about the matter, or parties concerned, previous to the assassination. I sent you a copy in the letter addressed to Jere. If you think it worth the trouble, you can inquire from knowing ones whether I ought to make a statement of any kind in my present condition. I have doubts about the matter, and concluded that it was better to seek information from those who are better informed, before so doing.

When you write inform me plainly what is the opinion of the public in regard to the course I should pursue. Congress, in my opinion, has acknowledged the illegality of our imprisonment and trial by asking and receiving an oath from us. Mention this idea to counsel and to members of Congress who may be favorably disposed. He informed me that he did not wish his visit here known to the public, lest it might frustrate the purpose which the committee have in view. I shall leave the matter entirely to your own good judgment. Owing to my not making such a statement as he required, he or some one will be sent again in a short time; therefore, I wish you to acquaint me at the earliest opportunity, so I may be prepared.

I have no news. Arnold has been quite sick with the dysentery. He is now out of danger, but very thin and weak. He was sick when he gave his statement, and the labor and excitement aggravated the symptoms. He and Spangler made full and detailed statements, which in my opinion does not shed much light upon the subject of the assassination; nothing more than was known and acknowledged on our trial. They seem to regret having given statements, but I can see no objection other than an impropriety.

My health continues very good, and I have increased several pounds in weight the past two or three weeks. I am now taking things as easy as possible, after finding all my endeavors fruitless and your promises of an early release mere speculation. You must not understand from this that I cease to regard you and all as formerly, but having been satisfied that I have been laboring under a delusion, I have concluded to act on the principle, that what can't be helped it is useless to grieve about.

A few nights ago, I dreamed I was with Tommy and Sammy. The emotion which it produced soon broke my slumber, and away fled all my happiness; such has been and continues to be my life, until I almost fear to hope. Try for the future, my good Frank, not to unsettle my mind with mere speculations, but tell me frankly and plainly the whole truth. Let me know all the correct news, and if anything new has developed in regard to the assassination.

Your devoted husband,

SAM.

Fort Jefferson, Florida, December 7, 1867.

My dearest Frank:

I received your last, dated November 7, which gave me much comfort. God grant your anticipation may prove correct. Judging from the tone of the papers, I fear there will be great difficulty to contend against. Our country seems now not to be governed by the Constitution, or by law, but by unbridled popular or public opinion, of which I have no doubt many others, as in my case, have been made victims.

I am very well, but yet in chains, with four others, under guard; and our duty now is to wash down the bastions of the Fort every day. I have gotten used to my present life, and do not feel much

239

incommoded. God grant that I may soon be in the fond embrace of you and our dear little ones. Good-by.

SAM.

Fort Jefferson, Florida, December, 1867.

Major G. B. Andrews:

I learn through my wife, by yesterday's mail, that the petition gotten up by the soldiers, with a view to my release, because of services rendered during the recent visitation of fever at this post, has not been received in Washington.

She was made acquainted with the fact through the Honorable Montgomery Blair, who stands high in the confidence of the present Administration. Mr. Blair informed her that such an instrument would have great weight in influencing a favorable action of the President.

Major, I can claim no exception to the general rule of nature. The drowning man catches at straws, the oppressed and exiled seek liberty, reunion, repose, etc.

Were I in other circumstances, modesty would compel me to refrain from the least notoriety, but in my present situation, not only my personal ease and comfort, but the anguish and distress of a wife and four helpless little children, cause me to throw off this humility, and solicit your kind office in my behalf.

I refer you to the hospital report to draw conclusions as to the services rendered. ¯With the exception of the first one or two cases (who died here) all were carried to Sand Key Hospital, over a hundred per cent of whom died.

Upon the sickness and death of Doctor Smith, our lamented surgeon, I was placed in charge of the hospital by Major Stone, who vested me with discretionary power in all that pertains to the duties of a physician. Immediately I discontinued the Sand Key Hospital, I used blankets instead of sheets, and had the windows of the hospital differently arranged.

There were in the hospital at the time some fifteen or twenty cases under active treatment, many of whom were delirious, and burning with the most intense fever. In less than six hours after, under my management, all were free from delirium, and perspiring freely, and seemed comfortable. All of these recovered. One afterward was taken with relapse and died. I considered all but one out of danger. This latter recovered sufficiently to walk about, but owing to negligence of the nurses, he was suffered to go out without my knowledge, in consequence of which he was taken with relapse and died. I refer you to Colonel Hamilton, who was here at the time, and to the non-commissioned officers of the companies. In proof of what I state, I was strenuously opposed by Major Stone in breaking up the Sand Key Hospital. Perhaps Colonel Hamilton is cognizant of the matter. I succeeded finally with Major Stone by telling him that if he left the disposition of the sick to my judgment, I would faithfully consult the greatest good to the greatest number, to which he consented.

Dr. SAMUEL A. MUDD.

The above letter, written by my father to the Commandant of Fort Jefferson, was not replied to. My father fully believed that Major Andrews destroyed the petition referred to.

Key West, December 13, 1867.

Dr. S. A. Mudd,

Fort Jefferson.

Dear Sir: You will oblige me by replying to the following questions:

1st. At what time did you enter duty during the last epidemic at Fort Jefferson? Did you attend Dr. Smith and Mrs. Smith, and what others previous to my arrival?

2d. What was the first case, and what time, whether from Havana, Key West, or regular at the Fort, and any other views which you may have bearing upon the origin, sanitary condition of the Fort, etc.?

The Surgeon-General desires a report upon the subject, and I desire and wish to do you every justice for the patient and noble conduct evinced by you during my stay at Fort Jefferson.

I would have written you at an early date, but my time has been much occupied, which I hope you will accept as my apology.

Very truly your friend,

D. W. WHITEHURST.

Port Jefferson, Florida, December 15, 1867.

Dear Doctor Whitehurst:

I received yours of the 13th asking a response to certain questions pertaining to the recent visitation of yellow fever at this Post. The boat leaving in a short time after, I had not time to write by the outgoing mail. Between now and the outgoing mail will permit me only to answer briefly your queries, viz:

1st. I was detailed on duty in the hospital, September 6. Dr. Smith was attacked suddenly the evening of the 5th. I saw him on the morning of the 7th. He was then delirious and unmanageable. He died on the morning of the 8th. Not having kept a record, have to refer you to the hospital report from the 6th of September to the 8th, when relieved by yourself.

2d. I am sorry to state my inability to determine positively the first case, or the manner of its inception. The first case of true yellow fever reported occurred on the 18th, and died the 22d of August. He belonged to Company K, and was taken sick in the quarters of his company, which were in the casemates on the southwest side of the Fort. Some two or three others, belonging to the same company, soon after were taken with the disease, which caused the surgeon of the Fort to believe that it arose from some local cause. He, therefore, removed the company on the eastern side of the Fort, immediately next Company L, and in front of Company I. After this change, several fresh cases took place, and the disease spread to the adjacent companies and prisoners. Company M was located on the south side of the Fort and adjoining Company L, and several days intervened before any cases occurred in that company. Most of the cases came in at night. I am of the opinion had Company K been removed immediately to one of the adjacent keys instead of the east side of the Fort, it would have prevented the spread of the disease. The poison being confined to that company, the winds being continually easterly, favored the propagation instead of cutting short the fatal malady.

So far as I am capable of judging, the first case originated here, but the poison may have been imported. Removal of the company not having checked the infection, on the contrary increasing, showed that they carried the poison with them. Captain Crabb is of the opinion he had the disease on his arrival here from Havana the last of July or first of August. Again about the middle of August the schooner *Matchless* from Tampa landed with two sick men aboard. I can't state whether it was before or after the 18th instant, or whether they had yellow fever. The two men were carried to the hospital.

In regard to the pathology of the disease as it existed here, although it answered minutely to the description given by learned men, I will now proceed to answer your kind note, viz: I was placed in charge of the hospital two or three days before your arrival (not having kept a record, I can't state the time with certainty). There were in the hospital at that time fifteen or twenty cases requiring active treatment. I attended these in hospital, and Dr. Smith and Mrs. Smith and Lieutenant Roemer until relieved by you. Dr. Smith was delirious and unmanageable from the beginning. I could by no means induce him to take medicine.

Very truly yours,

Dr. SAMUEL A. MUDD.

PRISON LIFE IN 1868

THE WITHHOLDING OF BOOTH'S DIARY-SURRATT'S RELEASE

Fort Jefferson, Florida, January 15, 1868.

My darling Frank:

We have received papers as late as January 7, but fail to see any indication of my speedy release.

I read a recent message of the President defending his course in turning out Stanton, and was astonished. He goes back to the period when he assumed the functions of a President, and omitted to charge the culprit or delinquent with wilfully withholding the diary of Booth. This seems more criminal than withholding the dispatch from New Orleans. His silence upon this point leads me to suspicion that he had a knowledge of all that was going on, and lent his approval to the cruel and barbarous wrong. It was a point which he should not have omitted to speak about, since every effort has been made to identify him with the horrible deed. Those who have done us a knowing wrong are the slowest to repair the injury or make suitable satisfaction; therefore, I look with no degree of confidence to those who hold the ship of state to redress the grievances under which we suffer.

I wrote to Mr. Stone some time ago, but have not received an answer. I have heard no report from the Butler Committee. When you write let me hear all that is going on, and what this committee will do with the statements they received from us. Would that it were in my power to promise you when I would be at home, definitely, it yet being in the unknown future. I fear to contemplate with any degree of happiness the time when we shall be again united in second bonds of wedlock, lest I should be visited by disappointment. Be assured, however, that time has produced no change in the affection which I have always manifested toward you and the children. Hoping to hear from you every opportunity, I am, darling Frank,

Your devoted husband,

Fort Jefferson, Florida, March 22, 1868.

My dearest Frank:

I received yours of the 26th of February and March 7 yesterday. I was much pained to hear of the accident to McColgan Mudd, and the sickness of our dear little children and servants. I can well imagine the distress, the loneliness of your situation, and the many difficulties you have to contend with. It is this appreciation of your many privations, helplessness, and insecurity that cause my principal suffering—mental anxiety.

I wrote to you on February 28 and March 13. I wrote to Jere on the 4th, and sent him some letters which perhaps he might use to my advantage. Faith and opinions are formed from known facts or certain evidences of the mind, and whichever way our honest convictions are led—be they good or evil—other virtues or vices will grow out of them. For example, if we are conscious of some meritorious act performed by a fellow-creature, our sense of love, honor, and esteem is immediately aroused; on the contrary, if insincerity, gross deception, etc., be practiced, sentiments of anger, hatred, and revenge arise. We are not always correctly informed, or we may draw erroneous conclusions; in either case it is the same. The surest preventative is to guard ourselves against such possibilities of misrepresentation. Take my advice, never incur a debt of gratitude—they are the hardest to pay. To avoid which, accept neither presents nor favors. If you have debts or bills to collect, after due notice, give them to a constable; the parties, knowing your situation, will not be offended.

Andrew ought by this time to be of some assistance to you. The innocent are not more exempt from a bad name and its consequences that the guilty. The most virtuous in the community are liable at any moment to be slandered, and they may go down to their graves with reproach. This is my experience and observation. Try and profit by it.

With a change of commander, new regulations are in force, among them: all letters written and received are to be examined. The two last were handed to me open. I am restrained, in consequence of this, from saying many things that I wish to say. My health continues as good as usual.

With fondest love for you and our dear little children, I am, Yours,

SAM.

Fort Jefferson, Florida, April 3, 1868.

My darling Frank:

I received yours of March 16 with Fannie's enclosed. Owing to the censorship that now prevails, I can't reply.

My health continues good. The weather is quite pleasant in the shade. There are a great quantity of ripe tomatoes, peas, beans and "collards" in the garden, now suitable for table use. The corn is in silk, and soon there will be roasting ears. This does not contrast with the season with you. In the interior of the State it must be delightful.

I am in hopes Andrew's sickness will not assume anything grave. I am growing more impatient daily to see you all. I have been thinking for a long time that the difficulties existing between the President and Congress are more pretended than real. In other words_a mutual understanding that such filibustering is to prevent a too sudden reaction, and perhaps disclosures deemed prejudicial to the welfare of the country at this time.

Remember me to dear Pa, and tell him my not writing is through no fault of mine. Thank him and all the family for the parental and brotherly sympathy and affection, and for the interest they have so kindly and generously manifested.

Hoping, dearest Frank, our unhappy separation will soon end, and with it nothing to prevent the happiness we anticipate, I am, as ever,

Your devoted husband,

SAM.

Fort Jefferson, Florida, April 14, 1868.

My precious Frank:

We have received papers up to the 31st of March. The impeachment seems only a farce. The part which each is to perform is likely well understood. In the *New York Herald* of March 21 you will see a favorable allusion to myself in a letter dated from Fernandina, Florida. I have seen the party who wrote it on two occasions here, but had very little to say to him, not knowing his disposition toward me.

I received at the same time a short letter, notifying me of this correspondence, to which I replied in a short note, and gave a few views of mine in relation to the recent visit of the yellow fever. He will likely publish the same; if so, it may cause some surprise among the medical fraternities, as I differ widely from most of the authors as to many of its most essential characteristics.

I make a distinction between the poison and the disease, the one being contagious, the other being harmless. This will revolutionize the system of quarantine should my views be adopted. I can bring undoubted facts in proof of the conclusions I have arrived at.

We have heard nothing from Grenfel since he escaped on the 6th of last month. All hands may have perished, it being quite stormy at the time,

If you do not receive letters as often now as formerly you must not complain, as the rule which prevails now is far more rigid than heretofore. I have written whenever it was in my power, and shall so continue. I think those to whom you showed my last letters misunderstood my meaning. I asked the question, What has been done? I could never see or hear that the President was ever approached on the subject, consequently concluded nothing had been done. I should have said nothing had been accomplished.

Affectionately,

SAM.

Fort Jefferson, Florida, May 11, 1868. My precious Frank:

247

Ere this reaches you the impeachment trial will have ended. I wonder what will next turn up to serve as an excuse on the part of my friends for not taking action in my behalf. With the change of commanders things have not resulted to our advantage. Since Major Andrews left there have been two commanders; each effected changes which have finally deprived us of even former privileges, and increased our degradation. The only privilege I possess now is the license to write to you, without knowing whether my letters leave the Post.

Your letters are read by Provost Marshal, then given to a corporal to be handed to us. He can in turn read them to the garrison if disposed before giving them into our possession. The post-office at this place is broken up. The military' have everything in their hands. Our mail is brought from Key West.

Your devoted husband,

SAM.

Fort Jefferson, Florida, May 30, 1868.

My precious Frank:

I have delayed writing several days. I have made up my mind to pass no more letters through the Provost Marshal's hands. From his manner toward us he has considerable prejudice. Such men I have met with before, being vengeful and unscrupulous; if therefore my letters don't come to hand as often as formerly, know that there is some good reason. He is expecting a furlough to go North by the next mail boat; should the furlough arrive we will have a respite.

We have seven more citizen prisoners from Alabama. Their offense hardly amounted to a breach of the peace. Their terms are one and two years. General Hill will, I learn, take command of this Post again in a few days. He is expected on the next boat. We suffered worse treatment under his command than any time previous or since; therefore, can't look with satisfaction to his coming.

I can't see the good reason for my friends holding back on account of the election. Mr. Johnson is a war Democrat, or was in favor of coercion. We were opposed to it. I am of the opinion, though, that he is already pledged to the support of the Republicans. The impeachment will end as it was intended. There can now be nothing reasonable to prevent bringing the question of my unjust imprisonment fairly and squarely before his Excellency, and learn his pleasure.

I don't see that anything can be lost, and we can have the gratification of knowing his mind.

Affectionately,

SAM.

The impeachment trial of Andrew Johnson, President of the United States, referred to by my father, took place in 1868, before the United States Senate, Chief Justice Chase presiding. Eleven articles were exhibited by the House of Representatives, charging the President with divers high crimes and misdemeanors. Thirty-five Senators pronounced him guilty; nineteen pronounced him not guilty. Two-thirds of the Senators not having pronounced him guilty, Chief Justice Chase proclaimed that the President of the United States stood acquitted upon the articles of impeachment.

Fort Jefferson, Florida, May 30, 1868.

My dearest Prank:

No doubt your mind has been subject to many conjectures owing to my long silence. To be candid, I have become disgusted and embittered because of the rule that now governs this Post. We have now acting as Provost Marshal an inquisitive and officious Yankee, from away down in Maine. He is one of those officious individuals fond of ruling, considering himself one of the elect, and adds daily new rules for the government of the prisoners, which tend to be more despotic than the laws of the ancient barbarians. All letters are carefully perused by him, not as a duty of his office, but because of his prying spirit and disposition to meddle with matters that do not pertain to his office. I have therefore concluded never to pass another letter through his hands. I correspond with you only, and I would sooner forego this satisfaction than again permit him to pry into another letter, to gratify his mischievous curiosity.

Surratt's trial it appears is again put off. This will continue to be done until he is released. The mendacious scoundrels who trumped up such a mighty conspiracy against him and us are too cowardly to acknowledge their error, and are seeking to screen themselves from responsibility and odium by availing themselves of delay, which unfortunately the law permits. I would like to know positively whether any action is contemplated in my case between now and the fall election. I am growing daily more bitter against tyranny and oppression. Life often feels a burden to me, but for the sake of you and the family I am restrained. Your devoted husband,

SAM.

Fort Jefferson, Florida, June 21, 1868.

My darling Frank:

We are in the midst of another warm and distressing summer. The atmosphere around the Fort, owing to the filthy condition of the moat outside, is terribly offensive at times and bids fair to breed another pestilence. This letter goes out by one of the seven men recently sent here from Alabama. They have been released, and leave to-day for their homes.

General Hill has assumed command of the Fort again. I have made up my mind that I will not pass another letter through the Provost Marshal's hands, so if you should not receive letters so often be not disappointed. The impeachment is over. What is to prevent action in my case? Try and give me some idea.

Your husband,

SAM.

Fort Jefferson, Florida, June 16, 1868.

My precious Frank:

I wrote to you last on the 11th. The Provost Marshal will leave on the next steamer from this place on a furlough. When he is gone I am in hopes I will be able to write you more regularly. The weather is growing quite warm and unpleasant. The engineers are digging out the breakwater, which gives rise at times to a most intolerable stench, often so offensive as to prevent sleep and our remaining in our quarters with any degree of comfort.

I wish when you write you would let me know what is the intention of those who have my case in charge. Congress is still in session; they may frame this as an excuse for non-action. Then the election takes place in November—this may be another excuse, and so on; but on my account I am in hopes you will urge the matter on immediately, and let me know the will of the President. It will give me but little concern either way, whether I meet with favor or otherwise.

Your husband,

SAM.

Fort Jefferson, Florida, July 5, 1868.

My darling Frank:

Suffering again with a terrible cold and wearied with the apathy and indifference of those who call themselves my friends, I cannot expect to impart comfort or detail matter of interest; yet duty and the small instinct of humanity permitted to remain prompt me to write, and at the same time to protest against this outrage upon the laws and every principle of justice, in my incarceration—robbing you and the family of the solace and feeble support I might be capable of affording. I hate to reflect upon the manner I have been accused and brought here—the falsehoods of suborned perjurers, and testimony of the most infamous characters, suffered to outweigh the evidence of men of undoubted veracity.

The last mail brought us news of the release of Surratt upon bail, and the abandonment of the prosecution of the first indictment. Had this been done long ago it would have been more creditable to the Government and the parties immediately concerned. Surratt having been virtually released finally, I can't perceive the slightest justification for holding me and others. Had Surratt been tried when we were he would undoubtedly have suffered the fate of his innocent and unfortunate mother. Your devoted husband,

SAM.

Port Jefferson, Florida, August 6, 1868.

My darling Frank:

Knowing the great trouble and expense of sending a lawyer down from Maryland to take legal action in our case, we concluded to engage one at Key West, who offers to undertake all the cases of civilians here for one hundred dollars in hand, and one hundred dollars each upon release.

I am in daily expectation of seeing the executive officer of the civil authority from Key West, although I have not the least idea how it will terminate. I have had no talk with any of the officers upon the subject, deeming it impolitic. Should I be released, I know not yet whether I will come home directly by sea, or by land by way of New Orleans.

Your devoted husband,

SAM.

Fort Jefferson, Florida, August 19, 1868.

My precious Frank:

The mail boat came in this morning bringing yours of August 3. Having to pass through the Provost Marshal's hands, I did not receive your letter until a few minutes ago. The boat will return again in an hour, so I have not time to tell you much. I am still in ignorance of what is going on. The lawyer to whom I wrote at Key West came here this morning on the boat, but I have had no chance yet to speak to him. He has made no attempt to my knowledge to call upon me, so I can't divine his object. I am sorry it is not in my power to make known some intelligence from him. The mail is gone abroad, and my hope is to send this per hand to Key West. The lawyer will return by the boat, but should I have a chance to speak to him before his leaving, I will endeavor to give him your address, so that he can inform you the course things are pursuing.

Your devoted and fond husband,

SAM.

Fort Jefferson, Florida, September 7, 1868.

Dear Jere:

Fearing you may not be acquainted with what has been done at Key West in our behalf, I send you a small clipping from the *Key West Dispatch* published at that place. We interpret the delay of the opinion of the judge as unfriendly, and that he only requires time to study out from the legislation of the past Congress a justification for his adverse decision.

General Hill told one of our number that the writ would not be granted, if so, it seems that he was in Key West at the time action was taken by counsel—he either made himself acquainted with the views of those in the interest of the Government, or he made known the wish of the War Department at Washington and exacted observance of the same. Time has elapsed sufficiently for us to have heard the ruling of the judge. We have very little hope of a favorable decision.

I would like to know, in case the judge refuses to grant the writ, whether an appeal will be taken, and if those representing the Government will suffer it to go before the Supreme Court. If they do, will it be done only to run me beyond the means of obtaining defense, or robbing me and family of every dime I might expect to make this side of the grave?

Very truly yours,

SAM.

Fort Jefferson, Florida, October 10, 1868.

My darling:

253

The papers received the last mail make short mention of the proceedings in Surratt's case. It is clearly no interest, of the Government to prosecute the man; and no reason therefor can be assigned, except to serve as an apology for the individuals who murdered his innocent mother. This is apparent and can not be disguised. They are like the horse in the mire—the more they struggle to hide their bloody deed the deeper they become involved. They tried him for murder and proved, without doubt, the innocence of his unfortunate mother. They will try him now, if they try him at all, for conspiracy and will prove no crime on the part of the son. It is a wonder the papers don't take up the subject of the legality of our imprisonment, especially since the developments made in the trial of Surratt. The judge at Key West was evidently instructed not to grant the writ in our favor. He gave no law nor good reason for sustaining his refusal.

My health is good, but I am far from being strong. Our fare is tolerable with what we are able to buy. Our sleeping quarters are the same miserable, damp casemates. My bed is made of moss gathered from the trees in Florida. It is very hard from long usage. I have shaved off my mustache and trimmed my goatee quite short, which has altered my appearance so much that I scarcely knew myself when I looked in the glass. I can perceive no wrinkles or gray hairs, although I believe my hair is much thinner than when I left home. Give my love to all and believe me,

Your fond and devoted husband,

SAM.

Baltimore, November 15, 1868.

My darling Sam:

I heard from you about the 28th of October. How sad it makes me to know you are so gloomy. Have courage a while longer; the darkest hour is just before day, and our lives surely will not be a continual night.

I truly believe Johnson will release you before he goes out of office; and if he does not, I have assurance Grant will, so for my sake bear up a while longer, and God will send you safely home to me and our dear little children.

I have been in Baltimore nearly two weeks, and will remain a week longer. I went to Barnum's Hotel on last Thursday to see a Mr. Kerr, who was on his way to the Tortugas as commander. We mistook the name, and failed to see him. I was very sorry, I think I might have influenced him in his treatment to you. Jere saw his father. He says he found him a fine old gentleman. He told him his son was a good boy. I hope he will show his goodness in his treatment of you. Don't let an opportunity pass without writing, I am now uneasy about you.

Your devoted wife,

Fort Jefferson, Florida, December 4, 1868.

General B. H. Hill,

Commanding Post.

Sir: The boarding up in front of our quarters and otherwise rendering our imprisonment more painful and odious, leads us to believe was the result of secret information which you deemed reliable. We very respectfully ask an investigation in order that the truth be made known. If we are to be held responsible for every rumor or falsehood that may be trumped up by the evil disposed, we are liable at any moment to be called out and shot. I have the honor to be,

Very respectfully, your obedient servant,

SAMUEL, A. MUDD.

No answer was made by General Hill to the above note.

Fort Jefferson, Florida, January 24, 1869.

My darling Frank:

To-day I received yours of January 1st, announcing the death of our mother, and a greater mother to our little children, thereby bringing us under a double debt of parental affection and love. Can I forgive those who have so inhumanly and maliciously caused our separation, and deprived me of affording all the consolation in my power—a debt of love and gratitude I owe—to the kindest and most loving of mothers? May the chastisement of Heaven fall upon and crush them to a sense of their wrong.

I am well, but feel low and dejected in spirit. Tears trickle at every thought of the death of my mother. Her holy and precious life is my only consolation; for I know she is now reaping the reward of her many virtues, freed from the pains and anxieties of _this miserable world. God grant we may terminate life with such hopes of the promises of eternal reward. Do not doubt the love I bear you and the children. It is all that has kept me alive. Hoping to see you soon, I am,

Your fond and devoted husband,

SAM.

Charles County, Md., January 30, 1869.

My darling Sam:

Your letter of January 8th I received on last Wednesday, the first for a long time. When I last wrote I was hoping that it would be the last letter I would write to you on that miserable island, but I now feel very, very hopeful that this will be my last. Every body seems to think that Johnson will release you, beyond a doubt, before his term of office expires; and for myself I can't see how he can possibly get out of it, after all the petitions and appeals which have been made in your behalf. I feel very sanguine of seeing you before the last of March. Should you be released, of which there is but little doubt, you must hurry home, for I assure you you are sadly needed.

I will send you a paper with the last petition from the Maryland members of Congress, and Mr. Merrick's and Mr. Stone's appeals in your behalf. You can judge for yourself your chance, but I hope, before this and the paper reach you, Mr. Johnson will have issued an order for your release. May our Lord protect us from another

256

disappointment, for I am really in no disposition to bear it. I put you under the protection of our blessed Lord. I think He will bring you home to me.

Your devoted wife,

THE PARDON

War Department, Adjutant-General's office, Washington, February 13, 1869. Commanding Officer,

Fort Jefferson,

Dry Tortugas, Fla.

Sir: The Secretary of War directs that immediately on receipt of the official pardon, just issued by the President of the United States, in favor of Dr. Samuel A. Mudd, a prisoner now confined at Dry Tortugas, you release the said prisoner from confinement and permit him to go at large where he will.

You will please report the execution of this order and the date of departure of Dr. Mudd from the Dry Tortugas.

I am, sir, very respectfully your obdt servant,

E. D. TOWNSEND,

Assistant Adjutant-General.

Headquarters, Fort Jefferson, Fla.,

March 8, 1869.

Special Order No. 42:

In obedience to communication from War Department A. G. Office, Washington, D. C., dated February 13, 1869, Dr. Samuel A. Mudd (a prisoner) is hereby released from confinement and permitted to go at large where he will.

By order Brevt. Major General Hunt.

J. M. LANCASTER,

Brevt. Capt. U. S. A., 1st Lieut. 3d Artillery, Adjutant.

LIBERTY

In pursuance of the above orders my father regained his liberty on the 8th day of March, 1869, having endured imprisonment for a period of four years, lacking about six weeks. Two days prior to the issue of the above order from the War Department, on the 13th of February, President Johnson wrote a note to my mother and sent it to her home by a special messenger, requesting her to come to Washington and receive my father's pardon. She left for Washington immediately, but being detained on the way, did not reach the city till the following morning. Once there, she repaired, in company with Dr. J. H. Blandford, my father's brother-in-law, to the White House. In a few moments President Johnson sent for my mother to come into the executive office. There he delivered to her the papers for the release of my father. My mother asked him if the papers would go safely through the mails. His reply, before he had signed the papers, was: "Mrs. Mudd, I will put the President's seal on them. I have complied with my promise to release your husband before I left the White House. I no longer hold myself responsible. Should these papers go amiss you may never hear from them again, as they may be put away in some pigeon-hole or corner. I guess, Mrs. Mudd, you think this is tardy justice in carrying out my promise made to you two years ago. The situation was such, however, that I could not act as I wanted to do."

After he had signed and sealed the papers, he handed them to my mother, who took them, thanked him and left. She had intended going to the Dry Tortugas and delivering in person the release to her long-afflicted husband. This, however, she was not permitted to do, as when she reached Baltimore, intending to take the steamer from that port for the Dry Tortugas, she found that the boat had departed a few hours before her arrival, and that another would not sail for two or three weeks. She therefore sent the papers by express to her brother in New Orleans, Thomas O. Dyer, who paid a Mr. Loutrel three hundred dollars to deliver them to my father at Fort Jefferson.

On the 20th day of March, 1869, sixteen days after President Johnson's term of office had expired, my father arrived home, frail, weak and sick, never again to be strong during the thirteen years he survived. It is needless for me to try to picture the feelings and incidents of his home-coming. Pleasure and pain were intermingled—pleasure to him to be once more in his old home surrounded by his loved ones, and pleasure to them to have him back once more; pain to them to see him so broken in health and strength, and pain to him to find his savings all gone and his family almost destitute.

Again we find him, after a brief period for rest, engaged in the struggle to regain in a measure his lost means and position. This he never accomplished. He found himself surrounded by exacting duties, yet handicapped by innumerable disadvantages. There were no laborers to cultivate the farm; the fences had fallen down or been destroyed by the Federal soldiery, and the fields were unprotected against intrusive cattle; buildings were out of repair, and money almost unobtainable. His hardships in prison, however, had in a measure taught him to be patient. Gradually things became brighter. When the warm glow of summer passed into harvest time, he was encouraged by the fact that a generous yield of earth's products rewarded him for his labor. He only partially regained his practice. While he was confined in prison many of the families he had attended employed other physicians. Many of these families sought my father's services on his return, but some did not. Apart from this, the people of the neighborhood had become comparatively poor by reason of their losses occasioned by the war. A great deal of his attention and skill was therefore given gratuitously.

During the four years they were together in prison Edward Spangler became very much attached to my father. As a consequence, a short time after Spangler's release, he came to our home early one morning, and his greeting to my mother, after my father had introduced him, was: "Mrs. Mudd, I came down last night, and asked some one to tell me the way here. I followed the road, but when I arrived I was afraid of your dogs, and I roosted in a tree." He had come to stay.

He occupied himself chiefly in helping our old gardener, Mr. Best, and in doing small jobs of carpenter's work in the neighborhood. My father gave him five acres of land in a wood containing a bubbling spring, about five hundred yards from our dwelling. Here Spangler contemplated erecting a building and establishing for himself a home. This purpose, however, was never to be realized. About eighteen months after he came he contracted a severe illness, the result of having been caught in a heavy rain, which thoroughly saturated his clothing. His sickness resulted in his death—rheumatism of the heart being the immediate cause.

He was a quiet, genial man, greatly respected by the members of our family and the people of the neighborhood. His greatest pleasure seemed to be found in extending kindnesses to others, and particularly to children, of whom he was very fond. Not long after his death my father, in searching for a tool in Spangler's tool chest, found a manuscript, in Spangler's own handwriting, and presumably written while he was in prison. This manuscript contained Spangler's statement of his connection with the great "conspiracy."

SPANGLER'S STATEMENT.

I was born in York County, Pennsylvania, and am about forty-three years of age, I am a house carpenter by trade, and became acquainted with J. Wilkes Booth when a boy. I worked for his father in building a cottage in Harford County, Maryland, in 1854. Since A. D. 1853, I have done carpenter work for the different theaters in the cities of Baltimore and Washington, to wit: The Holiday Street Theater and the Front Street Theater of Baltimore, and Ford's Theater in the City of Washington. I have acted also as scene shifter in all the above named theaters, and had a favorable opportunity to become acquainted with the different actors. I have acted as scene shifter in Ford's Theater, ever since it was first opened up, to the night of the assassination of President Lincoln. During the winter of A. D. 1862 and 1863, J. Wilkes Booth played a star engagement at Ford's Theater for two weeks. At that time I saw him and conversed with him quite frequently. After completing his engagement he left Washington and I did not see him again until the winters of A. D. 1864 and 1865. I then saw him at various times in and about Ford's Theater.

Booth had free access to the theater at all times, and made himself very familiar with all persons connected with it. He had a stable in the rear of the theater where he kept his horses. A boy, Joseph

Burroughs, commonly called "Peanut John," took care of them whenever Booth was absent from the city. I looked after his horses, which I did at his request, and saw that they were properly cared for. Booth promised to pay me for my trouble, but he never did. I frequently had the horses exercised, during Booth's absence from the city, by "Peanut John," walking them up and down the alley. "Peanut John" kept the key to the stable in the theater, hanging upon a nail behind the small door, which opened into the alley at the rear of the theater. Booth usually rode out on horseback every afternoon and evening, but seldom remained out later than eight or nine o'clock. He always went and returned alone. I never knew of his riding out on horseback and staying out all night, or of any person coming to the stable with him, or calling there for him. He had two horses at the stable, only a short time. He brought them there some time in the month of December. A man called George and myself repaired and fixed the stable for him. I usually saddled the horse for him when "Peanut John" was absent. About the first of March Booth brought another horse and a buggy and harness to the stable, but in what manner I do not know; after that he used to ride out with his horse and buggy, and I frequently harnessed them up for him. I never saw any person ride out with him or return with him from these rides.

On the Monday evening previous to the assassination, Booth requested me to sell the horse, harness, and buggy, as he said he should leave the city soon. I took them the next morning to the horse market, and had them put up at auction, with the instruction not to sell unless they would net two hundred and sixty dollars; this was in accordance with Booth's orders to me. As no person bid sufficient to make them net that amount, they were not sold, and I took them back to the stable. I informed Booth of the result that same evening in front of the theater. He replied that he must then try and have them sold at private sale, and asked me if I would help him. I replied, "Yes." This was about six o'clock in the evening, and the conversation took place in the presence of John F. Sleichman and others. The next day I sold them for two hundred and sixty dollars. The purchaser accompanied me to the theater. Booth was not in, and the money was paid to James J. Gifford, who receipted for it. I did not see Booth to speak to him, after the sale, until the evening of the assassination.

Upon the afternoon of April 14 I was told by "Peanut John" that the President and General Grant were coming to the theater that night, and that I must take out the partition in the President's box. It was my business to do all such work. I was assisted in doing it by Rittespaugh and "Peanut John."

In the evening, between five and six o'clock, Booth came into the theater and asked me for a halter. I was very busy at work at the time on the stage preparatory to the evening performance, and Rittespaugh went upstairs and brought one down. I went out to the stable with Booth and put the halter upon the horse. I commenced to take off the saddle when Booth said, "Never mind, I do not want it off, but let it and the bridle remain." He afterward took the saddle off himself, locked the stable, and went back to the theater.

Booth, Maddox, "Peanut John," and myself immediately went out of the theater to the adjoining restaurant next door, and took a drink at Booth's expense. I then went immediately back to the theatre, and Rittespaugh and myself went to supper. I did not see Booth again until between nine and ten o'clock. About that time Deboney called to me, and said Booth wanted me to hold his horse as soon as I could be spared. I went to the back door and Booth was standing in the alley holding a horse by the bridle rein, and requested me to hold it. I took the rein, but told him I could not remain, as Gifford was gone, and that all of the responsibility rested on me. Booth then passed into the theater. I called to Deboney to send "Peanut John" to hold the horse. He came, and took the horse, and I went back to my proper place.

In about a half hour afterward I heard a shot fired, and immediately saw a man run across the stage. I saw him as he passed by the center door of the scenery, behind which I then stood; this door is usually termed the center chamber door. I did not recognize the man as he crossed the stage as being Booth. I then heard some one say that the President was shot. Immediately all was confusion.

I shoved the scenes back as quickly as possible in order to clear the stage, as many were rushing upon it. I was very much frightened, as I heard persons halloo, "Burn the theater!" I did not see Booth pass out; my situation was such that I could not see any person pass out of the back door. The back door has a spring attached to it, and would not shut of its own accord. I usually slept in the theater, but I did not upon the night of the assassination; I was fearful the theater would be burned, and I slept in a carpenter's shop adjoining.

I never heard Booth express himself in favor of the rebellion, or opposed to the Government, or converse upon political subjects; and I have no recollection of his mentioning the name of President Lincoln in any connection whatever. I know nothing of the mortise hole said to be in the wall behind the door of the President's box, or of any wooden bar to fasten or hold the door being there, or of the lock being out of order. I did not notice any hole in the door. Gifford usually attended to the carpentering in the front part of the theater, while I did the work about the stage. Mr. Gifford was the boss carpenter, and I was under him.

DEATH OF DR. MUDD

My father died from pneumonia, January 10, 1883, after an illness of nine days. He contracted the disease while visiting the sick in the neighborhood in the nighttime and in inclement weather. He was buried in Saint Mary's cemetery, attached to the Bryantown church, where he had first met Booth. He was in the fiftieth year of his age at the time of his death.

BIG BYTE BOOKS is your source for great lost history!

Made in United States
Troutdale, OR
04/08/2024